The Rebel and the Kingdom

Blood and Oil (with Justin Scheck)

Billion Dollar Whale (with Tom Wright)

THE REBEL AND
THE KINGDOM

THE REBEL
AND
THE KINGDOM

THE TRUE STORY
OF THE
SECRET MISSION
TO OVERTHROW THE
NORTH KOREAN
REGIME

BRADLEY HOPE

CROWN
NEW YORK

Published in the United States by Crown,
an imprint of Random House, a division of
Penguin Random House LLC, New York.

CROWN and the Crown colophon are registered
trademarks of Penguin Random House LLC.

Credits for photograph insert appear on page 243.

LIBRARY OF CONGRESS CATALOGING-IN-PUBLICATION DATA
NAMES: Hope, Bradley, author.
TITLE: The rebel and the kingdom / Bradley Hope.
DESCRIPTION: First edition. | New York: Crown, 2022.
IDENTIFIERS: LCCN 2022026355 (print) | LCCN 2022026356 (ebook) |
ISBN 9780593240656 (hardcover) | ISBN 9780593240663 (ebook)
SUBJECTS: LCSH: Hong, Adrian. | Human rights—Korea (North) |
Human rights workers—United States—Biography. |
Asian American political activists—Biography.
CLASSIFICATION: LCC JC599.K7 H66 2022 (print) |
LCC JC599.K7 (ebook) | DDC 323.092 [B]—dc23 / eng / 20220729
LC record available at https:// lccn.loc.gov / 2022026355
LC ebook record available at https:// lccn.loc.gov / 2022026356
International ISBN 978-0-593-59421-6

Printed in the United States of America on acid-free paper

crownpublishing.com

2 4 6 8 9 7 5 3 1

FIRST EDITION

Book design by Barbara M. Bachman

For my parents, Mark and Linda

Behold! A new world is approaching
before our very eyes!
The age of might has receded,
and the age of morality has arrived.

—*KOREAN DECLARATION*
OF INDEPENDENCE, MARCH 1919

CONTENTS

AUTHOR'S NOTE

In late August 2011, I hitched a ride into Benghazi on a plane from Cairo chartered by the United Nations' World Food Program. I was arriving in the middle of a civil war, which had pitted troops loyal to the Libyan strongman Muammar Gaddafi against rebels, who were outraged by the country's corrupt government and inspired by the wider Arab Spring movement.

When I arrived, it felt like the civil war might be in its final weeks. A group of us reporters would make the long drive each day west along the coast from Benghazi toward Sirte—the final battleground—in the hopes of finding rebel commanders with updates on the fighting.

Rebel brigades blocked the road into Sirte about ninety miles east of the city. There, amid gaggles of fighters, journalists would spend a few hours each day conducting interviews. One day, as a fellow journalist named Kristen Chick and I were about to leave, we spotted a group of fighters gathered in a circle, laughing uproariously.

We headed over and, in the center of their circle, discovered an improbable sight: a grinning eighteen-year-old Korean American college student by the name of Chris Jeon. The young American had flown to Cairo, taken a train to Alexandria, and then hitchhiked his way into Libya. Jeon, who had just completed an internship at the financial firm BlackRock in San Francisco, was on his summer break. Clad in a blue Lakers jersey, Jeon didn't speak a lick of Arabic, but that had not deterred him from getting a taste of "one of the only real revolutions" in the world.

When I got back to Benghazi, I immediately wrote up the story of the mathematics student turned would-be rebel. Within minutes of being published online, the story exploded. Hundreds of news outlets around the world picked it up. Then, later that day, an email arrived in my inbox from an unfamiliar name: Adrian Hong.

"Great story," the stranger wrote, mistakenly referring to me as "Bob." And then he asked me if I could put him in touch with Jeon.

Adrian told me he was heading to Libya soon and wanted to help ensure Jeon got home to America safely. I connected Adrian and Jeon's father over email, but, curious, I began digging into Adrian's online trail. His full name, I learned, was Adrian Hong Chang, but he went by his father's last name. I saw that he was a Yale graduate who was active in North Korean human rights issues. Intrigued, I decided to strike up a separate conversation with Adrian himself. Why would a young North Korea activist like himself want to go to Libya?

He had a suave, confident way about him in our conversations. There was always a touch of mystery, too. He seemed to be extremely connected with the Libyan rebels. He also seemed connected to Syrian and Egyptian revolutionaries. But everything was vague. For the first time, but not the last, I began to wonder, is he really doing things, or is he pretending?

I was then living in Cairo and covering conflicts throughout the Middle East. I knew that war could act as a magnet—attracting all types of unlikely people, whether their aim was duty, altruism, or profit. My first thought was that he was an American spy posing as a businessman. But there was something about him—an air of authenticity mixed with a touch of the amateur—that kept me questioning. It was also highly unlikely a spy would contact an American journalist. There was too much risk of exposure. Was he an Ivy League do-gooder in over his head? Or could he, too, be a civilian thrill seeker, perhaps a more sophisticated type than Chris Jeon, but a thrill seeker nonetheless? Or was he something else entirely, some kind of rogue operative, with hidden motivations?

One thing I was certain of: The man seemed worth keeping tabs on.

WRITING ABOUT SECRETIVE PEOPLE and events is an enormous challenge. I have been tracking Adrian Hong and his activities for more than a decade and spent much of the last three years of my life reporting in depth on the story of Adrian and his organization, now known as Free Joseon. I interviewed scores of people around the world with unique insights, as well as obtaining documents, photos, and video footage unavailable to the public to confirm aspects of the story and fill in crucial details.

All my books have been catalyzed by questions that try to cut to the heart of how power and influence work in the twenty-first century. And I try to answer them by telling a good story. In *Billion Dollar Whale,* my co-author, Tom Wright, and I tried to understand how a young Malaysian poser could purloin billions of dollars, right under the noses of the financial world's watchdogs, while convincing politicians, Hollywood A-listers, and countless others that he was who he said he was. In my second book, *Blood and Oil,* with Justin Scheck, I wanted to understand Mohammed bin Salman, the enigmatic crown prince of Saudi Arabia, who had emerged from obscurity to embark on a quest to modernize the oil-rich nation while at the same time cutting a ruthless figure in his attempt to consolidate power and quash dissent. That book sought to probe how MBS was upending the simple bargain that had been at the center of U.S.-Saudi relations for more than eighty years—oil for military protection—and unpack the implications.

Here, the question that animated my reporting and writing is deceptively simple: Who is Adrian Hong? I wanted to understand how an idealistic Ivy League graduate had become a global fugitive. What had motivated him to do what he did? What made him think he could change the world? And, moreover, was it even possible for someone, a regular citizen driven by passion and good intentions (assuming they were good), working with a small group of collaborators, to effect a change to the global political order in the age of digital surveillance and autocracies? Those are the questions I hope you will keep front of mind as you read on.

A few things to note. First, I'm a journalist, not a historian. There are many fine books on the history of Korea, which offer far more comprehensive detail on pivotal events and figures. I sought to provide necessary historical context while placing current events and figures at the center of the book's narrative. My hope is that the pages that follow will offer insights both to seasoned readers of North Korean history and to those coming to the subject for the very first time.

Many of the sources for this book spoke to me at great personal risk. Adrian Hong, his fellow members of Free Joseon, and others connected to them have operated despite threats against their lives and myriad other dangers. In the book, I made the decision to not name anyone who has not already been publicly identified as a member of the group. I took special precautions to protect my communications with the book's sources and leave no traces for would-be assailants to identify them.

Finally, a note on names. The Korean names in this book follow the order of family name first, given name second. If the given name has multiple syllables, as it usually does, it is hyphenated. This does not apply to the names of Korean Americans, who typically follow Western naming conventions. For them, and non-Korean individuals, I typically use last names on subsequent references, with the exception of Adrian Hong.

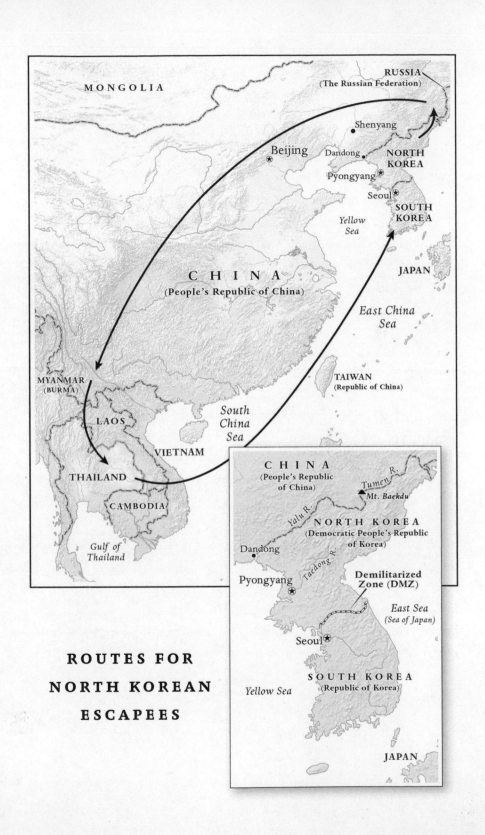

**ROUTES FOR
NORTH KOREAN
ESCAPEES**

THE REBEL AND
THE KINGDOM

THE BREAK-IN

MADRID
FEBRUARY 22, 2019

O N A COOL FRIDAY AFTERNOON IN LATE WINTER, A WELL-DRESSED man carrying two luxury gift bags walked up to the door of the North Korean embassy in Madrid and pressed the buzzer.

"¿Sí?" a voice said through the intercom after a few minutes.

"Good afternoon, my name is Matthew Chao," the man outside replied in good Spanish, explaining he'd been there several weeks earlier and had returned with a gift for "Señor So," citing the name of the embassy's highest-ranking official.

The embassy was a burnt-orange compound in Madrid's Valdemarín quarter, a posh district known for its parks and luxurious residences. The diplomatic compound looked more like the estate of a rich if perhaps paranoid Spaniard than the office-like quarters of the city's other embassies. The discreet entry gate was set back from the sidewalk and flanked by an imposing wall. Little could be seen from the road, and most people in the neighborhood walked by without giving the building a second thought. The embassy received few visitors.

Now, however, hearing the name of his boss, the North Korean worker, a thirty-year-old embassy employee called Jin Choe, who was gardening when the buzzer rang, cracked open the door. Seeing a smiling, dapper Asian man wearing a black suit with a polka-dot tie and his hair tied in a man bun, Jin allowed him in. "I'll find Mr. So," he said, pointing the visitor to a seat on a bench inside the door. The time was just after 4:30 P.M.

As Jin went in search of Mr. So, outside the embassy walls an older woman resting at a bus stop was observing a different scene, one that would have caused the junior diplomat to shut the door and run for safety. Concealed against a wall near the embassy's front door stood another five men dressed casually in blue jeans and sunglasses. Some of them wore large black backpacks. Several were crouching as if they were about to spring into the building.

A few moments after Jin disappeared, the man calling himself Matthew Chao rose from the bench and quietly opened the door behind him. The men waiting outside slipped inside. As they crossed the threshold onto North Korean grounds, several of the intruders pulled on black balaclavas and began running. They drew pistols and handcuffs from their bags, speaking to each other over a walkie-talkie app on their mobile phones and wireless headphones.

The intruders dispersed throughout the building, yelling at the startled staff to drop to the ground. After fastening their hands with plastic ties and handcuffs and placing bags over their heads, the masked men corralled the workers into a meeting room. Mr. So, whose full name is So Yun-suk, was initially pulled into a bathroom, while his wife—who had tried at first to barricade herself and their child in a bedroom—was guarded by a man upstairs without any restraints.

The intruders then went room by room, learning the layout of the embassy and ensuring no one was hiding in a closet or unused office. Most rooms were startlingly spare considering the building was home to four diplomatic staff as well as two of their wives and one young boy.

They charged into a propaganda room, whose walls were covered in North Korean ideological posters and stylized pictures of the three generations of the Kim dynasty, who have ruled the country since its founding in 1948 following the partitioning of Korea by the United States and the Soviet Union in 1945. The diplomats would be expected to gather in the room daily to read and recite ideological material praising their leader, Kim Jong-un, as well as his father and grandfather, as deities protecting the proud country from evildoers around the world, especially the United States.

Down one hallway, the embassy raiders came upon a chamber purported to exist in every North Korean embassy around the globe, a space few if any foreigners had ever set their eyes on: the intelligence center, featuring a computer, stacks of papers, and foil-lined walls intended to prevent the prying of Western intelligence agencies. Here the diplomats would receive orders from their superiors in North Korea via their own cryptographic system.

Within fifteen minutes, the group had taken control of the embassy and secured the premises. Or so they thought. Not all was what it seemed—both to the intruders and to the captives.

One of the North Korean hostages later told Spanish police that the man putting on his wrist tie couldn't figure out how it worked at first and required help from another of the men, an odd shortcoming for what he automatically assumed was the work of an elite paramilitary group seizing control of the embassy.

With their terrified captives tied up, the intruders dashed through the rooms again, sweeping everything they could, including USB sticks, two computers, a mobile phone, documents, and two hard drives, into a backpack. One of the hard drives was connected to the embassy's surveillance system, so taking it was meant to eliminate any evidence the men had been inside.

With the rest of the embassy staff terrified and tied up in the meeting room, Matthew Chao led So Yun-suk into the basement.

BUT THERE WAS A problem. What the intruders didn't know is that they'd missed someone, Cho Sun-hi, wife of one of the officials and the unknown, seventh resident of the embassy. Hearing men with South Korean accents storming into the embassy, she panicked.

North Koreans have been in a declared state of war with South Korea since 1950, so any unexpected interaction with a South Korean has the potential to create a visceral panic. From the time they are toddlers, North Koreans are taught that the United States and South Korea are "cannibals" bent on destroying the great North Korean state. As the men went room to room, kicking down doors, Cho escaped onto the terrace outside her room on the second floor. Fearing for her life, she decided to jump. Dropping onto the concrete below, she landed hard, injuring her head and leg.

In pain but undeterred, Cho hobbled across a paddle tennis court and out a side door with a small path onto the main road. By the time she reached the road, she was crawling on all fours.

A gym worker driving through the usually sleepy neighborhood of Madrid nearly swerved into the curb when he saw a woman with blood dripping over her face screaming beside the road. He pulled over to help, later telling police he thought she'd been badly assaulted.

He drove her to a clinic just down the road, where a staff member called an ambulance and the police. The woman was in a hysterical state, anguished words streaming out of her mouth, all but unintelligible to the Spaniards.

When police officers soon arrived, they struggled to determine where the distressed woman had come from. They tried calling the Chinese embassy, but realized she couldn't speak Chinese. One of the doctors used Google Translate to decipher her words. Finally, the officers understood; the woman was from the North Korean embassy, just up the road. But what she was telling them made little sense.

"Some people have entered the embassy and are killing and eating people," Cho was screaming. "There are children in there."

BACK AT THE EMBASSY, it had been only an hour since the masked men had stormed the building. During that time, Matthew Chao and his crew had tied up the staff, grabbed a ream of documents, and even quickly staged and filmed a video that involved smashing portraits of the former North Korean leaders on the ground.

About half an hour later, the intruders froze at the sound of the embassy's door buzzer. It was the police. Composing himself—and placing a "Dear Leader" pin, a red North Korean flag with portraits of Kim Jong-un's forefathers, on his suit jacket—Chao headed to the door.

Affecting the tone of a haughty and standoffish official, he opened the door to confront three Madrid police officers wearing sunglasses. They explained to Chao that an injured woman had been found on the street and was howling that something bad was happening inside the embassy.

Feigning bureaucratic nonchalance, Chao explained that if police wanted to interact with the embassy, they must go through the appropriate channels. Then he shut the door.

But who had called the police to the embassy in the first place? As the intruders raced to determine the leak in their airtight plan, it dawned on them: they'd missed someone. Someone had gotten away, someone they didn't know lived in the embassy until this moment.

They'd now been in the embassy for more than two hours. The original plan was to stay for no longer than forty-five minutes.

Ring. Ring. Ring.

Suddenly the phones in the embassy started to ring incessantly. The men tried to ignore them as they continued to try to convince So Yun-suk everything would be fine once they got on their way.

But whoever was calling was incessant, dialing again and again for hours. The sound filled the embassy's cavernous interiors, devoid of much furniture or carpeting. As afternoon turned to night, the masked men exchanged increasingly worried glances.

The North Koreans, sitting on the floor, shuffled uncomfortably. Did the ringing signal help or further danger? They were still unable to see because of the bags over their heads.

In the basement, So Yun-suk, the embassy's top North Korean official, stared with a pained expression at the man calling himself Matthew Chao.

"You can't keep me safe, Adrian," he declared, with an air of resignation. "You have to leave. Now."

A READY-MADE LIFE

In the camp, there was no difference between man and beast, except maybe that a very hungry human was capable of stealing food from its little ones while an animal, perhaps, was not.

—KANG CHOL-HWAN,
THE AQUARIUMS OF PYONGYANG

NEW HAVEN, CONNECTICUT
SPRING 2002

TOM NAKANISHI WAS SITTING AT HIS DESK IN HIS DORM ROOM AT Yale University doing homework when his roommate burst in clutching a stack of articles.

"You have to see these," the roommate practically shouted to his fellow sophomore, splaying out the papers onto the desk in the Berkeley College residence they shared. The articles detailed the real-world concentration camps in North Korea where prisoners were starved, tortured, and forced to perform backbreaking manual labor.

This was Adrian Hong Chang, boyish, clean-cut, and aged nineteen, on the cusp of a momentous shift in his life. At that time, saying you were going to change the world—from a dorm room in the Gothic brick Berkeley College building at Yale—felt like the kind of utterance any number of their classmates might make over a late-night joint. Though neither young man could fathom it, the fact was that, for Adrian, his growing obsession with North Korea was the spark that would lead to hundreds of rescues of international refugees and a confrontation with one of the most brutal regimes on earth on its own soil.

"We have to do something about this," Adrian told Nakanishi, in a moment that was still vividly imprinted in the latter's memory nearly two decades later. The world was ignoring an ongoing genocide in North Korea, he lamented. The irony stung: Americans were shedding tears over World War II films like *Schindler's List* and *Saving Private Ryan* while all but ignoring the concentration camps, extrajudicial killings, and mass starvation that were still happening.

The truth was, until recently, Adrian hadn't shown more than a passing interest in North Korea, whether at college or as a child growing up in California. In the early years of the twenty-first century, the casual observer might have a vague awareness that North Korea, like Cuba, was a place seemingly stuck in the 1950s. Those paying a bit more attention might have had a sense that these conditions were a by-product of World War II and the Korean War, which had established a family dynasty now led by a cartoonish man named Kim Jong-il, with a passion for cinema and brandy, and that he operated one of the world's last, terrifying, and sometimes darkly humorous dictatorships, with the self-importance of a real-life Bond villain. Someone who read the newspaper might have heard, too, of the country's devastating famine in the 1990s, during which millions of people died because of massive state negligence. They certainly would have heard about Kim's nuclear weapons.

The headlines could be scary, but often news reports about North Korea contained little nuance, and for good reason. Many so-called experts on the country had never been there at all because of its obsessive wariness of outsiders. Quirky and laden with third-world tragedies, North Korea for most Western audiences was not so distinguishable from the many places on earth where life is much harder than anything they'd ever experienced.

But beginning in the late 1990s and into the early 2000s, a raft of new reporting was trickling and then flooding out in newspaper articles, reports from humanitarian organizations, and books by escapees telling dark accounts of life in the "hermit kingdom." They told of a network of concentration camps that had been established throughout the country—camps that were reminiscent of Nazi-controlled Germany and Poland. North Korea wasn't just an insular country ruled by a dictator with delusions of grandeur, like Alexander Lukashenko in Belarus or Saddam Hussein in Iraq. It was like something out of a dystopian novel mixed with the systematic brutality of Adolf Hitler's Nazi Party. "Worse Than 1984," screamed the headline of an op-ed from 2005 by the British writer Christopher Hitchens describing North Korea.

The details were shocking, but simply too few people had been able to wrap their minds around the full scope of the regime's atrocities. It was a problem, Adrian believed, of awareness. Surely once people heard the details and saw the pictures, as he had, policy makers in Washington and others with influence would begin to act, he declared to Nakanishi.

Something was different about the cohort of these college roommates in 2002 compared with the irony-steeped Gen X generation that had come before them. Ten years earlier, Francis Fukuyama had published his infamous book *The End of History,* arguing that with the breakup of the Soviet Union liberal democracy had triumphed. But just the prior year, two weeks into their first semester at Yale, Adrian and Nakanishi had witnessed the world change before their eyes when Islamic jihadists crashed planes into the World Trade Center in New York City and the Pentagon.

Even before the pair arrived on campus, where they would witness the country's 9/11 reckoning together, they had bonded over the online messenger ICQ and Xanga, the social media website of choice for Asian Americans in the 2000s. They both came of age in California, sons of Asian families living in predominantly Latino areas, and both yearned to express themselves politically without yet knowing exactly what they wanted to say. Nakanishi hailed from Los Angeles, and Adrian had grown up in a suburb of San Diego.

During their online chats, Adrian intrigued his future roommate with his descriptions of his early life as an only child living in Tijuana, Mexico, where his family had lived until he was seven. His South Korean–born parents were Christian missionaries and continued operating an orphanage there even after they moved a few miles north to San Diego. His dad was a tae kwon do master and Adrian was, too. As his chat handle, Adrian had once chosen the moniker "tkdmaster001."

One of his father's main tae kwon do studios was just across the street from Bonita Vista High School, where Adrian was an A student and co-editor of the school newspaper, *The Crusader*. After school, an athletic and fresh-faced Adrian would often walk over to the sand-colored strip mall to the studio, next to a Fantastic Sams hair salon and a Massage Eden. Practicing since he was a small boy, Adrian was a black belt.

Classmates from those years don't remember Adrian mentioning North Korea, but he was proud of his Korean ancestry. On the Xanga account, he set his birthday as March 1, 1919, the date when a huge protest movement by Korean citizens kicked off to demand independence from Japanese rule and cultural hegemony. Some seventy-five hundred people died, with many more injured and arrested. The movement was a turning point in Korean society, but they weren't liberated from Japanese rule until the end of World War II in 1945. Today, in Korea, it's known as Independence Movement Day.

To Nakanishi, these intriguing elements of Adrian's story added up to an air of adventure, one detectable over late-night chat sessions in the months before they'd meet in person.

Once his family had moved north to San Diego, Adrian had spent most of his life in Chula Vista just to the city's south. The area had a distinctly low-key vibe: palm trees, strip malls, and the beach. Adrian had a high-octane personality, but he would occasionally let his SoCal origins slip through, talking in the laid-back, overly familiar manner of a Chula Vista "bro."

"Ah, the glorious life of a bachelor," he wrote on his Xanga page one afternoon while at Yale. "Sitting on a couch watching dvds alone, eating out of a can sigh."

Those around Adrian back then recall a confidence about him that was offset by a strong sense of empathy. Fellow students would re-member for years his ability to notice one person whose voice was being drowned out by louder students, taking them aside afterward and letting them know he heard what they were trying to say. And even from a young age, Adrian had seemed to hunger for something bigger than the chilled-out suburb he called home. Together with his best friend in high school, who would go on to become a key mem-ber of Adrian's clandestine work, he'd speak with fervor about civil rights leaders like Martin Luther King Jr.

Though he lived on a typical Southern California cul-de-sac filled with middle-class office workers who commuted into San Diego every day, Adrian's upbringing stood out for the sense of mission brought by his parents. Money earned by the tae kwon do studios his father ran was largely plowed into the Gloria World Mission, a charity his parents created to help poor and disadvantaged people in Tijuana. The family would frequently make the half-hour drive over the bor-der, spending weekends and religious holidays. The family car had the mission's name emblazoned on the side.

"Let us not live with words or tongue, but with actions and in truth" was the Bible quotation on the website of his father's studio, which described itself as the "fundraising arm" of the Gloria World Mission.

Adrian later told a friend that his parents had raised him with an obsession about getting good grades, but not about what to do after he got them. "I am just a normal dude, went to public school," he told the friend. "I did well, but when I got to college, I wondered what was the point?"

For much of his teenage years and first year at college, Adrian couldn't quite put his finger on which direction to take his life. Soon after arriving at Yale, he and Nakanishi began attending meetings of the Movimiento Estudiantil Chicano de Aztlán, a social justice group originally established in 1969, where there was vibrant discussion of the U.S. response to 9/11. Nakanishi's dad was a co-founder of the group as well as the Asian American Students Association decades earlier.

Students discussed what happened to Japanese residents of the United States and Asian Americans after Pearl Harbor. Would that happen now to Muslim Americans? Adrian was a spirited participant.

Adrian frequently showed a strong aversion to the status quo, the established wisdom on all topics, and the safe options for a young person making their way in the world. To him, there was a sense of meaning missing from so many efforts around him.

On AOL Instant Messenger he communicated under the user-name "areadymadelife," the title of a 1934 short story by the Korean novelist Chae Man-sik depicting middle-class Koreans with good educations but no direction. The feeling resonated with Adrian. He saw Korean and Korean American youths adrift without a deeper purpose.

As a plucky freshman at Yale, he wrote a sixteen-hundred-word op-ed in *The Korea Herald* lamenting the decline of values of his brethren and calling for Koreans at home and abroad to stop obsessing over material gains and foster a deeper appreciation of Korean heritage and its history of fighting oppressors. "Where are the college students of old, who rallied for democracy and freedom in the 70s and 80s?" he wrote. "Where are the aware, educated youth that would shake this earth? They have disappeared."

The article describes his personal journey to learn more about Korea and his heritage, including an impromptu trip to the Korean Mission to the United Nations, where he was denied entry. But here he was in January 2002—just eighteen years old, making him one of the younger members of his class—writing a long article about Korea without ever directly mentioning the North. The only references are to the concept of "reunification" and South Korea's long history of fighting communists.

Adrian was still a campaigner in search of a campaign. Then he encountered a book that would change the course of his life.

2

THE PRESENT IS
NO DIFFERENT

PYONGYANG
1968

KANG CHOL-HWAN WAS BORN IN 1968 IN PYONGYANG, NORTH KOREA'S capital, but his parents were brought up mostly in Japan. From the late 1950s, Zainichi Koreans—ethnic Koreans who had migrated to Japan during Japan's colonial rule over Korea or in the late 1940s in search of better opportunities—were steadily fed propaganda promoting North Korea as a socialist paradise. Kim Il-sung himself delivered remarks welcoming returnees, dangling a life with quality education and dignified work as rightful citizens. The call for repatriation was a joint effort. The North Korean state, with aid from other socialist countries slowly drying up, was looking to thicken its labor force, while the Japanese government wanted to weed out ethnic minorities thought to be incompatible with Japanese society.

The promises of material comfort and a campaign to rebuild the national identity were an appealing pitch for some in the Korean diaspora who faced discrimination in Japan and felt they could never reach equal status in the homeland of their former colonizers. But Kang's paternal grandparents, who had immigrated to Japan at a young age, were already wealthy from their business operating pachinko parlors and lived an opulent life in Kyoto's most upscale neighborhood. It was Kang's grandmother, a fervent socialist and Kyoto chapter director of the newly created Korean Workers' Party, who saw a higher calling and persuaded her husband to return to their homeland.

Arriving by ship in North Korea, the Kang family members were startled to find the country economically feeble and underdeveloped. North Korea was pummeled by the U.S. Air Force during the Korean War, but more than a decade later an air of lifelessness still lingered. Even worse, bureaucratic hurdles led to food shortages, and there was no freedom of thought. The onetime guerrilla leader Kim Il-sung had declared *juche,* meaning self-reliance, as North Korea's operating principle, pushing political and ideological unity that could justify the state's tight grip on all aspects of life.

For the first few years, the family didn't speak of the shocking difference between the reality on the ground and the picture painted to them by North Korean promoters in Japan. The shame of their getting conned by North Korean intermediaries in Japan was too much to bear.

Kang's family managed to maintain a higher standard of living than most in North Korea thanks to his grandparents' appointments to government posts and gifts from relatives back in Japan. He kept a collection of aquariums in his room, a symbol of the family's affluence and, later, the inspiration for the title of his book.

The family's political standing deteriorated over time, and one day in 1977 police arrived without any warning to arrest them. Kang never could definitively learn the event that sent his family to the gulag, but he believes it had something to do with a remark by his grandfather interpreted as treasonous by another official. Whatever the catalyst, in an instant, their lives were forever upended. The officers looted their possessions and escorted them to Yodok concentration camp 2915, where they were forced to live in a dirt-floor room and work in a dangerous gold mine, frequently witnessing deaths from disease and starvation. After ten years in the camp and another five struggling to make ends meet as a status-less worker, Kang managed to escape the country via China and make his way to Seoul.

Years later, he told his story to a French journalist, which led to the publication of *The Aquariums of Pyongyang*. First published in France in 2000, the book started percolating to a wider readership only in late 2001, when it was published in English, and would go on to become an international bestseller, published in more than two dozen languages.

At Yale, Adrian Hong consumed the book in a fury, feeling he'd found a cause so obvious and pressing that he was ready to devote himself to it. Not long after splaying the North Korea articles out in front of Tom Nakanishi and reading the book, Adrian started imagining how he, a teenage college student, could make an impact on something as intractable as a belligerent, hermit nation with a growing hoard of nuclear weapons.

AROUND THE SAME TIME as Adrian was first immersing himself in the literature on North Korea, a future acquaintance of his, the human rights investigator David Hawk, was putting the finishing touches on a pivotal 2003 report that pulled back the cover on the Kim regime's widespread human rights violations.

Hawk had earned a reputation as a steadfast human rights expert from his work to document Khmer Rouge atrocities in Cambodia in the 1970s and 1980s. While he was serving as the executive director of Amnesty International, the organization was awarded a Nobel Prize in 1977. In the mid-1990s, Hawk had turned his attention to the genocide in Rwanda, before focusing on North Korea's system of prison labor camps. He'd spend much of the rest of his life working to spread the word about the oppressive conditions facing millions of people there.

Released in October 2003, his 120-page investigation, *The Hidden Gulag: Exposing North Korea's Prison Camps*, used prisoner testimonies

and satellite imagery to conclude that North Korea was systematically imprisoning, torturing, and killing its citizens with abandon.
There were no trials, verdicts, or sentences from a judicial authority.
The ruling party simply decided who would disappear and sent them
to a camp in the North Korean hinterland. Hawk's report, which
would go on to see four different editions published in the years that
followed, was a persuasive, evidence-backed indictment of the Kim
regime's wholesale human rights violations. Hawk's report, along
with the testimony of people like Kang, brought North Korea's secret
culture of torture and imprisonment to the attention of the world.

The report generated instant headlines around the world. Of particular interest was Hawk's use of striking satellite imagery, which he
marshalled to bring credibility to the allegations.

Hawk's work, published by the U.S. Committee for Human Rights
in North Korea, was aided by growing communities of defectors and
escapees living in Seoul. During the famine in the 1990s, Kim Jong-il
had opened the gates to international aid groups who flooded into
North Korea to help millions of starving citizens. During the ensuing
years, North Koreans fled the country over the Chinese border. Hawk
as well as other academics and human rights campaigners sought
them out to learn about daily life and politics in the repressive North.
One of the most shocking topics were the camps, places some escapees were able to describe from chilling first-person experience.

What Hawk concluded was that North Koreans were undergoing
their own special kind of misery in the modern world. The Cambo-
dian and Rwandan genocides Hawk documented were bloody affairs,
where powerful forces sought to wipe out huge numbers of people
for political and religious reasons. In Cambodia, the killing went on
for three and a half years; in Rwanda, it was eight grievous months.

But in North Korea, the systematic degradation of human rights
had been going strong since the late 1950s. This was oppression carried out over generations, and many of the prisoners were from a
lower class. North Korea has a system called *songbun,* dating to a
major purge of "neutral" and "enemy" forces in society in 1957.

Under this system, citizens are subdivided into fifty-one categories and slotted into one of three broader classes based on their background as well as the behavior of their ancestors. The result is something like a merger of India's caste system with Joseph Stalin's ruthless sorting of society by political allegiance. Moving up is nearly impossible, but falling to the bottom is all too easy with as little as an ill-advised complaint. Having a parent who had been a landlord, merchant, or Christian minister or collaborated with Japanese occupiers was a recipe for a very low status.

The top quarter of North Korea's twenty-five million population today make up the loyal "core" class and are granted the best opportunities and privileges in society. These elites live a somewhat privileged existence, carrying smartphones and living in apartment buildings in what is jokingly referred to by some as Pyonghattan. These are what people often see when they watch footage from news crews permitted to visit North Korea. The "core" class are encouraged to intermarry so as to prevent any sullying of their impeccable blood. They are the ones running the country and filling the diplomatic posts around the world.

The "wavering" class is roughly half of the population. They serve the "core" class as technicians and laborers and live a quality of life that might be considered the upper end of lower class by Western standards—just enough to survive, with some rare perks. They are allowed to live in Pyongyang, working in servile and bureaucratic positions.

The final group, about 25 percent of all North Koreans, are the so-called hostile class, who are worked to the bone and live with barely enough for physical existence. Many descend from those who allegedly collaborated with Japanese occupiers or opposed Kim Il-sung in some way. These are the people whom hardly anyone sees. Even foreign diplomats living in Pyongyang are rarely given passes to leave the city or travel freely in the most impoverished sectors of the country. The homes of members of the "hostile" class are often without electricity or running water, according to reports compiled by human rights organizations. It's a medieval agrarian existence where nearly all of the fruits of their labor are given to the all-powerful overlord as a tax without any accompanying services or rights. Most of the roughly 100,000 to 120,000 people in prison camps come from the "hostile" class.

This wasn't genocidal, Hawk realized as he spoke to North Korean refugees. It was the state-driven grinding down of the human soul to next to nothing. For those confined to labor camps, death was viewed as the easy way out. Suicide was common. Guards would drive them to work harder with less food until their bodies simply stopped functioning. They were exhausted and starved to death, their dignity stripped away on arrival. Prisoners were at best machines for chiseling coal from the earth, harvesting crops, and manufacturing products to be sold to China for hard currency to support the regime.

The vast majority of citizens were effectively slaves, owned by the state, with no rights of any kind. Their purpose was only to further the Kim regime's wealth and secure its hold on power. The more privileged had better access to food and products, but they lived under perpetual fear of losing everything.

In an interview, Hawk told me that the story that stuck with him the most over the years was from a woman he spoke with named Kim Hye-sook, who was hauled to Camp No. 18 (known as Buk-chang) at the age of thirteen and spent twenty-seven years living there. Most of her family had been sent there four years earlier. The presumed reason: her paternal grandfather had fled to South Korea. This was the "guilt by association," or *yeon-jwa-je*, system in action.

The teenage Kim Hye-sook attended some school, but mostly she was part of a child labor brigade that spent most of their daylight hours cutting down trees and collecting wood. Soon after, she started work at the Hong-je coal mine, where the men and boys would break the coal and the women and girls would ferry it up in buckets, wheelbarrows, and trolleys that they'd manually push back to the surface.

While a prisoner there, she lost her father, mother, and a son. For a quarter of a century, she slept on the floor in one room with what remained of her family, sharing a single blanket. They subsisted on a meager corn porridge supplemented by grass or leaves they'd gather whenever they could. When she was finally set free in 2001, her brother and sister were so beaten down and brainwashed they initially opted to remain in the camp.

Her life was so difficult after leaving that she even tried to return to Bukchang again, but they refused her. Finally, she escaped to China and made her way to South Korea, where she encountered members of the international rights community, including Hawk, and shared her harrowing story.

One of the people Kim Hye-sook spoke to in 2013 was the then UN high commissioner for human rights, Navanethem Pillay, who, inspired by her story and others', appointed the landmark UN Commission of Inquiry on Human Rights in the Democratic People's Republic of Korea.

For as much as Hawk's 2003 report did to illuminate the horrors of North Korea's human rights abuses, when other countries paid attention, their diplomatic focus tended to go elsewhere: the country's nuclear weapons.

The origins of North Korea's nuclear ambitions can be traced back to the political philosophy created and championed by its founder, Kim Il-sung, who over decades forged an ultra-paranoid nationalist political system by marrying Soviet-style communism with *juche,* which entailed a philosophy of self-reliance. The primary ingredient of this system was a dose of mythology more at home in an ancient Persian civilization than modern-day politics: the idea that the Kim family were themselves deities with superhuman powers and, hence, the only ones qualified to lead the homeland.

By most authoritative references, the would-be deity had been born in 1912 in a humble North Korean village. As a young man in the 1920s, he escaped the yoke of Japanese occupiers who invaded and annexed Korea as they looked to expand the power of the Japanese empire. He and his parents moved to the Chinese province of Manchuria, where he became part of a small resistance group. As the

North Korean myth goes, Kim founded the Korean People's Revolutionary Army, the precursor to the official Korean People's Army, in 1932. Exaggerations aside, Kim actually was a guerrilla fighter by the mid-1930s.

In June 1937, a group of some 150 revolutionaries, supposedly led by the twenty-five-year-old Kim, blitzed Japanese-occupied public buildings, including police stations and post offices in Pochonbo, a town near the Chinese border. This elevated Kim's status enough to later earn him the rank of captain in the Red Army, where he commanded the Korean battalion. His ability to speak Russian and his relative obedience were noticed by Stalin, who eyed Kim as a convenient proxy leader for the Soviet Union after it went to war with Japan in August 1945, just days before Tokyo surrendered. If anything, Kim was adept at strategically positioning himself for advancement without coming across as lusting after power. Still, more than seven decades after he assumed control of North Korea, his history is so mixed up with the country's propaganda that sorting myth from truth is a formidable task.

With Japan's surrender, its thirty-five-year-long occupation of Korea came to an end. But before Koreans could catch wind of their own liberation, the country was arbitrarily divided down the middle at the 38th parallel, with the United States administering the south and the Soviet Union controlling the north. As was the case with so many centers of strife after World War II, the decision to divide Korea was made briskly by Westerners with little understanding of how momentous their decisions would be. In the case of the creation of two Koreas, it came down the night of August 10, 1945, when U.S. officials were working around the clock in a building next to the White House to figure out what to do in the weeks ahead with Japan on the verge of surrender.

Two mid-ranking officers, Charles H. Bonesteel and the future secretary of state Dean Rusk, were tasked with dividing the country with the Soviet Union, which had agreed to vague plans for a four-power trusteeship over Korea at the Yalta Conference in February

1945. Without much time to think things over and using a 1942 *National Geographic* map of "Asia and Adjacent Areas," they simply selected the 38th parallel because it looked like it intersected the country about evenly and placed Seoul, the capital, and several prisoner of war camps around Seoul in the American zone. Stalin, who wasn't too concerned with the details surrounding Korea, accepted the arrangement and ordered his ground troops to stop at the agreed-upon division line.

On the advice of his brutal secret police chief, Lavrentiy Beria, Stalin chose the reliable Korean Kim Il-sung as an administrative leader for what the Soviet Union called the Democratic People's Republic of Korea in the North.

Divisions of territories between the Americans and the Soviets were happening across the world, including in places like Berlin. But the Korean divisions proved an enduring flash point with few equivalents. Koreans on both sides never accepted the border or the idea of two sovereign states on the Korea Peninsula as legitimate.

In 1950, the tensions came to a boil. Kim Il-sung's Korean People's Army made the first move, rolling over the 38th parallel so powerfully and abruptly that they nearly won control of the entire country. But two months in, U.S. and United Nations forces managed to deploy enough troops to turn the tide. In the push and pull of the war, Seoul was seized four times.

North Korean land troops were driven back to the border, creating a stalemate with major powers backing the forces on either side. Cementing an eventual armistice in 1953 was the Americans' punishing two-year barrage from the air. Some 635,000 tons of bombs including napalm were dropped on North Korea, nearly 40 percent of the total munitions dropped by the United States in the European theater of World War II.

In that milieu, surrounded on all sides by the military might of interventionist global powers, Kim Il-sung became even more paranoid and aware of his own fragile hold on power. Though the ideas of *juche* are rooted in Marxism-Leninism, the ideology has evolved over time to incorporate the justifying principle that North Korea is different from other socialist countries and needs to protect itself at all costs. It's why North Korea is the only "socialist" country in the world run by a single bloodline of men descended from the founder, something completely anathema to Marxist political theory.

Thanks to aid from the Soviet Union and China and a firm hold on the economy, North Korea thrived well into the 1960s. But by the 1980s, the top-down controlled economy began to stagnate while South Korea started growing exponentially due to the government support for several key industries including steel, shipbuilding, chemicals, and electronics. When the Soviet Union collapsed in 1991, together with the death of Kim Il-sung in 1994, North Korea's problems came to a head, resulting in a four-year famine that saw hundreds of thousands, possibly millions, of people die of starvation.

Government propagandists painted this period as the third "Arduous March," referring to a winter in the late 1930s when Kim Il-sung marched through Manchuria with a group of anti-Japanese guerrilla fighters suffering from starvation and the bitter cold. Like Kim, North Koreans were to adopt a self-sacrificial attitude and band together to face adversities. They conveniently left out that the famine was entirely the result of the Kim government's mismanagement.

Yet much of the world failed to grasp the true scale of the humanitarian catastrophe thanks to North Korea's self-imposed isolationism. The term "hermit kingdom" has been applied to North Korea for much of its existence. It's not well-known nowadays, but the term dates back to the Joseon dynasty, the period from 1392 to 1910. After repeated invasions by Chinese and Japanese aggressors, Joseon rulers adopted a harshly isolationist policy that coincided with nearly two hundred years of peace, cultural development, and relative stability that in the mid-nineteenth century descended, as in neighboring China, into domestic unrest and foreign encroachment.

In 1888, *The New York Times* ran the headline "Trouble in the Hermit Kingdom" on a news brief about people seizing government officials and beheading them. The paper continued to refer to Korea as the "hermit kingdom" throughout the twentieth century, but after World War II, as South Korea evolved into an ultra-capitalist, open society and economy, usage of the term shifted to exclusively referring to the North.

Over North Korea's first few decades, Kim Il-sung, who never forgot how a U.S. general had requested nuclear bombs to use against his country during the Korean War, pursued nuclear weapons as the ultimate protection of North Korea from external meddling and would-be invaders. He leaned on Soviet engineers to build the Yongbyon Nuclear Scientific Research Center in the early 1960s, but even Kim's Soviet allies were wary of giving any further assistance that would help him construct actual nuclear weapons.

Western intelligence agencies later concluded that North Korea received clandestine support from Pakistan in the 1990s to weaponize its nuclear energy program. Abdul Qadeer Khan, the Pakistani nuclear engineer who helped his country develop weapons of mass destruction, is believed to have played a key role in providing technology for developing nuclear weapons to Kim Il-sung's engineers, the details of which emerged in a former Pakistani president's memoir.

By the mid-2000s, after many starts and stops, nearly all of U.S. foreign policy on the Korean peninsula was dedicated to persuading North Korea to give up any nuclear weapons program. But sanctions and warnings were not enough to tame the Kim regime's nuclear ambitions. In October 2006, an underground explosion was detected in North Korea's northernmost province, and the state news agency claimed that it had successfully tested a nuclear device. In the following years, North Korea continued its nuclear armament, conducting a series of nuclear tests and growing its stockpile of uranium and plutonium.

With the wary eyes of the world trained on North Korea's expanding nuclear arsenal, rather than its gulags, one of the few groups to advocate unabashedly for human rights in these years were Korean Christians, especially those in America. At churches in places like All Nations Church in Los Angeles and Adrian Hong's hometown of San

Diego, fiery pastors would hold shouting prayer meetings and invite escapees to tell their stories to the congregations.

To these pastors North Korea was a black-and-white issue. Human beings were suffering and it was their God-given mandate to try to liberate them.

TO ACQUAINTANCES, ADRIAN HONG appeared most interested in social justice and political freedom. But closer friends understood that beneath his political worldview lay a deeper religious conviction. At Yale, Adrian had a casual way of talking to people that suggested he could kick back like any college student, but in fact he avoided imbibing alcohol and drugs, without coming across as judgmental.

Some nights, he'd stay up late talking with Cole Carnesecca, a fellow Californian and Christian, about the biblical imperative to be involved in humanitarian work. Carnesecca helped run an event called All-Campus Worship that drew in Christian groups from across the university for one large service every month or so.

One of their debates was about whether church communities could mobilize to be part of larger movements as they had during the civil rights era in the 1950s and 1960s. For Adrian, faith and activism were two parts of his coalescing political identity, Carnesecca remembers.

By the time Adrian returned to campus for the fall semester in 2003, he had begun a full transition into a North Korea activist. He lost interest in classes and threw himself into understanding the region and its history. He began looking for ways to channel his desire for meaningful activism. During the week, he'd rush off to meet peers at Korean student associations at schools up and down the East Coast, crashing on couches. As the frenetic pace of his travels grew, friends would report sightings of him back at Yale with bemused excitement.

Adrian voraciously consumed books on North Korea and, never shy, called experts up out of the blue. One day he called Kongdan Oh, a kind academic with a strong sense of morality at the Institute for

Defense Analyses who briefed U.S. officials on Korean matters, to ask about North Korea.

As Oh often did with anyone interested in a topic dear to her heart, she gave him an impromptu primer on the history of the country and the complexities standing in the way of peace, not least of all the American fixation on nuclear weapons, which she thought was a recipe for preserving the status quo of North Korea's government and closed-door policies to the rest of the world.

Nuclear weapons ensured North Korea's safety in a world dominated by Western regime change efforts, so why would the country give up this trump card under any circumstances? No amount of trade and assistance was worth risking the Kim regime's hold on power, Oh told Adrian. Negotiation would lead to nothing. This realization made a big impression on Adrian.

Baby-faced and a year younger than most of his classmates, Adrian took to wearing a suit on his trips to campuses to appear older and more official as he liaised with Korean student groups. He began to grow more comfortable speaking to these groups, sometimes recruiting Korean singers and dancers to accompany talks he'd give about conditions in North Korea.

His vision grew bigger. On trips back to California, where his family and childhood best friend lived, Adrian tested out concepts for a new student group across the country. On one trip, he met up with a fellow Korean American called Paul Kim, known as PK, who was eight years older. PK was a stand-up comedian and co-founder of Kollaboration, a talent competition for Korean American artists. He'd come to Yale for a campus event, where they bonded over their interest in Asian American political issues. They were also avid Xanga users. Adrian told PK about his plans to create a national student organization.

Spitballing, one of them looked up at the name of the Korean-fusion bar where they were meeting on Wilshire Boulevard. It was called Blink, located on the second floor of a shopping center in Koreatown, PK told *The New Yorker.*

The name inspired an acronym: LiNK, for "Liberation in North Korea." The word suggested an aggressive stance, but it had a ring to it. Later, Adrian would be persuaded by other students to dial it down to Liberty in North Korea, though the concept of liberation better encapsulated his personal view.

LiNK was officially announced at the Korean American Students Conference (KASCON) hosted at Yale in March 2004, attended by hundreds of students from across the country. Adrian was on the committee that organized the event, arranging many of the guest speakers for the multiday gathering.

At KASCON, Adrian's friend PK was on hand along with a host of prominent Korean Americans. For many of the students, KASCON's annual gatherings were a defining event of their college search for identity. At the opening event, the conference flew the Korean Unification Flag—white with the peninsula's shape filled in with blue—to convey the oneness of the Korean people. For many young Asian Americans, KASCON felt energizing and all-encompassing. KASCON "subsumed us and was sometimes more important than school or career, and I think that was the case for Hong and he didn't shake it off like most of us did," recalled an acquaintance of Adrian's who attended.

Many of the nearly eight hundred students at the 2004 KASCON were entranced by the idea of LiNK, inspired by speakers who shared the stories of North Korean refugees, and horrified by a set of clips from an unfinished documentary showing malnourished children hunting for fragments of food during the famine.

This was a terrifying situation related to their own ancestry, and for many there was a growing desire to do something. As the event came to a close, Adrian had commitments from attendees to start dozens of new LiNK chapters at campuses across the country. He had the wind at his back. Public consciousness of the North Korean human rights crisis was spreading, at least among the intelligentsia.

Anne Applebaum, just a month before KASCON and shortly before she won the Pulitzer Prize for her book about the Soviet gulags of the twentieth century, penned a searing editorial in *The Washington Post* about North Korea on the occasion of the sixtieth anniversary of the liberation of Auschwitz.

"We shake our heads self-righteously, certain that if we'd been there, liberation would have come earlier—all the while failing to see that the present is no different," she wrote, going on to describe harrowing testimony in a new documentary about North Korea. Decades later, "it will surely turn out that quite a lot was known in 2004 about the camps of North Korea," she wrote. "It will turn out that information collected by various human rights groups, South Korean churches, oddball journalists and spies added up to a damning and largely accurate picture of an evil regime. It will also turn out that there were things that could have been done, approaches the South Korean government might have made, diplomatic channels the U.S. government might have opened, pressure the Chinese might have applied."

THE EARLY DAYS OF LiNK were equal parts disorganized and thrilling. Adrian was adept at the big picture of what the movement was about, but the on-the-ground mechanics of the organization, like raising public awareness and fundraising, were handled by a more organized collection of followers at the chapter groups on college campuses, including Cole Carnesecca.

Leadership of the national group, where the larger agenda was hashed out, included Adrian and a young woman who would go on to become a key member of LiNK over the life of the organization, Hannah Song, a Korean American from New Jersey. Song was a student at New York University and also deeply inspired by *The Aquariums of Pyongyang*. After hearing about the group a few months after KASCON, she pledged to help with LiNK and became a partner of Adrian's in charting the group's agenda for the chapters forming across the country.

Song's family, like many Korean families in the United States, had its own North Korean tragedy: her grandmother escaped Pyongyang just before the Korean War, expecting to be reunited with her husband and two children soon after. But as the war carried on and hardened into a simmering forever standoff, she lost all contact with her family. Heartbroken, she settled in Seoul and started a new family.

One of the main early events LiNK chapters around the country held was a screening of the 2004 documentary *Seoul Train,* which shed light on the Underground Railroad–like network of volunteers helping North Koreans escape, against the odds, as well as the tragedy of their sometimes failed attempts to get asylum.

A powerful example revealed in the documentary was the case of the MoFA Seven, an incident in which members of the North Korean Han-mi family tried to rush into the Japanese consulate in Shenyang, China, in 2002.

As they approached the gate, which was guarded by Chinese police, the two men dashed inside, leaving two women and a three-year-old child to be wrestled to the ground by the officers. All five members were turned over to the Chinese, but amid a groundswell of global interest in the case they were allowed to go to South Korea rather than be sent back to North Korea as China usually does with escapees, which it calls "economic migrants."

Not long after KASCON, Carnesecca watched Adrian begin drifting away from his classes and normal schedule at Yale. Alarmed, he came to see his role as keeping Adrian grounded and focused on his academics so that he wouldn't fail out of school. Adrian wanted to drop out, but Carnesecca persuaded him to push through and finish his degree. By this point, Adrian was visiting three campuses a week, spending Fridays and the weekend trying to seed new chapters of LiNK, but already he had a nagging feeling that all of this frenzied organizing wasn't enough.

Public awareness in the twenty-first century was increasingly becoming bite-sized—a new crisis, disaster, humanitarian issue every week and not enough time to make a difference. At times, friends would observe Adrian become completely consumed in his thoughts before suddenly reappearing to offer a new idea or solution.

One of these ideas became Adrian's new fixation: the notion of following in the footsteps of those in *Seoul Train*. Adrian was going to start rescuing North Koreans himself. But he had never even been to China, much less had firsthand knowledge of the logistics of assisting refugees in tense settings. He needed to embark on a reconnaissance trip.

"I can't talk about things I haven't seen," he told a close friend.

3

ACROSS THE TUMEN RIVER

Father, I stretch my hands to Thee,
No other help I know;
If Thou withdraw Thyself from me,
Ah! Whither shall I go?

—CHRISTIAN HYMN TREASURED BY
NORTH KOREAN ESCAPEE JOSEPH KIM

DANDONG, CHINA
NOVEMBER 2004

IN SEPTEMBER 2004, AN IDIOSYNCRATIC JOB POSTING BEGAN CIRCU-
lating among LiNK members in chapters around the country:

> if any of you out there [or anyone you know] are interested,
> willing and ready to spend a minimum of a year volunteering
> abroad in an unnamed East Asian nation [that is not South
> Korea, Japan or China], please send an e-mail.
>   warning: conditions will likely be terrible, work will all be
> pro bono, and it will not be pretty. Fluency in Korean abso-
> lutely necessary, some knowledge of Chinese a plus. . . . very,
> very serious applicants only need apply.

The author of the listing was Adrian Hong. Although he had still
not graduated from Yale, Adrian's ambitions were now spilling over
the confines of campus activism.

Later that year, Adrian, now twenty, led the group's first foray into China. He and a small group of LiNK members flew to Beijing and made their way to the North Korean border, wearing backpacks and baseball caps. This initial expedition was fact-finding in nature, but, even so, the chance to stand near the brown, slow-moving Tumen River and see firsthand the land that had come to dominate his thoughts and imagination gave Adrian a rush. Seeing fully armed Chinese soldiers at the airport and in the border regions, he thought to himself, "Wow, this is real."

Adrian reported back to LiNK members that the expedition had already had some "extremely close calls." "Things out here are much worse than we thought," he wrote in November 2004.

Through their growing network, they arranged to meet activists and religious leaders who operated secret shelters in China. To those veterans of the cause, Adrian and his youthful companions represented a fresh energy in the mission to help North Koreans—as well as a new source of funding.

The LiNK team spent much of their time talking to the escapees, taking their testimonies, and gauging their interest in making the risky journey abroad. Their only other option was living underground permanently with the ever-present risk of discovery and extradition back to North Korea. Adrian frequently asked if they wanted to come to America, a thought that many found so preposterous that it was like suggesting they travel to the moon.

Speaking to the young LiNK students in Korean, the escapees told stories that were often deeply disturbing. A child explained coolly that his mother starved to death while his father was in a concentration camp. A young woman explained how she escaped a farmer in the hinterlands of North Korea who'd imprisoned her and raped her for years.

For Adrian and the others, the trip cemented an understanding of the scarcity of routes a refugee could take to escape from North Korea and the options, once they did, for where to go next. On a map, the trip over the border with South Korea would seem the obvious way to gain asylum. By law, South Korea instantly grants any North Korean a passport because of South Korea's enduring position as the sole legitimate Korean government, with jurisdiction over the entire Korean peninsula and its adjacent islands.

But the reality on the ground makes easy passage an impossibility. The border between the two countries is an extraordinarily perilous place. Ever since two representatives, one from the United Nations and one from the communists, signed nine copies of the armistice agreement on July 27, 1953, and formalized a cease-fire line, a 160-mile-long and 2.5-mile-wide demilitarized zone (DMZ) has buffered the countries. On the North Korean side this entails a huge military presence, including thousands of artillery weapons pointed southward. Anyone trying to escape would be shot instantly if they were lucky enough to get as far as the border. Many land mines were removed in 2018, but there are still thick nests of barbed wire and large numbers of soldiers manning lookout towers.

The DMZ has other quirks. Inside it is a neutral zone known as the Joint Security Area, where North and South Korean soldiers carrying sidearms stand face-to-face. To its north, North Korea has loudspeakers that boom out propaganda, and to its south defectors turned activists launch balloons with anti-Kim leaflets and food. In the 1980s, South Korea built a 323-foot flagpole with a massive flag on its side of the border. The North responded with a 525-foot flagpole. The standoff was later referred to as the flagpole war. Untouched by human activity for decades, the DMZ is also home to rare and endangered species like the white-naped crane and Asiatic black bear.

An observer looking through strong binoculars on the South Korean side might also spot what appears to be a village on the northern side called Kijong, with colorful concrete buildings and street sweepers coming through at regular intervals. Zooming in from the border, analysts soon realized the buildings, constructed in the 1950s, were hollow inside. No one lives there. It is a real-life Potemkin village.

GIVEN THE EXTREME TENSION and scrutiny at the DMZ, crossing the North Korean border with China, in the north, has been the route favored by nearly all North Korean escapees. But this crossing has been perilous for a whole other set of reasons. The Chinese government took a position that no one leaving North Korea could be interpreted as a refugee, and therefore should be promptly arrested and sent back. The Chinese government ignored the near certainty that people returned this way would be thrown into labor camps for years as punishment.

Reaching the border in North Korea could be relatively easy for someone living in a remote, rural area. The border is erratically policed in those more distant areas. Much of the border is lined by the Tumen and Yalu rivers, which freeze over in the winter. Nearer the cities, there are roaming patrols on both sides of the border. On the North Korean side, discovery would lead instantly to being placed in a prison camp. On the China side, it would be a quick ejection back into North Korea and imprisonment. North Korean border guards were also known to shoot people whom they deemed too far across the river, spooking residents trying to wash clothes or bathe.

To get safely out of China, refugees needed a place to hole up, gain strength, and find trustworthy shepherds to get them to the next, equally perilous part of their journey. This is where volunteer groups came in. Often sponsored by Christian organizations, these groups organized networks of shelters in China near the North Korean border.

Some of these were overseen by a humanitarian worker called the Reverend Timothy Peters, an evangelical pastor. Adrian first encountered Peters in 2005, after the LiNK group had returned from its fact-finding trip to China. By the time of their meeting, Peters had been running his Seoul-based group, Helping Hands Korea, for almost a decade.

Peters first came to South Korea in the 1970s, and over the years his activities evolved into two distinct roles: outspoken critic of North Korea's human rights abuses and hands-on organizer of the Underground Railroad–like network that had been developed to assist in the escape of dozens of North Korean refugees every year. For the latter, Peters believed secrecy and zero publicity were critical components. The best opportunities for helping people escape existed because there was little discussion of what they were doing.

Peters met Adrian not in China but on a trip to the U.S. East Coast in late 2004, where he agreed to give a talk to the LiNK chapter at Brown University. In Adrian, Peters found "something special"— a young person with an extraordinary ability to raise awareness among university students and convince them that they could make a difference in something as big and intractable as the human rights abuses of a hermetically sealed totalitarian state. "The ability to get young people interested in human rights in North Korea was something rare," Peters recalled.

The vagaries of the political discourse on North Korea—with its focus on nuclear weapons and high-level diplomatic games—were, at best, oriented around how gradual change might slowly improve the situation on the ground in North Korea. For Peters and others like him, there was only one core truth: people in North Korea were suffering and they deserved help.

Peters learned early to run rescues by keeping a very low profile. The pathway out of the Chinese–North Korean border region required help from a network of volunteers—Chinese NGOs operating undercover, Christian volunteers, Westerners and Koreans alike. One of the hardest parts was getting an escapee off the street before they were reported to the authorities by a Chinese local or outright caught by ever-present Chinese law enforcement. Once they were identified by activists like Peters, escapees were hidden in a home or a shelter where they were generally well fed and given clothes and training in anticipation of the next phase of their journey, which involved traveling across the country and over yet another border, accompanied the whole way by intrepid guides.

North Korean escapees often brave perilous hikes through icy steppes into Mongolia before boarding a flight from Mongolia to South Korea. More common is a southwestern journey diagonally across China itself for days, even weeks, to the Yunnan province via trains, buses, and taxis. There they can hike across mountains into Laos or Myanmar and into Thailand, in the hopes of getting a flight from these countries to Seoul. At any moment on any of these paths through China, a Chinese officer could spot the suspicious-looking person—one who has never interacted with modern transportation, society, or technology for their entire life—and arrest them. Other risks include running across violent criminals, who are known to rob or rape escapees when they're at their most vulnerable.

Through their travels to China and meetings with activists like Peters, the enormity of this task was impressed on Adrian and the core LiNK members, who were keen to think of new strategies for helping escapees as well as financing shelters. The facilities were deeply imperfect—sometimes refugees would have to stay indoors for months at a time without exercise or sunlight—but they were a critical part of the Underground Railroad.

A major opportunity came in October 2004, when President George W. Bush signed a bill, the North Korean Human Rights Act, that focused attention on the "deplorable human rights situation in North Korea." The result of years of lobbying on the part of activists, Christian groups, and hawkish conservatives, the bill authorized $20 million a year to be spent on helping North Korean refugees and millions more for promoting democracy and providing information inside North Korea. For Adrian and his team, the interpretation was clear: the United States was opening its doors to North Korean refugees. The question was how to get them to U.S. soil.

Speaking to a State Department official soon after, Adrian candidly inquired, "Does the U.S. government have a plan for the North Korean people?" The official looked at him as if he were the most naïve person on earth. What about geopolitics, the balance of power, and nuclear weapons? Those were the focus.

Pushed again, the official admitted that the government was "years away from even thinking about a solution."

To Adrian, the message seemed clear: the grown-ups weren't planning to do anything about it, so the college kids would have to take over.

DIZZY AND ENERGIZED FROM his travels, Adrian found it difficult to focus in his final months at Yale but managed to attend the minimum number of classes to avoid getting kicked out. After Adrian had threatened to quit his undergraduate studies on many occasions, Carnesecca and other friends helped him get over the line on graduation day in May 2006.

College had come to feel sheltered and parochial. Fellow students would speak idealistically, but it felt theoretical. For all the lofty talk, most of his fellow Ivy Leaguers were on a glide path to the traditional trappings of success. He could see careers unspooling into the future: do-gooders who ultimately lean into their privilege and become well-paid lawyers and bankers.

Even after notching what should have seemed like a victory—hundreds of young Asian Americans joined the LiNK chapters during Adrian's first year—the young activist had become demoralized by what he saw as the ultimate indifference of people when they were presented with the terrible conditions of North Korea. He expected people to pour into the streets to protest the worst human rights violations of the twenty-first century, but instead found that most shrugged their shoulders. Even LiNK members didn't seem to care enough at times.

Why wasn't the planet up in arms to get rid of these scourges? To Adrian, life without bold action hardly seemed worth living.

What he saw as the indifference of South Korean youths was particularly galling. Since the 1950s, South Korea had evolved in utter contrast to its northern neighbor, going from a beaten-down agrarian society to one of the world's fastest-growing economies. Economists call it the Miracle on the Han River. By the early twenty-first century, teenagers and university students in South Korea seemed completely oblivious to the humanitarian disaster taking place miles away. Instead, they gorged on the so-called idol groups, the precursor to today's K-pop, and worked around the clock as part of a hyper-capitalist, ultra-materialistic society.

To those around him, Adrian's brooding over these issues made him more mysterious and a bit arrogant. Not everyone took well to Adrian's lofty views. He never outright criticized people for their choices, but his language sounded judgmental.

"People have come to their own compromises," he said once. "I don't begrudge them for filling in their own equations." After a beat, he'd then start talking about how "bad guys enable bad guys everywhere."

Even Adrian's family had grown worried. All these trips—was he saving enough money? Who would look after him if he got in trouble?

Adrian's all-consuming focus on the plight of North Korean lives had made it difficult to enjoy his own. One night, in his senior year at Yale, Adrian's girlfriend at the time gathered friends for a surprise birthday party. Cole Carnesecca's job was to bring Adrian to the venue, the upstairs of a deli near campus, but he couldn't get him to budge despite strenuous efforts. Finally, Adrian relented and they made their way to the deli. Just before they went through the door, Adrian turned to him and said he'd known about the surprise party all along.

Another time the two young men were talking about the situation

in Darfur. Adrian piped up: What if he got together ten retired marines who put their lives at risk to protect these refugee camps? People don't seem to care, he explained to Carnesecca, but maybe that
would help the world see the life being lost.

It was just a college thought experiment, but years later Carnesecca would recall the moment as an example of how Adrian's out-of-
the-box ideas for protecting refugees were beginning to drift into
something more dangerous.

4

SHENYANG SIX

I do not need my freedom when I'm dead.
I cannot live on tomorrow's bread.

—LANGSTON HUGHES

SHENYANG, CHINA
DECEMBER 2006

THREE DAYS BEFORE CHRISTMAS 2006, ADRIAN HONG WALKED INTO a Kentucky Fried Chicken in Shenyang flanked by two American women from LiNK. Accompanying them were six North Korean escapees, including two orphan boys aged sixteen and seventeen, three women in their forties, and a woman in her twenties.

From their table in the restaurant, the group could see the American consulate, a brown fortresslike structure surrounded by walls and barbed wire. If it wasn't for the American flag hoisted on a pole in front of the building, it might have struck passersby as a high-security prison. Adrian had come to Shenyang because it also was one of the biggest cities in proximity to the North Korean border. It was just about a three-hour drive from Dandong to Shenyang, but even faster by train.

This trip was risky, but it wasn't the first time Adrian had done it. Just two months before, he had followed the same playbook to help a trio of North Korean teenagers get into the U.S. consulate in Shenyang, including a sixteen-year-old named Joseph Kim.

Like many North Korean escapees, Joseph had experienced more hardship in his few years on earth than most people would in a lifetime. He had been just a small child when North Korea's great famine began. The famine was caused by a tragic combination of failures in food distribution, the socialist bloc's collapse, and devastating ecological disasters, resulting in deaths estimated in the millions. After years of having adequate food, his family began to struggle to put food on the table. His father would often forgo his share of food, telling Joseph that he was a growing boy and needed it more than him. When Joseph was twelve, his father died of starvation.

Joseph's mother sought jobs to provide the bare minimum to her family. Eventually, Joseph was separated from his mother and sister as he sought more food sources. At one point, destitute, he was living on the streets as one of the so-called *kkotjebi,* which translates to "wandering sparrows." North Korea's thousands of homeless children are said to have earned that nickname because of the way they searched the ground for rice grains and corn kernels to survive, pecking like birds for a meager morsel. (The term also could have originated from the Russian word *kochevnik,* meaning nomad.)

Much of Joseph's youth was spent surviving on his own, seeing his mother for brief spells as she struggled to earn enough money to support him and his sister. At one point she escaped to China, only to be sent back and imprisoned.

Finally, after a new period of homelessness and no family members to support him, Joseph made the decision to cross the Tumen River himself in a bid to make it into China and seek a better life. He walked for days to get to the Chinese border.

Just because he had made it to China didn't mean Joseph's problems were over. Any Chinese citizen could instantly report him to the police, which would lead to his arrest. After he had spent months begging and relying on handouts from local churches—sleeping wherever he could, including the forest and later the Tumen City church—an older Chinese woman, a Christian, agreed to let him live with her in the nearby city of Yanji.

In mid-2004, a Christian volunteer helped Joseph and the adoptive grandmother move to a shelter in Yanji. The shelter was run by fervent Christians and funded in part by LiNK. Inspired by the shelter's Christian leaders, Joseph spent his days reading the Bible. He'd start reading, along with the other escapees, at 4:00 A.M. and wouldn't stop until 9:30 P.M.

He had come to find the teachings comforting, but he also believed that the only way for him to escape from China was to prove to the shelter's operators that he was a motivated student and a genuine Christian. Even as others drifted off to sleep, Joseph would sit longer reading the Bible. "'Choose me,' I was saying," he wrote in his autobiography later.

Once again, Joseph bided his time. Months went by without any developments. Then, one day, a young American walked into the shelter and made a big impression on Joseph. "His hair was cut in a stylish way, and his clothes were American and very hip. Everything about him, in fact, was cool," Joseph wrote in his autobiography, *Under the Same Sky.*

THE MISSION TO HELP Joseph Kim and the other teenagers was the vanguard operation of LiNK's Project Safe Haven program. After graduating from Yale in May 2006, Adrian had moved to Washington, D.C., to intensify lobbying and build a national headquarters for LiNK, where he would oversee the group's increasingly ambitious efforts.

The fledgling group moved into a two-story residential house on Embassy Row where staffers—some low paid and others volunteers—worked on couches and at the kitchen table. Many of them had second jobs during the day to be able to afford their advocacy work at LiNK. Hannah Song worked for eight months in 2006 as a media supervisor at the marketing services company Mindshare before she quit to become Adrian's full-time deputy, giving up much of her salary.

Since the first LiNK trip to China a year earlier, LiNK had also partly funded several underground shelters in China to help look after the huge illegal North Korean escapee community. The group didn't have the capacity to actually operate a shelter, but it funneled money from bake sales, documentary screenings, and other fundraising efforts to buy food and supplies for shelters. The shelters gave food, clothing, and a place to live to thousands of people like the teenage Joseph Kim, who were operating without access to Chinese government services or the ability to work a normal job.

After hearing Joseph's story, Adrian had asked him in Korean, along with the two other escapees, if he would like to go to America. Joseph was shocked by how matter-of-fact Adrian was about this monumental possibility. His heart pounding, he said yes.

The only people who knew Adrian's plans were aides to the members of Congress who'd supported more North Koreans escaping to the United States. Even among LiNK the plan was closely held, and no one from the consulate knew precisely what was happening. The only others with awareness were advisers to political figures in Washington, D.C., who would push the State Department if they needed to.

In preparation for the effort to get the teenagers out of China, Adrian bought the North Koreans Western-style clothes and taught them how to act like spoiled Asian American kids. Joseph was told to act "rowdy" and adopt the look of a skateboarder.

All of Adrian's advice felt alien to the young North Koreans. Joseph and the others tried, awkwardly, to act out their assigned parts on short outings around town. Eventually, Adrian deemed the group ready, and they began their journey to the U.S. consulate in Shenyang from the shelter in Yanji. During a stay in a hotel one night in Shenyang, Adrian insisted the North Koreans sleep on the bed while he slept on the floor. Joseph wrote of how shocked he was about the luxurious duvets and the ability to call the concierge and ask for anything at a moment's notice.

"I felt like my life was going to change drastically," he wrote. "I was being carried along on a wave, not knowing what was coming next."

On the twenty-hour train journey to Shenyang, tensions ran high. So afraid of drawing attention from fellow passengers, the young men decided to pretend to be deaf and mute.

As the trip culminated in a final wait in a run-down hotel room in the city, the young men started to panic. Adrian left them to make calls to his LiNK colleagues, but they managed to lock their hotel room door and worried that they were about to get caught. Finally, Adrian returned and told them it was time to go.

They arrived at the U.S. consulate and were waved through by a young female diplomat. Even at the security station inside, Joseph worried that everything was about to fall apart and they would be arrested. About to bolt, he looked to Adrian, who told him, "You're safe!" he recalled later.

It wasn't all smooth at the consulate, however. At one point, Adrian became separated from the group and was taken into an interrogation room. The officials there noted his status as a Mexican national. Who had given him permission to start escorting North Koreans across China to the U.S. consulate? they demanded. Instead of hailing him for his efforts, the officials were treating Adrian as a security threat.

He retorted, brashly, "What about the Constitution?" The comment didn't go over especially well, but he was let free soon after.

The exfiltration of Joseph Kim and the two other young North Koreans was the kind of action Adrian believed would drive LiNK forward. Finally, two years after the group was formed, it was undertaking on-the-ground operations to make a true difference for North Koreans. Joseph ended up in Brooklyn and later got a job at the George H. W. Bush Library in College Station, Texas.

Soon, however, Adrian would conclude that a handful of rescues wasn't enough.

———

EVEN AS THAT INITIAL cohort of asylum seekers, including Joseph Kim, were still inside the consulate in Shenyang, awaiting permission from the Chinese to fly to the United States, Adrian returned to the city in December with the new group of six escapees from North Korea. In fact, one of the women he was now escorting was the mother of one of the boys from Joseph's group.

In the consulate, the tense negotiations between the United States and China over the fate of the North Koreans inside were under way, but the United States was holding its ground. It wasn't that Adrian had clout in the consulate as much as the staff there decided to accept the refugees and deal with the consequences.

No other groups advocating for human rights in North Korea were trying anything remotely similar to this. The only people who came close were the Christian-led shelter operators like Timothy Peters, who were quietly trying to help escapees slip over the border into Mongolia, Laos, or Myanmar.

This time in Shenyang, however, something was off. When Adrian dialed the same consulate number, explaining he had "more packages" to deliver, the prearranged phrase for North Korean asylum seekers, he got a cool response. The woman who answered asked for his number so that someone could call him back.

A few minutes later, a consular official called. They wouldn't accept the "North Korean refugees," he said, before dismissively suggesting they try the United Nations high commissioner for refugees in Beijing, more than seven hundred miles away.

This was a truly stunning development after months of carefully laid plans. Adrian struggled to maintain his calm, feeling his blood run cold as he considered the profoundly dangerous situation they were now in.

Adrian and the group had already traveled twenty hours on a train from Yanji. The trip alone was full of peril. Just one Chinese security official or ticket inspector could have gotten the whole group in serious trouble if they noticed the North Koreans on board. A further journey into the Chinese capital would be even riskier.

Even worse, Adrian believed, was the fact that the consular official had put a target on their backs by discussing "North Korean refugees" on an open phone line. Adrian had used a code phrase because it was well known that China's intelligence agencies listened in on any calls with U.S. officials in the consulate. Mentioning North Koreans was tantamount to calling the Chinese authorities to report illegal activity. The consular official later told a colleague that he felt Adrian had endangered the lives of the escapees by not asking permission before bringing them to the front door. Not only was it politically dangerous, but the consulate didn't have space for a flood of asylum seekers.

The true scale of the risks they were taking was starting to become apparent. Actions like using code words were tactics Adrian was making up on the fly as he operated on instinct. There were no spies on his staff, just college students. What they had in spades was the chutzpah to give it their best shot, but would it be enough to save the Shenyang Six?

Adrian knew that North Korean refugees discovered by the Chinese government on its soil were sent back as part of an agreement between Pyongyang and Beijing. China called asylum seekers "economic migrants," refusing to accept any claims of persecution, even though they would likely be imprisoned if they were hauled back to the border.

China's bellicose response to asylum seekers made escape from North Korea extremely difficult. Escapees couldn't go south, because the border was so well defended by North Korean soldiers, and if they went through China, they'd risk at any moment being sent back to North Korea by Chinese authorities without any ability to argue why they needed protection from the regime in Pyongyang.

For the U.S. consulate in Shenyang to assist in the flow of North Korean refugees to the United States via China amounted to a direct refutation of China's agreement with North Korea. For China's part, after years of carefully managing North Korea and using it as a buffer with South Korea and its thirty thousand American troops forty miles south of Seoul at Camp Humphreys, it didn't want the Kim regime to start saber rattling or tilting its nuclear weapons toward Beijing. The status quo of North Korea suited China well.

AS THE SECOND GROUP of escapees sat in the Shenyang KFC across from the U.S. consulate, Adrian tried to put on a brave face. The last thing he wanted was for those under his care to start panicking. Glancing out the window, he saw a van pull up. Burly men who appeared to be plainclothes officers jumped out and began looking around suspiciously. To Adrian, the sudden arrival of the van was a clear sign the Chinese had been listening to the call and were already deploying officers to capture any would-be escapees. It would be the MoFA Seven case all over again, in which several escapees were apprehended by Chinese police as they tried to enter the Japanese consulate in Shenyang in 2002.

Thinking fast, Adrian sent the group to another café farther away from the consulate while he stayed nearby to try another angle with his contacts in the U.S. government. This time he called the embassy in Beijing, where he connected with an officer who took his number and promised to follow up.

He received another call soon after from a senior official in the Beijing embassy. Verging on yelling, the diplomat declared that the consulate couldn't take any more refugees and accused Adrian of jeopardizing the escapees' lives by bringing them to Shenyang without prior coordination.

The message was clear: no more North Koreans could escape via the U.S. embassy, at least for now, and any efforts to do so would likely end up with their being arrested. It was a terrifying about-face after his successful ferrying of Joseph and his two companions just months earlier. How could the government change its policies so quickly?

Adrian implored the diplomat to consider the situation from the refugees' perspective. After all, they had taken the calculated risk to escape, believing the United States was true to its pledge to offer shelter to refugees from North Korea. And he argued that they were at even greater risk now that the Shenyang consular officer had said his name and referred to the "North Korean refugees" on an open line.

The truth was that Adrian wasn't getting permission in advance because he knew risk-averse officials could decline the plan at the outset. He felt that the North Korean Human Rights Act was an open invitation to bring refuge seekers to the consulate, and he wasn't going to give bureaucrats the choice over whether to honor the spirit of the law. It was better to ask for forgiveness than for permission, as he saw it.

But the plan had backfired. Now Adrian was responsible for a highly vulnerable group, North Koreans with no safety net whatsoever, nowhere to go, and with danger spreading all around. Adrian's contacts in Congress couldn't make a call that changed how the State Department handled cases in a matter of hours. Adrian needed a faster solution.

He pleaded one last time with the officer at the consulate to offer the North Koreans sanctuary. "We're a hundred yards away," Adrian told him. But there was no budging.

Adrian told his group they had two options: return to Yanji and go back into hiding or head to Beijing, as suggested by the consulate. It was unanimous: the refugees wanted to push on, fearing backtracking more than forging into the unknown. They wanted to get as far away from North Korea as possible.

Afraid his face had been recorded by Chinese state security because of his public work to help North Koreans, Adrian flew ahead of the group to Beijing and checked in to the InterContinental hotel to wait for the others to arrive. He arranged for a driver to take the rest of the group in a hired van, an approximately seven-hour overnight journey.

The next morning, Adrian woke early to prepare for the group's arrival. The plan was to show up at the UN building without warning, just as they'd tried with the U.S. consulate in Shenyang. But by mid-morning, he started to feel uneasy when they didn't show up. Hours rolled by with no sign of the North Koreans.

Suddenly there was a knock at the door of Adrian's hotel room. Looking through the keyhole, he saw a cleaning lady wearing an InterContinental uniform, but when he opened it, he found five Chinese police officers standing on both sides of her. He was immediately arrested and taken on a plane back to Shenyang.

The journey was terrifying, but the prison was a visceral shock. Seeing the inside of a Chinese prison—the overcrowded and decrepit cells, staying in close quarters with dozens of alleged criminals—was far beyond anything he'd ever experienced.

In Shenyang, Adrian learned his LiNK colleagues and the six North Koreans had also been detained midway on their drive. He kept his cool, despite the upsetting news, and at first even treated it as an opportunity to learn more about China's relationship with North Korea. During interrogations, Adrian would try to turn the tables on an officer and ask him about how many North Koreans came through the prison every year. The man told him it was a simple procedure: discover North Koreans, arrest them, and immediately ship them back. There were no efforts to ascertain why they'd escaped and what would happen to them once returned.

As the days passed, the interrogations didn't stop. At a certain point, Adrian, frustrated, decided to amplify the pressure on the Chinese by starting a hunger strike. After two days, the Chinese guards threatened to start forcibly feeding him.

Adrian and the others might have disappeared into the opaque Chinese judicial system. But with a quick-thinking, last-minute maneuver in the hotel room in Beijing, Adrian ended up saving the day. During his arrest, he hid his Razr phone with an American SIM card in the neck of his hoodie and offered up a local phone to the officers instead when they seized his possessions. On the journey back to Shenyang, he managed to slip the phone out of its hiding spot and send off a series of text messages to LiNK staff and congressional aides, before it was confiscated upon arrival in Shenyang.

One of those to receive a call about Adrian's arrest was a staffer for Jay Lefkowitz, George W. Bush's special envoy for North Korean human rights. Adrian had met Lefkowitz multiple times to discuss refugees and ways LiNK could bring North Koreans to America from China. The staffer called Jay immediately to give the news Adrian and two other LiNK members had been arrested in China.

If he had failed to alert his connections, Adrian and his colleagues could have spent months if not longer in a Chinese prison. Others helping escapees long before them were still languishing in other prisons in China after getting caught by the authorities.

During meetings at the White House over the Christmas holidays and conference calls, officials including Lefkowitz, working with Adrian's right-hand LiNK executive, Hannah Song, hashed out a plan with Chinese counterparts to return the three LiNK members and the would-be escapees.

At one point, Adrian's immigration status threatened to throw a spanner in the works. He was still living in the United States on a green card as a Mexican citizen, despite having spent almost his whole life in America. U.S. officials wondered whether they should be the ones helping rather than the Mexican government. But Lefkowitz and others succeeded in convincing the Chinese that Adrian was an American in all but passport; LiNK was American, as were the other two volunteers on the mission with Adrian.

The efforts partially worked. After ten days in detention, the LiNK members were deported to the United States from China. The North Koreans, however, remained in prison. Adrian later told an editorial writer at *The Wall Street Journal* that before he departed the Shenyang prison, he broke from his guard to run to the barred window of the cell of the two North Korean boys to yell words of encouragement.

"There is nothing like looking in the eyes of someone who thinks they are going to die," he said. "They both had that look—like there was no hope," he recalled.

5

BULL IN A
CHINA SHOP

WASHINGTON, D.C.
LATE 2006

Within the u.s. government, adrian hong's strategies for helping North Koreans had, by late 2006, become polarizing. On one side were those who believed any efforts to help North Koreans fleeing the brutal Kim regime were warranted even if not agreed upon in advance. Adrian and his colleagues had taken great personal risk to help innocent people try to seek a better life.

Among those supporting LiNK's methods was Sean Woo, then a foreign policy adviser to Senator Sam Brownback. Brownback, part of a Kansas farming family, was a charismatic Republican known for taking up evangelical Christian causes.

The senator had first become drawn to the North Korean cause after opening up a newspaper in 2001 and seeing the stunning images from the MoFA Seven, the group of North Koreans who tried to make a run for the Japanese consulate in Shenyang but were captured by Chinese police.

In the process of getting up to speed on North Korea, Brownback and his staff had met Adrian and other Washington-based LiNK members. "We thought there was some hope in being able to make this a bigger issue," Woo, the senator's aide, recalled.

But as Brownback and Woo met with officials in the State Department and elsewhere in the U.S. government, they were surprised to find huge resistance to changing tack on North Korean human rights. "I was absolutely stunned," Woo said. "After decades of effort getting poets and academics out of the Soviet stranglehold, I couldn't understand why the policy of the government was to toe the line on North Korean refugees." When Adrian and the other LiNK members were arrested in December 2006, Woo and Brownback were among those pushing the U.S. government to help.

Others in the U.S. government were far less eager to advocate for Adrian. This contingent consisted of a number of diplomatic realists within the State Department, notably Christopher Hill, who was the head of the U.S. delegation to the six-party talks initiated to persuade North Korea to lay down its "treasured sword"—the Pyongyang metonym for its nuclear program.

From the diplomatic realists' perspective, North Korea was a global threat so long as it possessed weapons of mass destruction. Human rights of North Koreans were being tread underfoot by the jackboots of the regime, but even worse would be a global thermonuclear conflagration in Asia with millions killed. Rogue efforts like LiNK, the realists believed, were even worse than doing nothing: such vigilantism couldn't be managed, which risked sparking a larger conflict and imperiling the objectives of diplomacy.

In fact, on the same day as Adrian's attempted rescue in Shenyang, Hill finished the latest round of the so-called six-party talks, which also included South Korea, Japan, China, and Russia. Little of substance had been agreed to, but the very act of holding these talks was evidence of the possibility of dealing with North Korea through diplomacy.

The fear of North Korea's nuclear weapons was all the more present in the minds of the world's national security establishments when, on October 10, 2006, North Korea's state news agency issued a statement that the country had successfully conducted an underground nuclear test the day before.

The North Korean statement announcing the test called it a "stirring time when all the people of the country are making a great leap forward in the building of a great, prosperous, powerful socialist nation."

And in the tradition of *juche*, the statement suggested that the test was conducted with "indigenous wisdom and technology" and demonstrated the "powerful self-reliant defence capability."

Over the ensuing years, North Korea alarmingly demonstrated its ability to improve its nuclear weapons capabilities and range. Even with stories about the country's network of concentration work camps, nearly all the discussion about North Korea related to nuclear weapons.

The timing of the December asylum mission near a major U.S. political initiative around North Korea and Adrian's bold, risky approach of simply showing up at the consulate were a combination that would plague Adrian in a much worse way thirteen years later in Spain. But the tragedy this time was how LiNK's asylum pipeline was profoundly disrupted so soon after it got started.

OVER THE HOLIDAYS IN 2006 and into early January, the Reverend Tim Peters, the founder of Helping Hands Korea, was quietly making his rounds at shelters in Chinese villages near North Korea.

Peters was working on helping a new batch of escapees take the long journey to Laos and Myanmar when a phone call came through from a trusted, secret ally in the area. "We need to meet right away," the contact told Peters.

Peters took a trip down from a mountainous area to meet with his contact in the boiler room of a building away from prying ears. The contact relayed the story of the LiNK arrests and explained that one of his own people had been involved, which led the police to show up at the NGO where he worked.

"You need to get out of town," the man told Peters.

Peters left China quickly and made his way back to Seoul. In the weeks that followed his hasty departure, Chinese police went into high alert to stamp out escapes, making the secret work to aid escapees on their underground network even more difficult. The trip Peters had been working on had to be put off by several months. Peters laid blame for the setback squarely on Adrian's shoulders.

"Adrian was like a bull in a China shop," Peters recalled. "This is an incredibly sensitive area. Intelligence people from every conceivable country are in that area. Of course the Chinese were on top of the situation in no time."

In fact, LiNK had been riling people up throughout 2006—the year when Adrian had graduated from Yale and turned full time to the North Korean cause. Not long after graduation, Adrian had led a LiNK group to Seoul to unleash Project Sunshine, an in-your-face plan to shock South Koreans into paying attention to the plight of their fellow Koreans to the north. Many of them had actual blood relatives across the border, including cousins, grandparents, and siblings, but South Koreans tended to minimize discussion of their embarrassing, totalitarian neighbor.

Hatched among LiNK members back in the Embassy Row office in Washington, Project Sunshine would entail holding a mock funeral in front of the Ministry of Foreign Affairs and Trade in Seoul to "mourn for victims of starvation, execution and torture in North Korea, continuing victims of public apathy and indifference," according to the press release at the time.

"The freedom, democracy and prosperity South Korea enjoys today bring with them an obligation to help those less fortunate, and we can begin with those family members just north of us, who are in dire circumstances," Adrian said at the time.

Images from the event seem to show curious South Koreans walking by, but most of them didn't stick around to hear the speech.

IN DECEMBER 2006, WORD spread fast in the North Korea watcher community about the arrest of Adrian, his colleagues, and the North Koreans.

Global newspapers began covering it, too, but it didn't quite rise to become a full-blown international incident. One reason might be the fact that it happened over the Christmas holidays.

Just before Adrian had ventured to China on the ill-fated rescue mission, he had been traveling with Jae Ku, an avuncular Korean American who was finishing up a stint as the director of the North Korea project at Freedom House before starting a new job as a professor at the Johns Hopkins School of Advanced International Studies.

Freedom House, a Washington-based nonprofit dating back to 1941 that is funded mostly by the government to conduct research and advocacy on democracy, political freedom, and human rights, had fronted LiNK about $10,000 early on to kick off its advocacy work, and Adrian often traveled with Ku to international conferences and symposiums. This time Adrian was accompanying Ku on a three-day trip to Japan to rally NGOs and meet with politicians about North Korea.

As the meetings were concluding, Ku asked Adrian what his plans were for the holidays.

"I don't want you to know," Adrian told him. Ku pushed for at least some information about where he was heading.

"I'm going to Vladivostok to look for new escape routes for defectors," Adrian replied. Ku wished him luck. It was the kind of thing he'd come to expect from the plucky twenty-two-year-old.

On Christmas Eve, Ku's phone rang. It was a call from a diplomat at the South Korean embassy in Washington, D.C., explaining the details of Adrian's arrest and asking whether Adrian held a South Korean passport. If so, they might be able to help with getting him out of China. But Adrian didn't hold a South Korean passport, which would have made him obligated to fulfill eighteen months of military service.

After ten days, U.S. diplomatic pressure persuaded the Chinese to release the three LiNK volunteers. But the fate of the six North Koreans still hung in the balance. After Adrian was deported to the United

States, he briefly saw his family in San Diego before picking up and heading back to Washington, D.C.

Back in Washington, Adrian and his allies pushed to save the North Koreans they'd been forced to leave behind, dangling the story to media outlets. They briefed a *Wall Street Journal* opinion writer on the situation, and on January 4, 2007, the *Journal* published an editorial with the headline "The Shenyang Six" about the North Koreans who were left behind.

Despite the diplomatic mess, it seemed nothing about his experience, including the ten days spent in the Chinese prison, had dampened Adrian's fervor. He pulsed between blazing anger and deep sadness over the events that had transpired, especially the way the U.S. consular official exposed their refugee mission by speaking about it on an open phone line.

In an email update to LiNK's supporters on January 26, he wrote, "It feels strange to be back here in Washington at LiNK headquarters, typing away at a computer. For those of you who have been following the news, the past few weeks have not been calm and restful—they have been rather dramatic and urgent." There was more to the story, he said, but he would have to leave it there. He told the supporters he had to wait until high-level discussions had resolved before saying anything else.

But by March 1, there had been little progress. Adrian decided to ratchet up the pressure. Edward Royce, a Republican congressman from California whose staff had become friendly with Adrian, yielded his time during a congressional hearing on the human rights situation in North Korea to read a statement from Adrian into the public record.

The statement narrated Adrian's experience with the U.S. consulate in Shenyang and embassy in Beijing before laying into them:

> I have confidence that underground networks can rescue thousands of North Korean refugees, if only they had a nation

willing to accept them. . . . It is absolutely unacceptable and shameful that a United States post will turn away legitimate asylum seekers, especially those that are targeted for capture and repatriation by local authorities. . . . That they are turned away, literally at the gates, and sent elsewhere is a betrayal of American principles, and perhaps laws.

Adrian spent the early months of 2007 pushing harder for the North Korean cause than ever. In March, he was in Geneva, giving a presentation about North Korean prison camps and attending a session of the United Nations Human Rights Council, and then in July he gave a rousing "Google Talk" on North Korea at Google headquarters in Mountain View, California. Then he was at the Shenzhou International Film Festival in Washington, D.C., accepting an award on behalf of the *Seoul Train* filmmakers. His attendance at all these events was proof of his growing skill at networking and the scarcity of young advocates for North Korean human rights—something activists operating in the space were keen to encourage.

Finally, in August, the U.S. government worked out a deal with China to allow the "Shenyang Six" to leave the country, but they were sent to South Korea instead of the United States. The Chinese called the gesture an "exception" to the policy; nothing had changed that would help the next asylum seekers. In fact, very few North Korean refugees would travel through that "corridor" again.

It would have been more difficult, anyway. Chinese police were beginning to step up their security around Western embassies and consulates in China to better intercept any would-be escapees before they could become a political football.

Still, it was a win of sorts, and LiNK pressed on with its publicity blitz, escorting North Korean refugees to campuses and meeting halls to tell their stories. Adrian met frequently with Joseph Kim, who had moved in with foster parents in California after spending more than four months living in the Shenyang consulate.

Kim was still deeply perplexed about why Adrian would be worrying about people he'd never met before. In his autobiography, Kim
revealed that he once thought Adrian must be among the richest people in America, which afforded him the leisure to focus on others.

But on a visit to the LiNK headquarters in Washington, D.C., Kim
was surprised to find the messy house "filled with twenty-somethings
sitting on couches and the kitchen table, tapping away at laptops," he
wrote. It was actually one of five different places LiNK worked from
during a three-year period after Adrian's graduation from Yale.

"I learned that some of the workers here held part-time jobs to
support their work with North Korean refugees, even though they'd
graduated from places like Yale and other top schools," he said. "They
were struggling to make ends meet. I was astonished. These people
were sacrificing the American dream to help people like me."

ANOTHER BIG EVENT THAT transpired in Adrian's life around this
time was meeting W., a young Korean American woman working in
children's development and entertainment who would later become
his wife. Adrian and W. found common ground with their interest in
helping others. She was a fellow idealist. But the deeper he got into
the North Korean cause, the more Adrian began to compartmental-
ize his life. He had developed a habit of showing up out of nowhere,
and he would share details about his personal life with only a small
group of friends.

It could be a challenging relationship at times. Adrian's travel
schedule was ramping up, rather than slowing down. And there was
a secrecy even between the couple about what exactly Adrian was
planning and doing.

In mid-2008, Adrian abruptly announced that he would be resign-
ing from LiNK during a trip to Seoul to visit the group's office there.
There was no succession plan in place, but Hannah Song, his deputy,
stepped up to run the group in the interim. She'd observed him drift-

ing toward a different kind of activism for months, but severing ties with the organization he founded was a shock, she later told other LiNK members.

"LiNK didn't need me," he told a friend later. "They could do what they were doing without me." And indeed, some of the six-figure donors he'd persuaded only months earlier to support LiNK weren't happy, but Song's leadership persuaded existing grassroots donors and major funders to carry on financing the group.

The deeper truth Adrian had realized, though he didn't dare state it publicly, was that he had come to believe that LiNK couldn't make enough of a difference. Something bigger was needed.

"We could rescue refugees for the next five hundred years, and it wouldn't change the situation on the ground," he told me later.

An op-ed he wrote in *The New York Times* a few months later, near the second anniversary of his arrest, offered insights into his changing perspective. In the piece, Adrian called the six-party talks an "abject failure" and called for more forceful action.

He said he was "wrong" to avoid calling for outright regime change previously. "Now I cannot deny what I wish were untrue—the North Korean elites will never bargain away the only powers that prevent them from losing authority." A few paragraphs later, he added, "If this government and its actions cannot be called evil, then the word has lost all meaning."

Around this time, Adrian began to confide to a close circle of friends that he was going to find a way to do something bigger, riskier, and perhaps even dangerous.

Soon after Adrian's statements about regime change were publicized, the writer John Cha, author of biographies about Korean and American leaders, criticized Adrian in comments included in an article published in San Francisco's *East Bay Express*.

"I think he's kind of a nut," Cha told the newspaper. "He's sort of hawkish and says stuff like, 'Oh we have to get rid of Kim Jong Il.' Well, that's fine, but how do you do it? He doesn't have any answers other than, well, 'I'd love to go in and remove him like we did with Saddam.'"

Reading Cha's withering assessment, Adrian wasn't angry. Instead, he contacted Cha to discuss North Korea. Cha told Adrian that liberating North Korea was an impossible task and the goal should be to democratize it over the long run through gradual change.

Adrian listened thoughtfully and gave his views. Before ending the call, they agreed they were on the same side of the problem, albeit with different approaches to solving it. Such openness to discussion would win him many followers over the years.

6

THE PEGASUS PROJECT

I imagine that the first question which the priest and the Levite asked was: "If I stop to help this man, what will happen to me?" But by the very nature of his concern, the good Samaritan reversed the question: "If I do not stop to help this man, what will happen to him?"

—MARTIN LUTHER KING JR., ON THE
PARABLE OF THE GOOD SAMARITAN

LOS ANGELES
1980s

As a kid growing up in Southern California, Christopher Ahn didn't think much about North Korea. His parents, who moved to the United States from South Korea before he was born in 1981, encouraged him to assimilate as much as possible in American culture.

His mother, aunt, and grandmother kept his Korean identity alive with songs and storytelling at family gatherings, along with serving traditional food such as *sogogi muguk,* or beef radish soup, and the Japanese omelet rice called *omurice.* But, for the most part, Ahn and his younger brother grew up like any suburban American boys in a California suburb, playing baseball and hanging out at the beach with friends.

In the early 1990s, Christopher's father, Young Chul Ahn, a former U.S. Air Force radar technician, opened a clothing store in the Los Angeles fashion district, near downtown and Skid Row. The business specialized in urban streetwear, just as the style was going global. The shop, which often featured a house DJ, was a success. But in 1992, the city was enveloped in unrest following a jury's acquittal of four officers of the Los Angeles Police Department in the arrest and beating of Rodney King. Footage of the brutal attack, filmed by an onlooker, had been broadcast across the world, making the acquittal all the more incendiary.

By the second day after the verdict, rioters had begun targeting Koreatown, a few miles west of the fashion district. Police blocked off roads to the more expensive, predominantly white neighborhoods like Beverly Hills and West Hollywood, but left Koreatown almost completely unguarded. Shopkeepers tried to hold off looters, some with their own guns, but in the end as much as half of the $850 million of damages in L.A. from the riots were in Koreatown.

While the Ahn shop wasn't directly hit by the mobs who ransacked Koreatown, the chilling effect of the riots spilled over into the fashion district. The flow of urban streetwear buyers completely dried up overnight, in part due to Black-Korean tensions after an innocent fifteen-year-old Black girl was shot and killed by a Korean shop owner who claimed she mistook her for a shoplifter. (Footage later showed she had money in her hand to pay for it.) With the shop facing a financial abyss, Christopher Ahn's father decided to reinvent the family business as a suit store with its own brand of trousers.

The Ahn family sold their house and moved into a rental, using the proceeds as seed capital for a dressy clothing company his father called Zannini. The name was intended to evoke high-quality Italian craftsmanship, though there was no connection to Italy. The resourceful Young Chul struck deals with Chinese manufacturers, and both Christopher's parents worked around the clock to get the new business running. Then, just as the family was on the path to financial recovery, Young Chul started complaining of stomach troubles.

A first biopsy came back with worrying results and another was ordered. It was stomach cancer. Just four days after seeking medical advice, Young Chul died, leaving seventeen-year-old Christopher as the man of the house. The sudden loss was a devastating blow to the whole household, which included Christopher's young brother, mother, and grandmother, who were all dependent on a family business not yet off the ground.

There was hardly time for Christopher Ahn and his family to process their loss. He and his mother were forced to focus on the business. The sudden change in circumstances carried enormous risk. They feared they'd lose their whole inventory in China if their suppliers learned that Young Chul had died suddenly, and they became nervous. Christopher and his mother, We Young Ahn, invented excuses every time one of the partners called to speak with them. Christopher took many of the calls, making decisions on fabric and quantities without batting an eye.

They kept up the charade for seven months, with Ahn attending high school by day and running the company by night. When the product finally made it to Los Angeles, Christopher and his mother flew to China, deciding it was time to come clean about Young Chul's death to their business associates. Their fears were unfounded. The men in charge at the Chinese suppliers wept over Young Chul's death and assured them they'd continue the relationship in his honor.

At school, Christopher had been known for a youthful, happy-go-lucky vibe, but after his father died and he took on the burden as part owner of the business, he became more serious. After high school and before he started college, Ahn joined the U.S. Marine Corps Reserve. "I wanted to find the fastest way of becoming a man," he recalled. Even while in boot camp, with his world expanding in some ways, Ahn's heavy early burden of responsibility remained. His mother sent clothing swatches to the boot camp mailroom so Christopher could make decisions about Zannini products. Seeing that he was helping run the family business during the intense and nonstop training, his drill instructors were taken aback.

After thirteen weeks of basic training at Marine Corps Recruit Depot San Diego, Ahn began his first semester of college in the fall of 2000 at the University of California, Irvine, studying political science.

One weekend every month he returned to Naval Weapons Station Seal Beach for training.

The Zannini business was chugging along and profitable during this time thanks to Ahn and his mother's efforts, but as the global retail market began to shift, they opted to sell it to the Chinese partners who made the clothes in 2003. That allowed Ahn to focus on his studies.

After finishing college, he was poised to take a sales job in Texas, which would have necessitated transferring to a new marine detachment there, when he heard that his fellow soldiers were about to deploy to Fallujah, Iraq, in 2005. The United States had just finished up one of the bloodier battles of the Iraq War there in what was known as Operation Phantom Fury, or the Second Battle of Fallujah. The city was badly damaged, reeling, and very dangerous.

Feeling loyalty to the men, many of whom looked up to him as an older brother figure, Ahn canceled the move to Texas and asked for a transfer back to his old unit. In 2005, a year after graduation, he went to Iraq, where he served as an intelligence analyst in Fallujah.

Over conversations with fellow marines during their downtime at their base, Ahn told the story of how his aunt was saved by a U.S. soldier during the Korean War. His grandmother was fleeing Seoul with her two daughters when she lost track of Christopher's aunt, who was just a toddler. Finding the soldier, she could only say in English, "Baby, baby!" The soldier understood and helped her find the child.

"That guy completely changed our lives," Ahn told them. "Our family looks at that soldier as a true hero."

It was one of the main reasons Ahn wanted to be a U.S. soldier, in addition to following in his father's footsteps. Young Chul impressed upon Christopher an appreciation of the opportunities available even to the newest immigrants in America. In Iraq, Ahn persuaded fellow marines to look at the local population as their main objective—protecting them, but also helping them rebuild.

After a nearly one-year deployment, he was finished with active service. Looking for something to do with his life after spending so much time in Iraq was a dizzying experience. In the end, he opted to do something that felt like a natural follow-up—an extension of his service—by joining a veterans advocacy group in Washington, D.C., called Vets for Freedom, which was run by David Bellavia, an army veteran and one of the only living Medal of Honor recipients. Bellavia and Ahn shared an apartment and would spend hours debating about war, but Bellavia gradually began to see things Ahn's way.

"I looked at the enemy as someone I had to pacify by killing them," Bellavia said. "For [Ahn], it was always about the people who were victimized. I've never met a person who wore the uniform who had so much empathy."

Funding for the organization dried up during the 2008 financial crisis, according to Ahn, and so he found himself for the first time in his life without a clear next move. What should he do with his life? Ahn considered applying to business school. Back in Los Angeles, his mother, We Young, was getting by on the proceeds of the Zannini sale and help from her sons. She still lived with her own mother, Ahn's grandmother. He felt adrift.

Most of all, Ahn felt energized to build something new. But what? That's when he met someone who would change his life.

AT MIDDAY ON APRIL 5, 2010, Adrian Hong ambled into a branch of Lolita's Mexican Food in northern San Diego. A few minutes later, Christopher Ahn, husky with an open grin, came in with a bearlike hand outstretched.

Over burritos in the no-frills chain famous for its carne asada fries, the two men started to get to know each other. They'd been introduced by a Korean American venture capitalist who knew both of them from different walks of life. He knew Adrian from his LiNK fundraising days. Ahn had written to the man out of the blue after reading his blog.

The two of them were in many ways the inverse of each other. To others, Adrian could appear cloaked in mystery and often spoke in the lofty tones of a civil rights campaigner. Ahn came off as humbler, more of an open-book type. Despite his powerful frame and ability to look imposing when he wasn't smiling, Ahn was a highly emotional and perceptive man with an entrepreneurial streak inherited from his dad. "I just want to help," Ahn would often tell people, rarely accepting compliments of any kind.

By then, Adrian had been out of LiNK for more than a year. Like Ahn, he was in the midst of figuring out a new phase. North Korea was on his mind, as always, but to make an impact he needed resources. Resources meant money.

Adrian had sought the guidance of a venture capitalist for a consulting business he had set up, Pegasus Strategies, the beginning of his long fascination with the mythical flying horse. This was Adrian's pure business side—helping companies get organized and setting up training—but he was plowing nearly all of the money he made into his extracurricular North Korea work. He was gifted at business, so much so that friends would later wonder what would have happened if he'd focused on building a technology company, rather than on North Korea.

During their lunch, Ahn, who had recently moved back to California after his advocacy job ended, asked Adrian for advice on getting into business. Should he do an MBA? Adrian was blunt. He told Ahn he saw no point in going to school, relating how he nearly dropped out of Yale because it was holding him back from doing what he wanted to do. "Business school is dumb," Adrian told him. "If you want to do something, do it now. If you have passion, people will share that passion with you."

Ahn couldn't help but smile at Adrian's confidence. They ate their food and shared a few stories. Ahn saw that Adrian was "quintessentially motivated to do good things." That appealed to Ahn, who was on the lookout for something "incremental that led to something positive."

Before they parted, Ahn turned to Adrian. "Hey, I know you are probably going to be doing a lot of other stuff in the future," he said, as the men gathered their belongings. "I'm interested in things like LiNK. If you need any help, let me know."

At the time, it seemed like an innocuous parting remark. Later, they'd realize it was the moment when their lives became intertwined and, later, upended.

Ahn ignored Adrian's advice and applied to the Darden School of Business at the University of Virginia.

But it would not be long before the men would meet again.

DESPITE HIS ANTI-BUSINESS-SCHOOL STANCE, Adrian wasn't entirely antiestablishment. After quitting LiNK, he was selected into the inaugural class of TED Fellows. A tech-savvy humanitarian with big ideas, he was a perfect fit for the program. By 2009, TED Talks were a household name thanks to the media entrepreneur Chris Anderson, whose nonprofit foundation had acquired the TED Conferences business from its two original founders eight years earlier and steadily built it into a juggernaut of videos and events featuring "the world's most inspired thinkers."

From that success the organization launched TED Fellows, a year-long program that funded a new generation of thinkers. With financial backing from Jeff Bezos, Google's charitable foundation, and others, the TED Fellows program followed the tradition of the great grant-giving programs for people looking to change the world, such as the famous "MacArthur Genius Grants."

But at TED, the focus was on younger achievers who were working on "world changing ideas." Applicants had to be between twenty-one and forty years old and have demonstrated "remarkable achievement" in their fields of endeavor. Instead of just showcasing ideas, TED was going to spur them. Of the fifty selected, twenty would be invited back as TED Senior Fellows for a three-year program where they'd receive support to attend conferences and continue to hone their ideas and projects.

"These men and women were selected for their achievement but especially for their promise," wrote Tom Rielly, the community director of TED Conferences, in a February 2009 email announcing Adrian's class of inaugural fellows. "Each of them shows real potential to create positive change . . . in their country, and even around the world."

In Adrian, the TED selection committee had been wowed by his planned Pegasus Project. In contrast to the business-consulting focus of the similarly named Pegasus Strategies, the Pegasus Project was squarely in the zone of Adrian's North Korea work. In articles and interviews over the years, he explained it in different ways. In 2009, he called it "part of an Underground Railroad for North Korean refugees," akin to the work LiNK had been doing.

But by 2010, when he was selected as one of the twenty inaugural TED Senior Fellows, he was emphasizing its technical focus, describing it in a TED brochure as "an initiative that uses cutting edge technology to penetrate closed societies and empower people in those nations to communicate amongst themselves, and with the outside world."

Using technology to fight the Kim regime was a thrilling and potentially transformative concept for Adrian after years of frustration trying to work from the outside—that is, through the byzantine constellation of nonprofits and religious groups focused on human rights in North Korea.

To Adrian, change in North Korea wasn't possible without widespread access to information. The Kim regime was so effective at controlling North Koreans because of its ruthlessness, but also its ability to keep the country fully disconnected from international culture and the true picture of life elsewhere. For ordinary North Korean citizens, it was easier to believe the state propaganda—something repeated and reinforced daily—than to stretch their minds to imagine the alien lands beyond the country's borders.

Thomas Schäfer, the former German ambassador to North Korea—who lived in the country for more than eight years at different points in the 2000s, the rare Western diplomat to be there that long—came to the conclusion that the system of North Korea was more powerful than the individuals in power at the top—the Kim family. That system had one core purpose: obedience.

"You exhaust them," he said, explaining the mentality of the regime. "You give them different tiring tasks all the time. You restrict them. That way they don't get any time to have novel ideas. They're so exhausted they conform."

There was, and is, perhaps no society on earth as closed as North Korea. It's been that way since the foundation of the country at the end of World War II, an inheritance from the megalomaniacal, controlling Kim Il-sung era.

Every day, North Koreans are expected to jot down in a special notebook how they failed to uphold their loyalty to the state and how anyone they knew fell short, according to escapees and North Korean human rights advocates. Then, once a week, after ideological lectures, they're required to publicly identify others who fell short. The system is both dangerous and utterly boring. The only way to survive is for people to agree in advance what little things they'll say about each other—serious enough to mention out loud but falling short of transgressions requiring disciplinary action.

On top of trying to pit neighbors against neighbors, the state weakens connections even within families. All North Koreans must join the military for seven years after finishing high school graduation, and it's usually the case that they don't see their families at all during that time, according to North Korean human rights groups. It's not uncommon for North Koreans to never once in their lifetimes leave the city where they were born, even to see a grandparent in another village or city.

The nation's past leaders are worshipped with religious fervor. North Korea's founding leader, Kim Il-sung, is known as the Great Leader, and his son Kim Jong-il as Dear Leader. Every day at 6:00 A.M., an instrumental version of a song called "Where Are You, Dear General?" blasts through loudspeakers in Pyongyang. The song was originally part of a 1971 opera called *A True Daughter of the Party;* later, government officials rewrote history to say that it was composed by Kim Jong-il himself. No adult citizen would be caught going out without their "Dear Leader" pin affixed to their chest.

Propaganda is unceasing. One side of the propaganda operation is to reinforce the nation's leadership mythology. The other side is to block out the rest of the world, something that feels inconceivable in the great interconnectedness of the late twentieth and early twenty-first centuries, when information beams across the globe nearly instantly.

The only news sources are state-controlled newspapers, including *Rodong Sinmun* (Labor Paper), the official mouthpiece of the Central Committee of the Workers' Party of Korea, the country's top government body. In news footage from North Korea, riders on Pyongyang's subway are shown standing around a copy of the day's edition of the newspaper taped inside a glass case. The infallibility of the regime is blasted at all times on the radio and television. Nothing passes into the minds of a North Korean citizen that isn't first bent and twisted by the regime's propaganda machine.

Most North Koreans have no access to a computer, much less anything like the internet. Only the top echelon of society would be able to access the domestic-only network called Kwangmyong. According to testimony from escapees later given to human rights groups, some citizens of distant agrarian areas are even barred from visiting big cities like Pyongyang because of their "hostile" status. They barely have a sense of the contours of their own country, much less an awareness of such a thing as the internet.

The internet is accessible to only a tiny group of officials and foreign diplomats living in Pyongyang. The infamous North Korean hackers almost exclusively work from locations abroad in coordination with intelligence and officials at embassies, according to a *Wall Street Journal* investigation into the practices of the hackers. At the time of Adrian's initial work with the Pegasus Project, the country had only just gained access to the internet at all via a joint venture with a Thailand-based company. By the end of 2014, there were only 1,024 IP addresses in North Korea—enough to support thousands of internet users within government ministries.

Yet information seems to find a way. Many of the televisions in North Korea come from China and have USB ports that allow people to watch films and TV shows on flash drives. This has created a booming business in smuggling in and trading illicit media, especially near the Chinese border, where North Koreans can see with their own eyes just across the Yalu River the bright lights of the city of Dandong.

Entertainment, Adrian and others believed, was a powerful tool in weakening the regime. Even Kim Jong-il understood the power of the silver screen, devoting significant resources to the production of North Korean films that were emotional and patriotic at the same time.

The best way to show North Koreans a glimpse of life outside was South Korean TV shows and movies. They were easier for their intended recipients to understand and possible to sneak into North Korea through smuggling networks. Activists in South Korea were also known to try more outlandish mechanisms of distribution, like floating balloons over the border.

At one point, Adrian connected with like-minded activists in South Korea, in particular a group called Fighters for a Free North Korea that gained attention for its controversial project to attach DVDs, transistor radios, and USB flash drives to balloons and send them into North Korea from strategic locations in the South. The group drew the ire of North Korea for challenging the regime, but also of South Korea, for endangering the residents living near the border and needlessly bringing North-South tensions to a boil.

With gaps forming in the great firewall, Adrian's hope—the idea that animated his TED fellowship—was to find new ways to beam even more information into North Korea in the hopes of inspiring North Koreans to rise up. With political organizing at an impasse, technology as the solution seemed like a refreshing direction.

One of Adrian's ideas was to get well-resourced donors to help finance a kind of pirate internet in North Korea—transmitting it from a satellite so that anyone with a Wi-Fi-enabled device could access a truer picture of what's happening in their own country and the world. But as was often the case for his projects, ideas were the easy part.

In a speech at the Hackers for Human Rights gathering in New York in July 2010, wearing a blue shirt, clean-shaven and hair-gelled, he told an audience of activists and technologists about his vision for empowering human rights workers around the world with safer ways of communicating and operating in dangerous environments.

He called on members of the conference to help build tools to circumvent firewalls and anonymize their communications to prevent dissidents and activists from being arrested for expressing their views. He asked for people to speak to him afterward so he could share more specific actions, because he couldn't reveal them "on camera."

Once he finished with his discussions about human rights in the world and technology, Adrian gave his most distilled views yet on how he was approaching his lifelong quest to make a difference for the North Korean people. Referring to his own journey, he said that two years earlier—around the time he was leaving LiNK—he had an epiphany.

As inspiration for their efforts, many activists would invoke the oft-repeated refrain "What would their children think of their actions when they looked back years later?" For Adrian, he explained to the audience, the question wasn't about the next generation; it was about the very purpose of mankind.

"What have we done with this great civilization, gleaming skyscrapers and modern technology, if people are still having limbs hacked off while their families watch just because they speak a different language," he told the audience. Doing nothing, to Adrian, was not much better than supporting the evil side of humanity.

The second part of his realization in 2008, he said, was based on Martin Luther King Jr.'s final speech before he was assassinated.

Dr. King gave a novel interpretation of the parable of the Good Samaritan from the Bible, where a down-and-out traveler is lying half-dead along the road. First a Jewish priest walked by and then a Levite came by, but they avoided the man. The third, a Samaritan, stopped to help him.

The traditional interpretation was to look at the Samaritan as the hero because he stopped to help, but Dr. King gave a deeper interpretation. Both the priest and the Levite might have had good reasons to not stop, worrying about making it in time to give a sermon or fearing he was dangerous. They thought, if I stop to help this man, what could happen to me?

The Samaritan's innovation, Dr. King argued, was to ask a different question: If I do not stop to help this man, what will happen to him?

For Adrian, this was the question he wanted to answer. The idea would drive him to pursue liberation in North Korea, no matter the consequences. It was an idea that "changes everything," Adrian told the crowd of hackers in New York.

With technology beaming human rights abuses to the world in real time, how could we—the passersby—not stop to help, no matter the risk? he implored.

"If we don't stop to help these people, what will happen to them?" he asked.

FOR ADRIAN, IDEAS WERE flowing, but funds and willing partners were harder to find. The tension between his aspirations and the reality of twenty-first-century activism caused Adrian a lot of headaches.

One of those who saw Adrian struggle with this tension up close was Michael Horowitz, a Jewish human rights activist who ran the International Religious Liberty Project at a conservative think tank called the Hudson Institute. Horowitz and Adrian had bonded over Adrian's efforts to pressure the Bush administration to treat North Koreans as refugees.

Horowitz was well known in Washington for his ability to persuade disparate parties from different faiths and political persuasions to coalesce around a unified project. After the 2004 North Korean Human Rights Act, Horowitz wanted to push activists, priests, and humanitarians to fight the Kim regime even harder and to focus on the conflict over the atrocious human rights abuses under way in North Korea.

In Adrian, he saw a potential leader, someone who could help put a bigger spotlight on these efforts. Horowitz even told him he could be the first Korean American president, seemingly not realizing Adrian's Mexican birthplace would bar him from running.

Their exchanges could sometimes be testy, albeit respectful. "I was constantly ragging him," Horowitz recalled. "Adrian, you have the intelligence, the drive, the skill, to become a historic figure. We can take down this regime. . . . But for him it was just a bridge too far. He was reluctant to be the spokesman for it."

Horowitz appreciated Adrian's sacrifices, even if the younger man wasn't willing to be a public face in the mold Horowitz hoped for. To Horowitz, it was clear Adrian could have made a killing if he'd simply gone into banking or law. Yet here he was with his Ivy League credentials throwing everything into the cause.

One exchange between the two men from November 12, 2009, is a window into Adrian's mindset. After prodding from Horowitz earlier in the evening about the lack of leadership among Korean Americans on North Korea, Adrian responded at 10:12 P.M.:

> no one voted me president of the korean american community. I don't have an answer to your gripes about the broader community, and I share the disappointments on a deeper level than even you. I am trying to get them on board, and I'm not holding my breath either. I realize you're frustrated, but you should know that taking out your frustrations with scathing attacks of the messengers will win you no allies.

Horowitz responded at 10:49 P.M.:

> when will you—or any korean american leader—risk isolation and failure by risking acts of leadership that don't involve backward looks to see where others may be?

Sounding chastened, Adrian responded at 11:17 P.M.:

> I have stopped holding my breath years ago. I ended up in a jail cell in china for it, but I have no regrets, and would do it again in a second. when you say "don't wait, just do", I'm not sure what you really mean. we've dived into the underground boldly—perhaps too boldly, and paid the price for it, but we continue to work there. but how can we lead in a community movement without SOME waiting? I can issue as many press releases and call for as many meetings as I'd like, but if no one shows up, where are we then? there is a slow churn in the korean american community, and has been for years. many of the funders and backers of pioneers in the underground have been korean american. and the people I am waiting on are not church leaders or coalition presidents, they're people who can very literally help us get the fuel to move the car forward. my own lingering in the community is because of a very personal heartbreak—they are quite literally my family, so the moral ambivalence (and cowardice) is all the more devastating.

Perhaps weighing on Adrian's mind, and adding to the pressure he felt, was the fact that he had just gotten married to W. in August, a few months before this exchange with Horowitz. There was no doubt he'd pursue his dream of fighting for the liberation of North Korea, but he also had to think of his new family.

Adrian was a man of growing stature in the world, someone with an expanding contact book of important people, but to his old mentor Jae Ku, the man who'd fronted Liberty in North Korea money when it was first starting out, Adrian was still a young guy trying to make it in the world.

Whenever Ku saw Adrian, even as Adrian notched his TED fellowship and other recognition, Ku continued to see the young man as a college student and ended their lunch by giving him whatever money was in his wallet.

"I figured, hey, you don't have much of an income, hopefully this will pay for a couple of meals," he remembered. "I think he really appreciated that."

Then, one night a few months after one such visit in 2010, Adrian was up late on his computer with the television playing in the background. On came an advertisement for a box of tools for woodworking—Ku's hobby.

Adrian ordered it immediately and had it shipped to Ku. "I thought you'd like it," he told him.

The act was characteristic of Adrian's impulsive generosity—a trait that left a mark on many people who entered his life, no matter how briefly.

7

HORREYA

Now that we have come out of hiding,
Why would we live again in the tombs we'd made
out of our souls?

—KHALED MATTAWA

DUBAI
2011

"THIS IS HOW THE REGIME GETS HARD CURRENCY," ADRIAN WHISpered to his new acquaintance, Ousama Abushagur, from across the table.

The men were meeting in Dubai, inside a restaurant called Pyongyang Okryu-gwan, which translates to "jade stream pavilion." The restaurant sat in the heart of Deira, the old part of Dubai. It's a short walk to the Emirati city's famous creek, which is still full of wooden dhows that travel back and forth to Iran laden with televisions, washing machines, and other wares.

The restaurant, which later closed during the COVID-19 pandemic, was actually a branch of a long-running Pyongyang establishment that specializes in *Pyongyang naengmyeon*, buckwheat noodles served in chilled broth. The original location in North Korea's capital seated more than two thousand patrons, and branches have been opened throughout Asia, in Kathmandu and Beijing. A *Washington Post* piece from 2016 put the number of North Korean restaurants abroad at over a hundred. According to a report in the South Korean newspaper *Chosun Ilbo*, each branch contributes up to $300,000 to the regime in North Korea. Though a relative pittance, even that much money is important to the heavily sanctioned government.

Selling buckwheat noodles was one of the stranger activities affiliated with the North Korean government's secretive "Room 39," a bureau charged with bringing in hundreds of millions of dollars a year for the regime. It's one of three "third floor" bureaus, called that because they originally were on the third floor of the Workers' Party building in Pyongyang, according to testimony from the former North Korean general and politician Kim Kwang-jin. To get foreign currency for the Kim family and the regime's inner circle, Room 39 pursued moneymaking ventures including selling heroin, insurance fraud, and counterfeiting from its network abroad.

There was no communist kitsch to be found inside the Pyongyang Okryu-gwan restaurant in Dubai. Instead, the proprietors emphasize natural imagery. There was a large painting of Mount Baekdu—a volcanic mountain that straddles the border with China and is the mythical cradle of the Korean people and the North Korean leadership—and another of a tiger. Waitresses wore pink dresses, seemingly in pointed contrast to the stereotype of austere North Korean diplomats. At the end of a dinner, the all-female waitstaff picked up guitars and microphones, belting out North Korean songs in an hour-long show.

Inside the Dubai location in May 2011, Adrian and Abushagur dined on kimchi and *galbi,* a popular dish of barbecued beef short ribs. Leaning a little closer, Adrian informed his companion that North Korean spies and arms dealers were known to frequent the restaurant to strike deals. Abushagur could tell Adrian enjoyed the thrill of visiting an establishment where a tinge of danger hung in the air—where the staff and patrons, some of them a tad suspicious looking themselves, had no idea Adrian had dedicated his life to dismantling their Dear Leader's regime.

The two had first met only weeks earlier over Twitter.

In April, Adrian was sitting in his Brooklyn walk-up apartment when he came across a story about Abushagur, the tech-savvy son of a Libyan dissident, in *The Wall Street Journal.* The article described how Abushagur had worked with other rebels to obtain aid from the United Arab Emirates. and Qatar to set up their own phone network in Libya, a crucial step that allowed the ragtag militias fighting the regime to communicate over cell phones without worrying that spies for the nation's feared ruler Muammar Gaddafi were listening in.

First sparked in Tunisia, pro-democracy demonstrations had spread across the Middle East like a wildfire. Decades of built-up anger over corruption and autocratic governments exploded on the streets as massive protests that included violent confrontations with police. Seemingly all-powerful men like Zine El Abidine Ben Ali in Tunisia and Hosni Mubarak in Egypt had no choice but to step down, while others like Libya's Muammar Gaddafi and Syria's Bashar al-Assad cracked down viciously on their populations.

From the beginning of the Arab Spring, Adrian was an unabashed supporter. He wrote an op-ed in *The Christian Science Monitor* on January 31, 2011, calling on the administration of Barack Obama to offer its support to the protesters and rebels rising up across the Middle East.

In the piece, he asked, "Does the United States exist as any nation does—simply to protect its own citizens, borders, and strategic interests? Or are we something more—a nation and people that considers, as President John F. Kennedy once said, 'the survival and success of liberty' to be a foundational objective?"

The creation of rebel mobile networks in Libya using donated equipment, stacks of cash, and savvy engineering was of particular interest to Adrian because he foresaw something similar happening in North Korea. When—never *if,* in Adrian's telling—the Kim regime fell, he was fascinated about what he and his growing band of volunteers could do on the ground to stabilize the country.

After reading the *Journal* piece, Adrian got in touch with Abushagur, saying he wanted to meet and help in whatever way he could. Abushagur told him he was based in the U.A.E. Days later, on April 24, 2011, Adrian showed up in Dubai to meet him. "He was the kind of person to make a decision and go," Abushagur remembered.

The pair immediately hit it off. They were both driven by a passion to help the citizens of oppressed regimes to shake off the yoke of dictatorship and believed technology could play a critical role. Adrian's ambitions felt a bit bigger and riskier. He immediately drew Abushagur into his collection of global contacts with different skills and networks, a core component of Adrian's underground work.

Abushagur had studied engineering at the University of Alabama in Huntsville and had worked for years in telecommunications and software. Now serving as a TED Senior Fellow, Adrian also spoke the language of technology. His Pegasus Project, set up to help spread information in closed societies, was the kind of project Abushagur was eager to embrace.

Adrian was especially fascinated by his new friend's father. Mustafa Abushagur, a lifelong opponent of the Gaddafi regime, was a founding member of the National Front for the Salvation of Libya. A professor of electrical engineering and entrepreneur, Mustafa had earned a PhD from Caltech in 1984. Over dinners and weekends throughout his childhood, Ousama had watched his father debate with friends about how to take on the Gaddafi government; it seemed all the more amazing because they were living in places like Huntsville and Rochester in the United States and working day jobs to support their families at the same time. For Adrian, this was validation of a longtime belief: anyone could play a part in shaping history if they committed to a cause, no matter how small they start out.

Now with the Gaddafi regime on the run, Mustafa Abushagur and his old friends were suddenly being treated by governments around the world as the rightful representatives of Libya. There was no formal process for being recognized except for their stating confidently that they were the National Transitional Council (NTC) of Libya and that they'd hold elections once the civil war was won. (Mustafa Abushagur would briefly serve as the country's prime minister in 2012, after the fall of the Gaddafi regime.)

After their meeting at the North Korean restaurant in Dubai, Adrian and Ousama Abushagur communicated frequently over email and Google Chat about projects they could launch in Libya. Abushagur explained his next project was to set up another rebel phone network closer to Tripoli in Misrata, a crucial step to allowing the NTC forces to organize their final series of assaults on Gaddafi redoubts. Adrian tried to find donors for the project, but in the end Abushagur received donations from the Abu Dhabi telecommunications company Etisalat. At the time, the U.A.E. government was supporting the rebels against Gaddafi.

In July, Abushagur took a thirty-hour ride on a fishing boat from Malta to Misrata. With satellite dishes, batteries, and "rapid-deployment kits" designed for getting communications going during natural disasters, Abushagur brought the system online in a month. At one point, he was forced to wait for a week on the fishing boat until a missing component was quickly flown from the United States to Malta and transported into Libya on another fishing boat.

By then, Adrian was getting a serious itch to join the fray, even if initially he was just an on-the-ground observer. The civil war in Libya was cresting, and for Adrian it could have been a rare chance to see a closed society enter the global order again, minus its strongman dictator. Across the region, there was hope and vibrant debate over the shape of the future and what their uprisings might mean for others shackled by autocracies around the world.

When Tripoli fell to the rebels in late August, Adrian and Abushagur agreed they'd travel into the capital together as soon as possible.

ON SEPTEMBER 18, 2011, Adrian stepped onto an airplane at Malta International Airport. It had propellers and just enough room to fit two dozen people at most. On the tail were the letters WFP: World Food Program, the branch of the United Nations that focused on food-security issues around the world.

Adrian, still just twenty-seven years old, and Ousama Abushagur, thirty-one, were headed to Tripoli, the onetime stronghold of Muammar Gaddafi that had fallen to rebel forces just three weeks earlier.

The WFP plane, operated by the United Nations Humanitarian Air Service (UNHAS), allowed humanitarians and journalists free passage when it had extra space. UNHAS had only just started flying into Tripoli carrying aid, UN staff, and international diplomats. Abushagur, as part of the Libyan opposition, had secured two spots for the men.

It was a heady and thrilling time in Tripoli. Gaddafi's forces had made a rapid escape to Sirte in the middle of the country, where they'd hold out for just one more month before the dramatic end of the first phase of the Libyan civil war, when Gaddafi was chased out of a drainpipe and killed by rebels.

In Tripoli, tough-looking Libyan fighters (mostly in their teens and twenties) spent much of their days posing on top of pickup trucks and bickering with each other over territory—an early harbinger of the debilitating infighting between them over the country's future in the years to come.

This was Adrian's first time anywhere near a war zone. Tripoli was relatively quiet after Gaddafi's forces were routed by Operation Mermaid Dawn, a secret invasion of the city by armed rebels who triggered a massive, widespread uprising that was wildly successful. But there was gunfire night and day by rebels pointing their guns skyward. Dozens of people were hit by the falling bullets during those joyous first few weeks. Hotel rooms often had a smattering of bullet holes in the windows.

From the lens of a North Korea watcher, the situation on the ground in Libya was hugely inspiring. Here was the Middle East's own hermit kingdom completely overrun by its citizens while its autocratic leader, with similar delusions of grandeur as the Kim dynasty potentates, was running away in fear. The mechanisms of mind and physical control fell apart more rapidly than anyone could have imagined.

If Libyans could do it, maybe North Koreans had a chance, too.

During the week Adrian was in Tripoli, he met with members of the transitional government and enjoyed seeing the fruits of the revolution. Adrian began organizing with another TED Fellow named Suleiman Bakhit to get injured fighters from Misrata to Jordan for medical treatment. Misratans underwent some of the worst fighting of the whole civil war, and many were missing limbs and dealing with other grievous injuries.

In the evenings and late into the night, Adrian and Abushagur would talk about the lessons of the Libyan experience, including the way that information about the West seeping into the country over the years began to weaken the bedrock of the regime. Young Libyans were much more exposed to the world than any North Korean. They had Facebook. They were fans of Justin Bieber, and, oddly out of time, the television show *Friends* had become a phenomenon in the 2000s in Libya.

One night they drove down to Abushagur's family's hometown of Gharyan for a party celebrating the fall of Tripoli. It was an immensely refreshing and inspiring visit, seeing all the previously cloistered citizens waving the new flag of Libya and chattering excitedly until the early hours of the morning.

As Adrian met NTC members, however, he was interested in all the mundane details as much as the big sweeping concepts. He wanted to know how they were funding themselves, keeping track of money, and distributing it, as well as how they were interacting with foreign governments and establishing their legitimacy. Years later, Abushagur reflected on how the gears were turning in Adrian's head.

"He realized that no one is going to do something for the betterment of your country other than the people inside it," Abushagur said. "No one is going to do the hard part for you."

One of Adrian's biggest challenges had always been financial. He was awash in big ideas and ambitious projects, but had little funding to pull any of them off. His credit cards were maxed out to the tune of more than $10,000 from self-funding his North Korean projects, friends said.

Adrian took notice of the way that foreign governments were pouring money into the NTC. If he could just spark some kind of movement, he was confident money would start to flow and groups like his banding together could take out the Kims once and for all.

One day toward the end of the trip, Adrian dragged Abushagur along for a meeting at the North Korean embassy in Tripoli. Gaddafi developed close ties with North Korea during the 1970s and 1980s as part of his efforts to create a bloc of countries opposed to Western dominance. Libya was one of the larger buyers of North Korean weapons, and several hundred North Koreans lived in Libya, mostly as cheap construction labor that brought foreign currency home to North Korea.

When they went inside the embassy, Adrian introduced Abushagur as a member of the new government and asked about North Korea's ability to supply construction labor for the rebuilding of Libya.

The meeting was a ruse. It technically brought Adrian onto North Korean soil and gave him a chance to study the behavior of North Korean diplomats up close.

Adrian was using Libya as a training ground for his bigger ambitions. The country's civil war allowed him to operate in a wilder territory and liaise with government figures and rebels, all the while thinking through the parallels for North Korea.

AROUND THE TIME THAT the Arab Spring was kicking off, there were murmurs from North Korea watchers about Kim Jong-il and the country's succession plans.

The Dear Leader hadn't been himself since a debilitating stroke in 2008. The way the country had shifted in the aftermath had convinced the German ambassador to North Korea, Thomas Schäfer, that the established perspective on rule in North Korea was completely wrong.

For years, countless observers had described the country as being ruled by a powerful dynasty whose leaders wielded nearly unfettered and uncontested control. Yet, living in Pyongyang, reading in between the lines of the state propaganda outlets, and parsing the words of his interlocutors in the city, Schäfer began to believe that the real power brokers were the unsmiling, anonymous cadre of top officials behind the throne.

For example, in the autumn of 2007, Kim Jong-il—still in good health—reached an agreement at the inter-Korean summit to allow private investment into North Korea. The deal was done—or so it first appeared. Soon after the announcement, the state newspapers began describing foreign investment as a way to undermine North Korea's government. It was a hidden threat to the *juche* mentality, editorials argued.

A few months later on New Year's Day 2008, a new decision was handed down: economic gains and profits for North Korean enterprises were good, but foreign investment wouldn't be allowed.

"Kim Jong-il agreed to a policy that was questioned later, and then he was rebuked by what you might call the leadership of the country," Schäfer said. "The policy was reversed."

Then, late that summer, Kim Jong-il had his stroke. Immediately, one of his sons, Kim Jong-un, stepped into the light as the likely heir. As with his father before him, Kim Jong-un started taking on bigger roles and responsibilities. The military pledged allegiance to him in December 2008. On January 8 of the next year, Kim Jong-il informed his control tower on personnel matters, the Organization and Guidance Department, that his youngest son, Jong-un, would be his successor.

But, again, Schäfer was startled to watch the policy changes that blossomed during a period of weakness in the Kim dynasty. Throughout 2009, the military and ultraconservative forces in the government pushed through a markedly different agenda from what Kim Jong-il had been angling toward before his stroke.

There was an uptick in ballistic and nuclear tests. The long-running six-party talks were canceled. The country's economic policies tightened, including a currency reform that gave a hard blow to the new class of traders who were instrumental in bringing market-like experiences to North Korea. And the population came under stricter control, with more military leadership appearing on television and in state newspapers.

From Schäfer's perspective, it was not just the beginning of a drift toward more hard-line views in the country but an affirmation of the hidden politics of North Korea. The misunderstanding of that power dynamic was at the root of failed diplomacy with North Korea over decades.

ON DECEMBER 17, 2011, Kim Jong-il died of a heart attack. Twelve days later, a painstakingly choreographed funeral procession wended through the snow-dusted boulevards of downtown Pyongyang, with mourners lining each side, howling with grief. The chosen successor, his son Kim Jong-un, walked alongside the hearse.

The dictator's death created what many observers saw as a possible period of weakness in the government. Would Kim Jong-un assume the mantle of his father and grandfather? Or did the vacuum create an opening, as some more hawkish North Korea thinkers hoped, for a change—something that would weaken the grip of the all-powerful Workers' Party of Korea on the necks of citizens?

In fact, the world's top intelligence agencies were often taken aback by developments in North Korea, former officials said. Family dynamics and national security decision-making are so closely guarded that the best insights tend to be accidental. Most of the best insights into these officials are from teachers and classmates who met them without knowing who they were. The Kim regime does seem to know that its leaders can't simply drink the government's Kool-Aid. As a child, Kim Jong-un, together with his brother and sister, was sent abroad to Switzerland to get a deeper understanding of what the world is really like.

Back in Cairo, I wrote to Adrian to ask him what he was thinking. The impromptu interview would end up providing one of the fullest insights into his thinking ever published. Soon after, he began avoiding media requests and events as he moved deeper into the shadows.

At 1:32 A.M. in New York, he logged on to Google Chat to talk while his wife, W., slept in the next room.

On the Pegasus Project, he explained that it worked in closed societies. "A lot of the work I do ends up being vague publicly by default because of the subject matter and risks involved," he wrote, by way of explaining his history with LiNK and his arrest in China.

On North Korea, his view was that Kim Jong-un's rise to take over as Supreme Leader had long been planned, so the transition would be smooth. The death might have hit the world by surprise, but the party leadership had known long before that it was a likely scenario. They'd hoarded food for months so that one of Kim Jong-un's first acts would be increasing rations and goods—an immediate win for the new leader.

Explaining his work in the Middle East to me, he said, "I consider the Arab Spring a dress rehearsal for North Korea."

Adrian: North Korea is a far more lethal, prepared and massive opponent for the people than Syria, Libya, Egypt, Tunisia or Yemen. By far.

> In every category. Pervasiveness of public security and secret policy, size of military and mobilization, hopelessness and general impoverished and malnourished state of the people.

Me: Yet, do you get the feeling or do you know that there are internal movements interested in regime change?

Adrian: There are and have always been, but they have been crushed or in hiding.

> This month there was a report [*sic*] armed North Korean soldiers defected to China and disappeared.

> There are also tens of thousands of refugees that are in exile who are all invested in change in Pyongyang, many with family left behind or imprisoned in concentration camps.

He went on to explain how he believed that no North Korean leader would ever reform the country by choice.

> *Adrian:* They've gone too far—public executions, mass concentration camps, systematically starving segments of disloyal individuals.
> > North Korea is the International Criminal Court's wet dream.
> > They know any opening with reforms would also mean an opening to crimes against humanity charges on a staggering scale, domestically and internationally.
> > They've also seen what happened to Ben Ali, Mubarak and especially Gaddafi this year.

Before logging off, Adrian offered me an indication of what he was planning to do next.

> *Adrian:* Governments and critical agencies have been perpetually unprepared for a potential collapse or instability in North Korea. This is time to revisit those plans and make sure they're up to par.
> > The next six months will afford an extraordinary opportunity for dissidents and freedom activists as well to press for change.

Years later, it would become clear that Libya's transition was not the success story it seemed at the time it might become. A brief unity government fell apart as infighting between militias in different regions over the future and the country's money divided it into a patchwork of fiefdoms. As of early 2022, Gaddafi's son Seif al-Islam had gone from being a prisoner of a group of freedom fighters to their leader as he began a quest to become the second Gaddafi to rule Libya.

———

SOON AFTER RETURNING FROM his first trip to Libya, Adrian, working with his friend Ousama Abushagur, set in motion plans to host a TEDx conference in Tripoli. This was another way to get involved in the country's unprecedented chance to rethink what its future might look like now that it was free from the old regime and a way for him to overtly bring North Korea into the discussion.

The event kicked off on February 13, 2012, in the upscale Rixos Hotel in Tripoli. Speakers included the Harvard Business School professor Bruce Scott, who gave an inspiring talk about capitalism and democracy, as well as Hannah Song, the head of LiNK since Adrian's resignation, who made the trip over to talk about the possibility of a similar kind of regime change in North Korea.

As Song began her presentation, a slide bearing the title CHANGING NORTH KOREA loomed behind her. Below the headline were two words and an arrow:

Impossible → Inevitable

"Many people have written off North Korea, saying it is hopeless, it's unchanging and impossible, but I'm here to tell you today that North Korea is changing and that it's being driven by the people," she declared.

For Adrian Hong, listening in on Song's presentation, "inevitable" did not imply wait and see. Like the vegetable seller in Tunisia who set himself on fire, helping trigger the Arab Spring, Adrian believed that individual actions must be the sparks of change.

8

ABOVEGROUND, BELOWGROUND

The aim of totalitarian education has never been to instill convictions but to destroy the capacity to form any.

—*HANNAH ARENDT*

WASHINGTON, D.C.
SEPTEMBER 2012

NEXT TO THE DIMINUTIVE JOSEPH KIM, ONE OF THE FIRST NORTH Koreans LiNK helped bring to the United States back in 2006, Adrian Hong looked like a giant. He also looked the part of what his friends liked to call "the suit."

His hair slicked back and beard trimmed into a goatee, wearing a black suit and striped salmon-colored tie, Adrian gave his standard stump speech on North Korea—one he'd given hundreds of times by now—while still sounding energized and impassioned.

"This is not a problem that will go away," he told the crowd of onlookers at the Hudson Institute in Washington. "At some point it will have a hard or soft landing. At some point those people will be free. The question mark is how many people will need to die until we get to that point."

The event was ostensibly to celebrate the publication of the journalist Melanie Kirkpatrick's book *Escape from North Korea,* about the underground network helping escapees get to South Korea or the West. It was a classic think tank policy breakfast in a big wood-paneled room, complete with free coffee and Danish at a table. The crowd included policy bigwigs, current and former diplomats, and academics. It was a world Adrian knew all too well by now. It was the "aboveground" world he occupied all the time.

But there was also an underground, an inverse life of "the suit." Adrian had become accustomed to passing back and forth between these two worlds, but the balance of time he spent in each was beginning to change.

By late 2012, Adrian had launched a secret organization he called Cheollima Civil Defense. Cheollima is a mythical horse of Korean lore, frequently depicted in posters with wings like Adrian's favorite Pegasus from Greek mythology. Cheollima means 1,000 *li,* a Chinese unit of distance that is roughly 0.31 mile, or half a kilometer. The mythical horse could race 1,000 *li* in a day—an impressive distance, but not outrageously high.

Until now, Adrian had separated his life into two buckets: his business consultancy, Pegasus Strategies, where he earned his money; and his nonprofit Pegasus Project, which developed creative means of spreading information in totalitarian states. Now he had added a third bucket—a far more secretive one.

By now, Cheollima Civil Defense counted just a handful of people as members, including a childhood friend of Adrian's and other hardcore activists, academics, and even a few businesspeople who shared the same driving desire to make a difference. The common denominator was an immense sadness about North Korea and a frustration with the way the "aboveground" organizations were progressing with the cause. Many, Adrian felt, had become addicted to donations and government funding, which they used to operate policy breakfasts and write reports.

By now, a decade had passed since Adrian had read *The Aquariums of Pyongyang* and become fixated on the North Korean cause. With the intervening years, however, little had changed. Western policy makers were still focused on framing the issue as a rogue state with nuclear weapons. At think tank events like the one at the Hudson Institute, Adrian and others, like Joseph Kim, would field invitations to talk about North Korean human rights, but to Adrian it felt like window dressing. Policy makers still approached North Korea as a puzzle best addressed with a dose of game theory—mathematical models used to study conflict and cooperation among decision makers.

With North Korea, game theory suggested the United States should engage in a series of bluffs with Kim Jong-un's government in order to push it toward choosing to denuclearize. Diplomats argued that a steady, firm approach would eventually yield results. Yet those efforts had failed across the board. Not only did denuclearization talks fail, but the country amassed even more warheads, more powerful rockets, and systems for using nuclear weapons.

For North Korea, belligerence was working. "They want both nuclear weapons and normal relations with the United States," said Joseph DeTrani, a former CIA official who spent much of his time between 2003 and 2016 working on the U.S.–North Korea talks. "They feel they will accomplish that by staying the course."

Over the course of 2012, the U.S.–North Korea roller-coaster ride was a perfect example of the circular nature of talks between the great powers. In January 2012, North Korean citizens were banned from using their mobile phones for a hundred days in honor of the late Kim Jong-il. By February, an eighteen-foot statue and a nearly four-hundred-foot rock carving were unveiled on what would have been his seventieth birthday.

Then there was a flicker of hope about the possibility of a new round of talks in February. On the twenty-ninth, North Korea even went so far as to announce it was suspending its nuclear-weapon and ballistic-missile tests and uranium enrichment while also granting international inspectors access to its nuclear sites.

Like clockwork, it all came undone with a new round of provocations. Just two weeks later, North Korea announced a long-range rocket launch, and Barack Obama, on a visit to Seoul, said, "North

Korea will achieve nothing by threats." In April, the rocket test failed, and North Korea declared the nuclear suspension it announced in February off the table, again.

While the civil war in Libya inspired Adrian to dream about an eventual uprising in North Korea, the same conflict inspired North Korea to distrust any long-term promises of the United States. The United States, the U.K., and other world powers had improved relations with Libya starting in the late 1990s. Gaddafi even condemned publicly the September 11 attacks on the United States by al-Qaeda and pledged Libya's assistance in the forthcoming "War on Terror."

By 2006, Libya was removed from the U.S. list of state sponsors of terrorism. At the time of the outbreak of the civil war in 2011, Gaddafi's son Khamis was on a tour of the United States as part of his internship at AECOM Technology Corporation. Another son, Seif al-Islam, armed with a degree from the London School of Economics, was marketed as the reformer who was going to turn the country into a replica of the United Arab Emirates—a place of modernity and moderation.

The reversal came quickly. Soon after the uprising, the United States dropped its support for the Gaddafi regime and gave the rebels the key military support that made it possible for them to seize the country. A NATO air strike allegedly struck a convoy with Khamis just eight months later, killing him.

For the North Koreans, these events were considered crucial intelligence on how the sweet-talking Westerners actually viewed their new "friends" who came into the fold and played ball on American terms, according to former intelligence officials who focused on North Korea. Not only second-class, they were also disposable when the opportunity came knocking.

That experience, together with the rise of the young Kim Jong-un as heir, further emboldened North Korea to tighten its grip on its nuclear weapons. The hard-right military contingent was clearly ascendant in the waning days of Kim Jong-il's rule and early days of his son's rise, more proof for the then German ambassador to North

Korea, Thomas Schäfer, that the country's true power lay out of view, just behind the leader.

After Kim Jong-il's death, there was a huge intensification of the "military first" policy. Schäfer observed increases in Pyongyang's control over its population, with fewer refugees able to escape and more interference from government minders on diplomats like himself. Suddenly North Korean officials started complaining about embassy officers using Wi-Fi within the embassy compound. "They were afraid North Koreans might get onto the internet," he said.

The purge got started in earnest even before Kim Jong-il's death in 2011. Some thirty officials involved in North Korea's talks with South Korea either were executed or died in "staged traffic accidents" in 2010, according to Amnesty International. The disappearances came on top of an earlier cohort of two hundred, who were rounded up immediately after Kim Jong-il's death and vanished.

It was clear North Korea was entering a dangerous new leadership phase.

For idealists such as Adrian, the obsession with viewing North Korea as a "prisoner's dilemma" saga of global implications was excruciating. As his speech at the Hudson Institute suggested, he believed the fall of the Workers' Party of Korea was inevitable and coming soon. Why wait if it means another generation of North Korean children are brainwashed and enslaved?

Cheollima Civil Defense was Adrian's antidote to such navel-gazing and war-gaming. In the beginning, it was about intelligence gathering. If there's one thing Adrian was talented at, it was traveling long distances, meeting people from across the spectrum, giving them his time, and developing relationships. For every North Korean escapee, humanitarian worker, and official, Adrian would be ready to respond, and they, in turn, would be eager to share what they knew.

The result was the flickering to life of a broad intelligence network. Adrian was skilled at turning one connection into another, and then another, building up his network, node by node. By late 2012, it was strong enough that he was obliquely boasting about having access—usually indirect—to people inside the North Korean regime itself. It was the kind of insight that is of great interest to foreign intelligence agencies, not to mention the American government.

Perhaps unsurprisingly then, it was during this time that Adrian started debriefing members of the FBI's counterintelligence division in New York on findings from his international travels. Federal agents had first shown up at his door in late 2011 after discovering that a young Mexican citizen with a green card had been spending weeks at a time in civil war–era Libya.

"They had a few questions," he later joked to a friend about the visit from the FBI. But Adrian flipped what began as an adversarial approach into a relationship that might prove mutually beneficial. Of course, he knew his work would unlikely be formally sanctioned by the U.S. government, which would never risk a confrontation with a nuclear-powered country to help rescue some defectors. But if he found himself in trouble, being connected to the FBI meant he always had someone to call. The intelligence materials he was developing through his growing network could also sometimes best be put to use by informing foreign governments of secret weapons shipments and business cutouts helping launder Kim regime funds. He also believed there were those in the government—policy making as well as intelligence—who shared his views on a muscular approach to North Korea. If push came to shove, they might bail him out, he thought.

After a trip abroad, Adrian made a habit of meeting up with agents and giving a debriefing. Sometimes he'd discover a name of a businessman playing an important role in sanctions evasions in a place like the United Arab Emirates. Other times it might be a perspective on what's happening on the ground in North Korea. Adrian frequently met with high-profile defectors and businessmen connected to North Korea, people not necessarily in contact with U.S. intelligence. FBI agents would dutifully write down his information, giving nothing in return. They were jovial and friendly, but they knew their craft required them always to be receiving, never giving. They seemed like friends, but were they?

———

THE NEXT MONTH, OCTOBER 2012, Adrian took trips to Seoul and Tripoli. In Libya, he was heartbroken to see how quickly the whole project for a new country was falling apart amid infighting and territory grabbing.

His friend Ousama's father, Mustafa Abushagur, owing to his experience building an opposition from the ground up and gaining international acceptance for a new revolutionary government, had been a mentor to Adrian. But the elder man's own political journey was hitting major obstacles. Abushagur had been selected as prime minister by the democratically elected General National Congress in September 2011, only to be fired from the job before he was able to make a decision. Two others had been fired the prior month.

In an op-ed in the *Libya Herald*, Adrian called on the Libyan government to allow Abushagur to select his cabinet and focus on the well-being of the country. If they didn't, Adrian warned, the country would drift toward becoming a failed state.

"What happens in Libya now will have serious ramifications not only on the success of the Syrian revolution, but on all democratic efforts to replace dictatorships in the future," he wrote. "The 'Libya Model' will either be a positive example, or a warning against change for oppressed peoples worldwide."

Adrian's fears began to play out. Libya became the site of proxy battles for power for bigger countries across the world. Some of the most powerful players were the Gulf states who'd helped tip the scales against Gaddafi, only to undermine the country's democratic transition immediately after.

Countries such as the U.A.E. and Saudi Arabia are innately biased in favor of strongman states. It wasn't that they were opposed to one-party, one-man rule; it was that Gaddafi himself had questioned the legitimacy of the Gulf monarchies. Across the countries of the Arab Spring, the U.A.E. and Saudi Arabia sought to destabilize democratically elected powers in favor of military dictators and autocrats.

The experience was chastening for Adrian. He'd been such an unabashed believer in the Arab Spring. Now it was drifting into an Arab Winter and who knew how long it would last.

"He had the realization that other countries will not solve your country's problems," Ousama Abushagur said. "Democracy post-revolution is not always the best strategy."

Adrian's belief that North Korea's government was on the cusp of disintegrating wasn't shaken, but the on-the-ground experience with Libyans, Egyptians, and Syrians was a lesson about the need to take charge.

One of his favorite projects was imagining taking over the North Korean phone system just as Ousama Abushagur had done for the Libyans. The two of them would think through the plan, where they'd need to gain physical access, and what they could do with control of the physical communications infrastructure.

It was a kind of blueprint. Blueprints would soon become a key feature of Adrian's planning for North Korea.

ONE OF ADRIAN'S BEST talents was spotting potential sources and allies in unexpected places. A particularly enticing candidate emerged in early 2013: Kim Han-sol, the son of the pudgy and controversial black sheep of the Kim family, Kim Jong-nam. Kim Jong-nam was the eldest son of Kim Jong-il, and for the better part of the 1990s, until 2001, he was seen as a contender for heir apparent for the Dear Leader.

Succession in North Korea was a strange blend of the medieval concept of a divinely chosen monarch and Soviet-style command and control of the population. The next leader would have to come from *Baekdu hyultong,* which means Baekdu bloodline, named after the tallest mountain in the Korean peninsula, Mount Baekdu, and refers to the descendants of "Great Leader" Kim Il-sung.

Kim Jong-nam's mother was Song Hye-rim, once North Korea's

leading actress and one of four women the cinephile Kim Jong-il had children with. Kim Jong-il's relationship with Song was extramarital and kept secret from Kim Il-sung, his father, until several years after Jong-nam was born in 1971.

Kim Jong-nam, like his younger half-siblings later, was educated abroad. Kim Jong-il sent his children abroad in part to protect the secrets and the mystique of his royal family from his children's prying peers. Kim Jong-nam lived with an aunt and went to a French international school in Russia called the Lycée français de Moscou, and to the International School of Geneva and the International School of Berne in Switzerland, becoming more aware of the world and culture in the process. Like his father he was enamored with films, and he even had his own movie set so he could make his own shorts.

After Kim Il-sung's death in 1994, when Kim Jong-nam was twenty-three years old, he was allowed to enter the public sphere, and he began a series of government jobs. On the sly, he'd take trips to Japan to experience the global culture and cuisine he'd come to love as a teenager.

Finally, in 1998, it appeared that Kim Jong-nam was in the running as heir to his father. He was appointed to a senior job at the Ministry of Public Security and head of the North Korean Computer Committee. He joined his father on a prominent state visit to China.

But his status cratered a few years later when he traveled to Japan, accompanied by two women and his four-year-old son. The Japanese authorities discovered he was using a fake Mandarin name, Pang Xiong (translation: Fat Bear), on a forged Dominican passport. He claimed that he was taking his son to Disneyland in Tokyo, but was detained by Japanese authorities for three days.

While the Japanese press gleefully reported on the event, Kim Jong-nam, upon his release, bought out the entire first-class cabin of a double-deck plane to avoid the swarm of reporters and, instead of returning to Pyongyang, flew on to Beijing wearing a diamond-encrusted Rolex watch on his wrist, according to Japanese news articles. The event was painfully embarrassing for the tough-talking image projected by North Korea and foreshadowed Kim Jong-nam's immediate loss of favor.

In another sign of the powerful backbench of the Workers' Party in North Korea under Kim Jong-il's instructions, it appears that a movement was started to undermine Kim Jong-nam as the rightful heir. The army began a campaign using a carefully worded—if a bit awkwardly long—slogan: "The Respected Mother is the Most Faithful and Loyal Subject to the Dear Leader Comrade Supreme Commander."

For observers on the ground, the implication was clear. Succession depended on the identity of the mother more than the status as oldest in line. By shifting attention to Ko Young-hee, a Japan-born opera star and the mother of Kim Jong-il's three youngest children, the supreme leader was readying the public for a shift in succession. The younger of her two sons is Kim Jong-un, who later succeeded his father. The elder son, Kim Jong-chol, made a poor candidate, because he was more interested in video games than politics and was thought to be "too effeminate" to be a leader by his father, Kim Jong-il, according to a once-secret U.S. government cable later released by WikiLeaks.

Effectively exiled, Kim Jong-nam set up in Macau, the former Portuguese colony that had turned into China's gambling hub, bringing along his wife and children, including his son Kim Han-sol. His life was largely a mystery in those years, but it later emerged he liaised with intelligence agencies in the United States and China both and lived a well-financed lifestyle. He could sometimes be found in Geneva, hanging out at the bar with a local luxury watch salesman.

In early 2012, a journalist with the Japanese newspaper *Tokyo Shimbun* published a book based on extensive interviews and email correspondence with Kim Jong-nam, whom he'd met in 2004 and twice in 2011. Kim Jong-nam's comments would have been forgettable if he wasn't the former heir apparent of North Korea, telling the journalist that "the Kim Jong-un regime will not last long."

"Without reforms, North Korea will collapse, and when such changes take place, the regime will collapse," he was reported as saying, according to the book. "I think we will see valuable time lost as the regime sits idle fretting over whether it should pursue reforms or stick to the present political structure."

It's impossible to know exactly how the comments were viewed in Pyongyang, but by all signs it was an explosive development. The system that had emerged over decades was a totalitarian state with communist tendencies ruled by a dynasty that is portrayed as deity-like, so for a family member to step out of line, so publicly and blatantly, would have been anathema to the regime leadership. After years of being effectively ignored by Pyongyang as he lived out the debauched life of an exile in Macau, Kim Jong-nam had, it seemed, made himself a target.

IN 2013 IN PARIS, Adrian's networking scored a new prize. Through a businessman with connections to Kim Jong-nam and others in the powerful North Korean diaspora, he was introduced to Kim Han-sol, the son of Kim Jong-nam. Adrian flew into France for the chance at a one-on-one meeting with him and spent several hours getting to know him at a Paris brasserie. Adrian later told a writer for *The New Yorker* that the young man—who was just eighteen at the time—was dripping in wealth, including a pair of Gucci sneakers. In a separate discussion with a friend, he clarified that he didn't mean the comments as disparaging. "I'm just a normal guy from California, so seeing that kind of money feels a bit crazy," he explained.

Source of wealth didn't matter to Adrian. This was the kind of person he could work with. That Kim Han-sol's dad was likely corrupt and seemed mostly interested in drinking and gambling wasn't a problem. The aura of Kim Jong-nam's birth—and therefore his son's—could be a tool in the fight against the regime.

A year before they met, Kim Han-sol, still a high school student, gave an interview on Finnish television that was highly critical of the regime. Asked of his future, he told the interviewer, "I would like to engage in more humanitarian projects and also work to contribute to building world peace.

"I've always dreamed that one day I will go back and make things better," he said, speaking in English with a British accent.

Such talk was music to Adrian's ears, especially when Han-sol mentioned in the interview that he was particularly interested in the Libyan revolution and had learned about it from a Libyan roommate at the United World College, a boarding school in Bosnia-Herzegovina he attended for high school. Afterward, he attended Sciences Po university in France.

The two young men had a natural chemistry. They opened a communication channel to stay in close touch and started brainstorming ways to work on North Korea together.

IN 2012 AND 2013, the powerful layer of the North Korean leader and his top officials who ran the country were still focused on internal purges—less so on outcasts like Kim Jong-nam.

Kim Jong-un's position was solidifying, and he was getting into the swing of the position, although his hefty frame and buzz cut, which was modeled after his grandfather's look, became ripe fodder for editorial cartoonists in the international press.

Behind the scenes, the hard-liners in North Korea were especially concerned with the one man all the world powers hoped Kim Jong-un would listen to, his uncle Jang Song-thaek. Jang was married to the only daughter of Kim Il-sung, a hugely important union. As the vice-chairman of the National Defence Commission, he was viewed as second in charge to Kim Jong-il for much of the 2000s. Some even viewed him as a contender to succeed him, his prospects buoyed by his decades-old marriage into the Kim family.

After Kim Jong-il had a stroke and was weakened substantially for years afterward, foreign intelligence agencies believe Jang became more influential in decision-making, battling against the hard-liners for a slightly more moderate approach. When Kim Jong-il died, he appeared in a four-star general's uniform at the funeral and served as Kim Jong-un's right hand during the transition between leaders.

Jang was a frequent visitor to China over the years and had come to believe North Korea needed to open its economy up gradually to be able to survive into the next century. China managed to do that over the course of the second half of the twentieth century while maintaining its control on the population. Why couldn't North Korea do something similar?

At one point in 2004, Jang's relationship with Kim Jong-il grew complicated. Jang apparently suffered a major loss of power and was placed under house arrest, only for Kim Jong-il to reinstate him the next year. Jang's apparent return to favor gave many North Korea watchers in the United States, Europe, and China hope that the country could be persuaded to drop its nuclear ambitions in exchange for access to global markets and investment from wealthier countries.

But his China visits soon began to become a problem. On one trip in 2012, he visited China on his own and was given a reception fit for a head of state—a dangerous image to be broadcast before Kim Jong-un's team back in Pyongyang.

Not long after, he suffered a "promotion"—named to become the chairman of the newly established State Physical Culture and Sports Guidance Commission. To North Korea watchers, it was clear he was being shunted out of important areas of governance. In 2013, despite some signs of Jang's position getting restored, Kim Jong-un sent a military leader to China instead of him—another sign he had made a cardinal error of taking on too much of a public persona and was being put in his place.

Then things took a decidedly North Korean turn. Two of his top aides were executed in November 2013.

Then, on December 8, 2013, North Korean state television broadcast live images of Jang sitting at a meeting of the politburo of the

Workers' Party of Korea wearing a suit in a row just behind the top military brass. Kim Jong-un, wearing a Mao-style suit and glasses, watched on.

Suddenly, as cameras rolled, three military officers stepped up to him and ordered Jang to his feet. They grabbed him by the arms and almost dragged him from the room.

Days later, a television presenter read out the charges: Jang was a traitor to the country. "He was a despicable human scum, worse than a dog, the man who perpetrated thrice cursed acts of treachery."

After a trial by military tribunal, he was reportedly executed by machine guns.

The public nature of Jang's fall seemed to suggest an unmistakable and Machiavellian message both to North Koreans and to the world: Kim Jong-un was firmly in control.

9

BLUEPRINTS

The most difficult task can be resolved when one starts with the easiest thing.

—*DOSAN AHN CHANG HO*
(AS FIRST TWEETED BY THE
JOSEON INSTITUTE ON
MARCH 28, 2015)

**NEW YORK CITY
OCTOBER 2014**

ONE DAY IN THE FALL OF 2014, A MESSAGE ARRIVED IN SOO KIM'S inbox from her old classmate Adrian Hong. He wrote to her on Facebook, no formalities, just a simple "Hey are you there?"

Kim had known Adrian socially at Yale. They weren't close but were both interested in Korean affairs and saw each other at events hosted by the Korean American Students of Yale. She hadn't put much stock in his activism back then. She chalked it up to the kinds of youthful passions and curiosities they all had, not the life calling it would later become.

In fact, Kim's own passion around Korean affairs had been kindled at Yale in much the same way as Adrian's, and it had become a career path. Born in the United States to first-generation immigrants, Kim learned everything she knew about her motherland, which wasn't much, through the prism of her household. At Yale, it felt like she was finally opening her eyes to the full significance of the division between North and South Korea—and the human cost. This was an experience many Korean Americans told me they felt when attending college. It was the first time they properly delved into their history and heritage beyond the food, music, and language, all the while meeting other Korean Americans on similar quests.

After she finished a master's degree at Johns Hopkins University, that newly stoked passion led Kim into government service. She joined the CIA as an analyst, using her Korean-language skills to help the U.S. government understand one of the most complex security challenges in the world.

A year out of Yale and already in her classified job, Kim one day spotted Adrian in a Starbucks in Washington, D.C., but kept her greetings brief. In her new job, which he didn't know about, she was required to keep a low profile. Still, Adrian intrigued her. Kim had begun to reconsider his commitment to Korean issues. All his high-sounding rhetoric in college looked more meaningful in retrospect, especially after his arrest in China, which she had learned of through classmates. Former Yalies had shared stories of Adrian's travails with pride, almost as if they had hung out with a future celebrity before he became famous.

As the years ticked by, Kim kept an eye out for news about Adrian and his work. He seemed to believe strongly in what he was doing. His dedication spoke to what she considered the ultimate question about the leaders in Pyongyang: If North Korea doesn't follow rules and international norms, then what about North Korea makes or justifies getting equal treatment that the United States, South Korea, or other open countries get?

In the fall of 2014, a friend asked Kim if she'd stayed in touch with Adrian, because he'd written to her asking for Kim's contact details. Kim was surprised, but refrained from sending him a message. Then, a short time later, he pinged her on Facebook.

Adrian refused to say anything over Facebook Messenger, speaking cryptically and asking if she had plans to be in New York anytime soon. By coincidence Kim was traveling there a few weeks later, and they scheduled to meet up for coffee.

In the café in Manhattan, Kim couldn't make out what was going on. He was asking her questions but not explaining the context of why he was asking them. "Who do you see are the movers and shakers in North Korea?" he asked. It felt, to Kim, like he kept dancing around a deeper question.

It felt like he wanted to know if she wanted to do something about it.

Kim was noncommittal in their meeting and kept it secret from most friends and mutual acquaintances. After a few days, she sent him a message on Facebook saying she was interested in helping but needed more information about what it was he was trying to do.

Kim wasn't the only one who suspected Adrian had something up his sleeve. Not long before their meeting, Adrian had traveled to Seoul and met with the Reverend Tim Peters, the Christian missionary who was forced to flee the Chinese border with North Korea when Adrian was arrested in 2006.

Peters was surprised to receive the email from Adrian, which he sent using an account for his consulting business, Pegasus Strategies. There was still a simmering resentment about the impact of his arrest in China years earlier on Peters's own rescue work. Adrian told Peters he wanted to talk—that he had a proposal for a new way to approach North Korea.

During their meeting at a café in the city, Adrian had the same circumspect demeanor—dangling a thought but holding back on the details. He hinted at having serious connections that could make this project possible, which Peters interpreted as Adrian suggesting he had the backing of an intelligence agency.

"We're planning something much bigger," Peters recalled Adrian saying to him. But when Peters asked for details, Adrian demurred: "I can't talk about that."

The dance annoyed Peters, and he spoke bluntly in reply, reminding Adrian that his operation in China during the Christmas holidays in 2006 put in danger not only North Korean refugees but all the operations along the border. He warned Adrian about the perils of not thinking through a plan completely. If he didn't, many people could be impacted or even hurt.

Afterward, Peters wrote to Adrian, thanking him for visiting and buying him a latte. Adrian wrote back that he felt discouraged by their meeting.

Throughout 2014 and 2015, Adrian had meetings like his coffees with Kim and Peters in the hopes of rapidly expanding the Cheollima Civil Defense network. Only those who pledged their commitment to the cause would receive a fuller briefing. And if things went well, there was a kind of initiation where the new member vowed secrecy and began to communicate with Adrian confidentially on his projects, both real tasks on the ground and ambitious plans—large and small—that might add up to toppling the regime.

For a guy who prized secrecy, Adrian had also developed a tendency to drop hints of his thinking online. His writings and Twitter posts from December gave an insight into his coalescing worldview as the year was ending. On December 10, 2014, he tweeted, "There will soon come a day when the world must account for its collective apathy & inaction in the face of massive suffering in #NorthKorea."

A day after this post, Sony released the weakly reviewed comedy *The Interview,* starring James Franco and Seth Rogen as Americans who stumble into a chance to assassinate Kim Jong-un, played by the actor and comedian Randall Park, on behalf of the CIA. Weeks before the release, a group of hackers calling themselves Guardians of Peace, which the U.S. government later said were North Korean operatives, hacked into Sony's systems, leaking embarrassing information about executives and destroying some of the company's IT systems.

Adrian penned an article in *The Atlantic* excoriating the movie and its premise, which traded in similar stereotypes to other famous spoofs of the North Korean regime on *Saturday Night Live* and the infamous *Team America: World Police,* which Adrian said were replete with "cheap and sometimes racism-tinged jokes."

"This film is not an act of courage," he wrote. "It is not a stand against totalitarianism, concentration camps, mass starvation, or state-sponsored terror." Adrian argued that the notion of a film striking the same tone about "Islamic state slavers" or "genocidaires in the Central African Republic" was inconceivable. "North Korea is not funny," he concluded.

Some commentators defending *The Interview* had likened it to Charlie Chaplin's 1940 spoof of Adolf Hitler in *The Great Dictator,* which ended with an earnest and emotional speech about the perils of fascism. Responding to those observations, Adrian pointed out that in Chaplin's 1964 autobiography he wrote that he regretted making the film: "Had I known of the actual horrors of the German concentration camps, I could not have made *The Great Dictator;* I could not have made fun of the homicidal insanity of the Nazis."

As the year drew to an end, he continued to air his feelings on Twitter in a series of messages. On December 21, he tweeted,

> The problem in #NorthKorea is not a lack of awareness of how bad their situation is—they know all too well.
>
> You cannot watch your children starve or see family sent to concentration camps & for too long believe your government is capable & good.
>
> Real problem in #NorthKorea is a lack of breathing room to organize; heavy surveillance hand of the state stifles organic social networks.
>
> so dissent can only be carried deeply in one's soul, never shared & energized with the kindred sympathies of potential collaborators.

Then, on New Year's Eve, he posted the second-to-last message he would ever tweet from that account, quoting Martin Luther King Jr.:

> We will have to repent in this generation not merely for the hateful words and actions of the bad people, but for the appalling silence of the good people.

———

THE NEW PLAN OF action Adrian had hit upon was multipronged. On the surface, he was forming a new think tank, the Joseon Institute, that would prepare blueprints for every possible situation that international powers would need to deal with after "Year Zero"—the inevitable moment when the Kim regime fell. Out of view, he was also clandestinely searching for ways to hasten that downfall.

What was brilliant about the concept is how it allowed Adrian's diffuse network to row in the same direction. Perhaps more difficult was the task of keeping the levels of secrecy within his network straight. During college and afterward, he collected a following of young people wishing they could do something to make a difference. They'd heard his speeches and watched the videos. The stakes were clear, but what could they do? For those willing to take a risk, they could join his incipient Cheollima Civil Defense.

But some wanted to "volunteer" in a more traditional sense. The Joseon Institute was the answer. In a dingy Koreatown office in New York City, Adrian laid out the challenges before a room of recent college graduates whom he had come across in his years of activism around North Korea. Many were Korean Americans, but there was a solid minority of activists and volunteers without Asian ethnicity, too.

What could be done to reform education in North Korea after so many years of inculcation? How could a team take over the power grid from the government if the government fell? How could the mobile phone network be seized and turned into a means of letting the outside world in? The group dug into these deceptively simple questions.

"The Joseon Institute believes that dramatic change on the Korean Peninsula is imminent, and has been undertaking research in preparation for that end for the past several years," a job advertisement that appeared later read, summarizing the group's mission.

Christopher Ahn, the retired marine, flew in from Los Angeles to attend a few sessions and was struck by how enthusiastic the volunteers were about the notion that they could do something tangible to address something as intractable seeming as North Korea.

Adrian had also tapped some of the high-level relationships he had been working to establish over the past couple of years, such as that with Kim Han-sol. Kim Han-sol, who was living mostly in Macau, agreed to be a secret part of the Joseon Institute. He wanted to focus on helping North Korea build a culture of entrepreneurship from zero and led the group's Start-Up Committee.

The group put together a hundred-day stabilization plan that totaled hundreds of pages. Each topic had a planning commission, or a task force, helmed by members of the group. The commissions ranged from food security and public health to national heritage and energy planning. There were task forces for mobile banking and microfinance, demographics and digital mapping.

Under Adrian's framework for the Joseon Institute, an ordinary primary school teacher could take her real-world experience and mash it together with research about totalitarian states to create the beginnings of a plan for what to teach young North Koreans the day after the fall of the regime.

"People were excited," Ahn said. "These were people tired of hashtag advocacy. They loved the idea that an average person could make a micro push, and all of them together creates momentum."

Adrian asked Ahn if he would be willing to take part in any planning around what to do about North Korea's military in the event of regime change, but the veteran demurred. "I'm not the strategic thinker," he told him. "My job in the marines was just to make sure my men shaved in the morning and stayed safe."

Adrian's raising of aspects like the North Korean military suggested a far bolder appetite for action than most think tanks would dare have. And, indeed, some other North Korea–focused institutions distanced themselves from Adrian's positioning.

Adrian's old mentor Jae Ku suggested he discuss possible collaboration with Jenny Town, co-founder and director of a website called 38 North devoted to North Korean affairs. But Town, who had met

Adrian years earlier and was aware of his more radical stance on North Korea, ruled it out. On paper they might have seemed destined to work together. In her first few years after getting her master's degree from Columbia University, Town had worked in advertising and briefly at the College Board in Washington, D.C., before the pull of North Korea persuaded her to join Freedom House to work on its human rights in North Korea project.

But over the years Town had come to an altogether different perspective on North Korea. Like Adrian, she was appalled at the human rights situation there and believed in devoting her life to making a difference to the country's everyday people. She also shared his view that technology could help the cause. But as Adrian's ambitions for action grew, Town's focus was many tiny changes on the ground, particularly at the socioeconomic level, which, in aggregate, she believed could destabilize North Korea and nudge it toward change.

What mattered to her were things like the explosion of cell phones and greater trade and market activity. Something as simple as the government allowing people to earn some money outside their government jobs could have long-lasting ripple effects. "All of those are signs the social fabric and social contract is changing," she said.

One hope shared by many North Korean analysts was that the country would follow in the footsteps of China, which improved the lot of its citizens through enhanced economic engagement with the world while retaining the political and societal control it considered so crucial to its view of how life should be governed. The thinking goes like this: If North Korea would get hooked on trade with the rest of the world, it would be easier to influence and less likely to act rashly. It would treat its people better because it would have the resources to do so.

Adrian, however, found this to be wishful thinking. His worldview of North Korea was black-and-white not because of naïveté or missionary zeal but because of his experience meeting defectors and escapees over many years. To him, it was clear: the leaders in Pyongyang enslaved millions of North Koreans to preserve their own power.

He also was willing to dispatch with accepted wisdom, such as the idea that North and South Korea should be reunified—a view widely held in the Korea watcher community in the United States at the time. The idea was that Koreans were one people divided by the vagaries of history.

For Adrian, the only thing that mattered was ridding the world of the gangster state overseen by Kim Jong-un and helping the people of North Korea break free from their shackles.

"The human rights of the North Korean people, an end to decades of perpetual hunger by large segments of the population, the elimination of Pyongyang's proliferation and the export of terror, the closure of North Korea's concentration camps—all these are moral imperatives," he wrote in a 2016 op-ed in *The San Diego Union-Tribune.*

In the article, he detailed some of the Joseon Institute's plans for the days and months after the Kim regime fell. South Korea could send teachers, engineers, aid workers, and medical staff, as well as trainers for police, firefighters, border security, and a coast guard.

The Korean People's Army should be repurposed to work on infrastructure, policing, and national projects, while the command economy apparatus continued distributing food until the beginnings of a market economy could be installed.

This was the first time Adrian had spelled out publicly just how much he'd shifted from an advocacy-focused NGO creator to a believer in the imminent fall of the Kim regime. The undertone was that such a fall could come faster than people thought with some help.

IN ADRIAN'S OFFICE IN Manhattan's Koreatown, he was frustrated about the cool reception his group was getting in the North Korea watching community, a mixture that ran the spectrum from liberal activists to conservative think tanks as well as many others passionate about the issues but with the perspective that incremental progress was the way to go.

Even worse, that uneasiness was impacting his fundraising plans. Despite his hopes to hire twenty full-time staffers at the Joseon Institute, it languished in a Koreatown office space with just a handful of full-time people and relied almost entirely on volunteers. He earned some income from the institute, but supplemented it with his private sector consulting work.

To his closest friends, fundraising was always Adrian's biggest problem. He had blueprints for operations big and small that might strike a blow against the North Korean regime, but very few people would hand him money for anything that could blow back into their face or risk getting them in hot water with U.S. authorities.

In desperation, Adrian began to toy with controversial approaches for raising money. In conversations with business owners in parts of Asia including China, Japan, and Thailand, he suggested that the transition government of North Korea could award contracts to those that helped free the people from the Kim regime. There was interest, but no takers.

By now, Adrian had shifted away from the kind of one-on-one networking he had been doing with potentially sympathetic acquaintances like Soo Kim and Timothy Peters. Much of his travel around the world was now intended to facilitate meetings with international businessmen and private security and intelligence types—people who might have radical ideas for how to change the equation about North Korea.

Some Joseon Institute members were growing frustrated, too. They were fired up to help and glad to have helped with the white papers, but what next? There was a nagging itch to take things a step further.

On March 23, 2016, Adrian arrived at Parliament Hill in Ottawa, Canada, to speak about North Korea before the Standing Senate Committee on Human Rights. He was wearing a black suit, glasses, and a new beard and mustache that made him look much older than he did back when he would traipse from campus to campus giving speeches at LiNK chapters. More than ever, he was pushing his belief that engagement and gradual change were pointless in North Korea.

"North Korea is not a normal nation with a government seeking to serve and protect its citizens," he told them. "It is a brutal totalitarian regime, ruled by a royal family and a class of vassals, both in tenuous concert with one another."

That brutality was about to be reinforced on the world stage in shocking form.

10

PRUNING THE FAMILY TREE

Death is the solution to all problems. No man—no problem.

—*JOSEPH STALIN*

LANGKAWI, MALAYSIA
FEBRUARY 2017

IN EARLY FEBRUARY, KIM JONG-NAM PACKED HIS BAGS AND BOARDED a plane in Macau for the almost four-hour flight over the South China Sea to Kuala Lumpur.

Since his exile from North Korea, Kim Jong-nam, once considered the front-runner to succeed his father, Kim Jong-il, as North Korea's leader, had been living in Macau, China's over-the-top answer to Las Vegas. In Macau, he had adopted a lifestyle that suited his dissolute surroundings. It required hundreds of thousands of dollars a year to maintain the lifestyle to which he and his family had become accustomed. Kim was known to undertake expensive travel to places such as Geneva, buy expensive watches, and hang out in high-end bars. He was an avowed gambler.

Out of favor in North Korea and with little treasure amassed there anyway, he was always in need of cash. For Kim Jong-nam, foreign intelligence agencies had become a key source of income, according to reporting by Warren Strobel in *The Wall Street Journal*. He had little ambition related to North Korea, but he would feign enthusiasm for his paymasters, whom he would meet in neutral territory like Malaysia.

For the CIA, it was a small price to pay to have a living descendant of Kim Il-sung's outside North Korea and on retainer for the U.S. government. If North Koreans believed in the importance of the Kim dynasty, here was one key family member open to saying things that could threaten the authority of his younger brother Kim Jong-un, who together with Pyongyang's backstage power brokers was continuing the country's brutal, hermit kingdom policies.

Lately, Kim Jong-nam had been feeling a little more paranoid than usual. He had an unnerving feeling he was being surveilled when he traveled. He'd received warnings from his network that he wasn't safe from his half brother and his Reconnaissance General Bureau, the North's main spy agency. But he decided to shrug off these concerns and head to Malaysia for one of his regular cash pickups, as he had done dozens of times over the years in cities across Asia and Europe.

After arriving in Kuala Lumpur from Macau, Kim Jong-nam spent two days in the capital resting and zooming around the city with his trusted chauffeur before flying on to the archipelago of Langkawi to meet his Korean American CIA handler in a hotel for a brief meeting. He uploaded files he'd gathered in the previous months onto a USB stick and handed them to the case officer, took his money, and headed back to Kuala Lumpur for a few more days of rest and relaxation, the *Journal* and others reported later.

As he arrived at the airport on February 13 to fly home to Macau, he would soon learn his sixth sense about surveillance was spot on.

NORTH KOREA'S RECONNAISSANCE GENERAL Bureau had been tracking Kim Jong-nam's movements for years, carefully crafting a plan to end his life. To the Kim regime back home, Kim Jong-nam was a loose end that needed to be eliminated. In fact, Kim Jong-nam had narrowly avoided previous assassination attempts. In 2012, he was attacked in Beijing by a man who appeared to be a North Korean agent. He survived when a Chinese police officer came to his rescue. A separate hit squad was also caught by the Chinese police and sent back to North Korea. South Korea's National Intelligence Service later revealed that Kim Jong-nam even wrote a pleading letter to the regime, begging his half brother to spare him and his family, according to an article in the South Korean newspaper *Segye Ilbo*, citing Korean intelligence officials.

But Malaysia was the perfect place to go after him. The Southeast Asian country lacked the extreme surveillance culture and political sensitivities that had hindered efforts in China, and, conveniently, Malaysia had a no-visa policy allowing free travel to and from North Korea.

Despite North Korea's reputation for limited resources and seemingly outdated technology, it had racked up quite a few espionage coups over the years, surprising casual observers and superpowers with its effectiveness at assassinations, international crime, and theft. To earn foreign currency, North Korea had at times been one of the most sophisticated producers of counterfeit U.S. bills. The country didn't have open access to the internet, yet its computer hackers had cut off huge conglomerates like Sony at the knees and stolen hundreds of millions of dollars from banks and other institutions.

This time, however, the strategy involved little in the way of technology. Months before, North Korean operatives had begun brainwashing two young women into believing they were participating in a low-budget practical joke TV show where they'd smear an unsuspecting victim's face with a cosmetic cream in a public place while the whole thing was caught on hidden camera. Neither woman knew about the other.

Siti Aisyah, an Indonesian living in Kuala Lumpur, first met a handsome, young man calling himself "James" on the street who asked if she'd be interested in starring in a film project. She was flattered. "Why not?" she thought, according to testimony she later gave to Malaysian authorities.

They practiced the stunt, which involved rubbing cosmetic cream on unsuspecting victims, in various locations around town. James praised her skills. When he told her to meet him at the airport in February several weeks after they'd first met, it felt like any other time she'd carried out the stunt. This time, if she did a good job, there'd be a bonus, James told her.

On the day of Kim Jong-nam's flight, Siti met James in a café at the modern Kuala Lumpur International Airport. He scanned the room, looking for the target as she sat wrapped in a shawl with her sunglasses on her head.

Arriving wearing a light-gray jacket, jeans, and a purple shirt, with a black backpack, Kim Jong-nam headed to the AirAsia self-check-in kiosk to get his boarding pass.

"There he is," James said, after spotting Kim Jong-nam looking at the departures board. "The guy in the gray jacket."

Suddenly he carefully applied some kind of oil on her hand—not the usual cosmetic cream they'd used on previous attempts around Kuala Lumpur. He took pains not to get any on his own hands. Unbeknownst to her, it was one half of a chemical mixture that when combined with another became the deadly VX nerve agent.

VX, which stands for "venomous agent X," was discovered in the 1950s by scientists at a British firm investigating possible pesticides. But this particular chemical turned out to be extraordinarily good at killing humans, so it was discontinued in agriculture. The U.K., U.S., and Russian militaries subsequently developed chemical weapons based on the chemicals. Cuba later used it against Angolan insurgents during its civil war, and Saddam Hussein used it in the infamous Halabja chemical attack in Iraqi Kurdistan, killing thousands of people and injuring thousands more.

Siti approached Kim from behind a pillar and jumped up on him, smearing it across his face, before running away shouting, "Sorry! Sorry!"

Seconds later, a Vietnamese woman, Đoàn Thị Hương, wearing a sweater emblazoned with "LOL," rubbed her hands across his face as well and ran away. She thought she was part of the same practical joke show.

CCTV footage shows Kim Jong-nam looking confused by what had just transpired.

He starts to head toward the bathroom, but then changes direction to approach airport workers, his demeanor seemingly changed. Speaking animatedly, he starts gesticulating about what had just happened to him moments before. "Very painful, very painful, I was sprayed liquid," he told them. An officer guided him to the airport medical clinic.

Within moments of the two liquids becoming mixed, the nerve agent began spreading through his body and causing painful muscle spasms. On his walk to the clinic, his knees became stiff and he had trouble walking.

By the time he got·inside, he collapsed onto a chair in extreme distress. Sprawled out, with his belly partially exposed, he started gasping.

An ambulance was called, but it was too late. He was already starting to have a seizure. His lungs contracted violently, making it impossible to breathe. Medical officers rushed to give him oxygen and get him to the hospital. But on the way, just fifteen minutes after the attack, he died.

Malaysian investigators later examined CCTV footage to discover a whole North Korean team in the airport, dressed as travelers with suitcases: a chemist, lookouts, and an apparent boss, nicknamed Grandpa, who could be seen smoking cigarettes in the background.

The chemist was later apprehended and caught on camera getting his story straight with North Korean officials, seeming proof it was a deadly state-sponsored assassination. However, he was later released, after officials cited a lack of sufficient evidence. A Malaysian court dropped charges against Siti, who was allowed to return home to Indonesia. Hương pled guilty to a lesser charge and was also released from custody.

———

ON FEBRUARY 14, VALENTINE'S Day, Christopher Ahn was leaning up against the rooftop bar of the Z Hostel overlooking the Manila skyline at about 9:00 P.M., smoking a cigarette and drinking a beer, when Adrian's call came through.

Ahn hadn't meant to be alone in Manila. A Filipino American friend had convinced him that they should travel to the Philippines together from their homes in Los Angeles for a short, cheap holiday. But at the last minute, his friend canceled because of a work problem. Ahn decided to go on by himself.

Ahn found the city a perfect blend, both foreign and oddly familiar to a Korean American. Thanks to World War II's unexpected consequences, Filipinos have deep familiarity with American culture. He had spent a pleasant few days hanging out at the hotel pool, walking around town, and talking with locals.

Now, seeing the name flash on his phone on the encrypted communication app Signal, Ahn grimaced. He knew this wasn't going to be a friendly check-in. Adrian and Ahn had spent more time together since they first met over burritos some seven years earlier, but they weren't close friends.

Encountering Adrian at events and occasional coffee meet-ups, Ahn saw him as a man shouldering an increasingly heavy burden. With money always running low and a belief that if he gave up he couldn't count on someone else to pick up the slack, Adrian was massively overstretched.

"Where are you?" Adrian asked Ahn breathlessly when he finally picked up. When he learned he was in the Philippines, he sounded relieved. "That's perfect."

There was no small talk. Adrian cut to the chase: Was Ahn aware of the assassination of Kim Jong-nam, the older half brother of the North Korean leader, Kim Jong-un, in Malaysia just a day earlier, on February 13?

"Kim Han-sol is freaking out," Adrian told Ahn, referring to Kim Jong-nam's son, who had, from afar, become involved in work at the Joseon Institute. "Can you help him?"

For Adrian, this was both a humanitarian mission and a strategic one. With his father gone, Kim Han-sol was the last remaining male in the bloodline who could legitimately claim to be descended from Kim Il-sung and Kim Jong-il. Like his father before him, Kim Han-sol could have some role to play if the North Korean regime began to tip over.

As soon as news broke about Kim Jong-nam's murder, Adrian called Kim Han-sol to encourage him to seek safety outside Macau. Kim demurred, saying he thought the family was safe. Only about six hours later, he called back with a new view: "Help us escape." Kim Han-sol explained that his family's usual bodyguards had disappeared and he feared they'd be killed if they stayed in Macau.

Adrian already had a team in Europe to help the family seek asylum in the U.K. or the Netherlands—countries they'd worked with before at LiNK and increasingly with Cheollima Civil Defense. But the family needed assistance, and none of Adrian's contacts could help them stay safe on their way to Amsterdam. "Can you meet them?" he asked Ahn.

Despite Adrian's ambitions and audacity, his underground organization was nothing more than a collection of his contacts working together over encrypted messengers. There were no resources to rely upon except the meager savings of Cheollima members. Adrian was winging it, but Ahn agreed to help nonetheless.

Once Ahn made contact with Kim Han-sol, he went online to buy three plane tickets for Kim Han-sol, his mother, and his sister, to fly from Macau to Taipei the next morning. Wasting no time, Ahn also bought himself a ticket for later that night. He arrived in Taipei after midnight on February 15 and took up a watch post next to a noodle stand inside the arrivals hall.

"People say we're the Underground Railroad, but it was really just me buying tickets with my credit card on Expedia," Ahn says.

Arriving a few hours later that morning, the family of three wore masks to hide their faces. The masks aroused no suspicions. People in Asia frequently wore masks when traveling, even years before COVID-19 made mask wearing a global practice.

Seeing an American-looking Korean man standing near the entrance, Kim Han-sol greeted him with the prearranged code name "Steve." Ahn quietly took them to a VIP lounge where they could lie low until Adrian and his team gave an update on the next move. Ahn saw his job as keeping everyone calm and relaxed. As they got to know each other, Ahn, ever the laid-back Los Angeles native, spoke softly to Han-sol's mother in Korean and gave his iPad to Kim Han-sol's teenage sister to watch Netflix. Kim Han-sol was spooked but in control, while his mother and sister were clearly anxious to find safety.

The airport swirled with activity, but other travelers seemed to pay little attention to the group camped out in the lounge. Finally, Adrian called with news: the Netherlands would grant them asylum.

Ahn bought another round of tickets on his credit card and waited with the family, opting to have them board the flight to Amsterdam at nearly the last possible moment. He then escorted them to the gate, where the attendant's eyes widened when he saw the family's North Korea passports. Ahn dialed Adrian and put him on speakerphone as he tried to persuade the attendant to let them board. It didn't work.

Not sure what else to do, Ahn took them back to the lounge to regroup. While they were waiting there, two men showed up in the lounge and asked to speak with Ahn. They told him they were from the CIA. The younger one, who introduced himself as Wes, appeared to be Korean American.

"Do you guys even know what you're doing?" the older one asked him, incredulously. Ahn told the men to "talk to Adrian."

"I'm just helping out this family," Ahn explained to the agents, declining to give any details. "I'm a proud American and I haven't done anything wrong."

The CIA officers said they would take care of the travel issues. Not long after, an airport official came to notify Kim Han-sol and his family that they would be allowed to travel onward to the Netherlands. Ahn bought yet another set of round-trip tickets on Expedia.

While they waited in the lounge overnight, Ahn shot a short video on his phone as an insurance policy to protect him and the group. It was proof of life in case someone questioned what happened later.

The next morning, the CIA agent named Wes showed up to join them on the flight. Ahn gave Kim Han-sol a big hug and wished them luck on their journey before heading back to Manila, his head spinning with the events of the last twenty-four hours. This was among the first "kinetic" operations of Cheollima and by far the biggest and most important. It was scary and thrilling at the same time. To Ahn, it felt good.

Adrian had worked out the details. By the time the group would arrive, after the lengthy fourteen-hour flight from Taipei, a Cheollima team, including a lawyer specializing in political asylums, would be in place at the arrivals area of Schiphol Airport in Amsterdam, waiting for Kim Han-sol, his mother, and his sister to arrive.

At the appointed hour, with the Cheollima team in place, there was no sign of Kim Jong-nam's family members. They never walked out of customs.

Later Adrian and the Cheollima team would learn that the family had arrived in Amsterdam but left with "Wes" through another exit and promptly boarded another flight out of the country—likely to the United States.

Kim Jong-nam was killed days after receiving money from his CIA handler. Now, it seemed, the CIA was putting the family into protective custody.

Adrian was crushed. He later said losing the family was the biggest mistake of his years of underground efforts. Kim Han-sol could have been an invaluable asset when Cheollima took more decisive action. If Adrian was the rebel organizer, Kim Han-sol was the unlikely prince who could have helped form an opposition government to one day begin a new era for North Korea.

EVEN THOUGH KIM HAN-SOL and his family had slipped through Adrian's fingers at the last moment, Adrian decided Cheollima had reached a critical milestone. This was the kind of action that would put them on the map, which was all the more important because their aspirations were much greater than simply running an underground network for people to escape the wrath of the Kim regime. They wanted to take on the regime itself in the places and times they chose.

Back in New York City, Adrian convened a special meeting of the Joseon Institute at their Koreatown headquarters. Until that moment the Joseon Institute was mainly a producer of edgy white papers from volunteers—the aboveground side of Adrian's activities. Cheollima was the name Adrian used for his loose confederation of allies in the activist world who were keen to take on edgier work—propaganda operations at the border, gathering intelligence from defectors, and developing sources with information about North Korea.

Standing before a room of more than forty volunteers—teachers, businesspeople, a few creative types—he explained that it was time the organization known as the Joseon Institute disappeared and for Cheollima Civil Defense to rise up in its place. For years, Adrian had been convincing these volunteers with little or no specialist training of any kind that they could actually make a difference in the world by pairing their passion for the cause with direct interventions on the ground.

Adrian praised the actions of Ahn, who had flown in from L.A. to join the meeting. Without Ahn's quick movements, it's possible Kim Han-sol, his mother, and his sister could have been captured in Macau by North Korea operatives. This, he told them, was the kind of action Cheollima Civil Defense could do going forward. With nothing more than credit cards and the will to help, they'd assisted in rescuing high-profile targets of Kim Jong-un's. What could they do with resources?

Adrian was in his element, idealistic and inspirational, but he also had something concrete to show for his vision. He framed their group as part of a long history of Koreans resisting oppressors, including fighting against the Japanese occupiers mostly in the twentieth century. It came across as a combination of battle cry and human rights sermon. At times, he struck listeners as a lawyer making a moral case for a client's actions; the twist was the client hadn't committed the acts yet.

In practical terms, Adrian also laid out core tenets of the group, including secrecy and compartmentalization. After this meeting, efforts would be segmented into groups with only those who "need to know" given all the details. Different groups also worked on problems like how to set up a Bitcoin wallet for donations to the group, anti-regime propaganda efforts, and secrecy protocols for the group. Everyone was to use disappearing messages on apps like Signal to communicate. They'd hold conference calls using a piece of software called Silent Circle.

Afterward, Adrian led the whole group to Dallas BBQ, a discount barbecue restaurant popular with thrifty twentysomethings in Manhattan who wanted to eat and drink to their heart's content. He had an odd affection for the venue, even though he knew the food wasn't great. The group, which was overwhelmingly made up of Korean Americans, took up an entire floor of the restaurant's upper level.

"I couldn't remember being around so many Korean Americans in public, except at church," Ahn recalled.

The cast of characters in the barbecue joint included businesspeople, academics, and activists—the types of people who worked hard in high school, went to good universities, and got great jobs after graduation. The types of people who, perhaps, once would have been called yuppies.

And yet there was something else about the ragtag, underfunded, hyper-ambitious group. They had more heart than your average person, and they were tremendously inspired by Adrian, who had promised them they could make a difference and then proved himself right with the Kim Han-sol operation. Having a steady paycheck, a mortgage, and a young family was all they'd fought for growing up, but the Cheollima call to arms answered a deeper feeling. It gave them meaning.

Even the name, Cheollima, felt transcendent. For centuries, Koreans heard stories of the mythical horse that could travel 1,000 *li* in a day. North Korea had adopted it for its own communist agenda, printing propaganda posters to encourage workers to meet high production targets. Under Adrian, Cheollima was reinvented as a mythical savior, moving fast to rescue the North Korean people.

Celebrations completed, the group moved rapidly to raise its public profile.

On March 8, 2017, cheollimacivildefense.org flickered to life with a dual English and Korean statement about the Kim Han-sol operation. At the top of the page was a secretive logo, almost like a mission badge in the military. At the center of the first post was the dramatic video of Kim Han-sol that Ahn had filmed at the airport back in Taipei.

Speaking softly in English, with a Hong Kong–style English accent, and sitting against a white background while wearing a dark black zip-up top, Kim Han-sol is shown speaking and showing his passport with his details blacked out: "My father has been killed a few days ago. I'm currently with my mother and my sister and we're very grateful to . . ."

The sound cuts out briefly when he's saying the name of whom he's thanking. His voice comes back on with a final comment: "We hope this gets better soon."

It would be two years before the full audio was released. Kim Han-sol thanks "Adrian and his team" in the part silenced on the initial version of the video.

Posted on the new website, Cheollima Civil Defense's inaugural statement was at once vague and grandiose. It suggested that the group had a wide reach and network of contacts. The group thanked the Kingdom of the Netherlands, the People's Republic of China, the United States, and a "fourth government to remain unnamed."

"We also recognize our colleagues who remain in the North or within its system who provide critical assistance in extracting such individuals," the statement read.

Who exactly those "colleagues" in North Korea were would begin to become clear in the years ahead.

11

FACE-TO-FACE

When the situation was manageable, it was neglected, and now that it is thoroughly out of hand, we apply too late the remedies which then might have effected a cure.

—WINSTON CHURCHILL

WASHINGTON, D.C.
NOVEMBER 2016

FROM THE OUTSET OF HIS PRESIDENCY, DONALD TRUMP, THE NEW York City real estate tycoon turned U.S. president, viewed geopolitics through the lens of deal making. And there were good deals and there were bad deals.

His business career was a mixed record. He'd become rich, but gone bankrupt more than once and been forced to sell some of his prized possessions along the way. In the same way he conducted business, pinballing from opportunity to failure and back again, there was no focused foreign policy agenda in his administration. Many White House operations were dedicated to managing the daily crises, which were sometimes caused by Trump and his coterie of advisers' insistence on throwing out precedent.

However, no topic sent chills through the ranks of the National Security Council and foreign policy establishment more than his hot-and-cold approach to North Korea. For most of the veteran foreign policy hands, that Trump thought he could make a difference on such a long-running, sensitive, seemingly intractable issue was a nightmare that reminded them of the Stanley Kubrick film *Dr. Strangelove.*

One of the last transition meetings between the administration of Barack Obama and the incoming Trump team was dedicated to conveying just how perilous the North Korea problem had become. In the eyes of Obama, it was the single greatest danger posed to the United States, as the outgoing president confided to Trump in a one-on-one meeting at the White House in November 2016.

The established view over decades among America's foreign policy elite was that North Korea was a nearly unsolvable puzzle. It was too dangerous to ignore but too small and often too quiet to focus on. Journalists came up with the phrase "strategic patience" to describe the Obama administration's strategy of pressuring the country with sanctions while remaining "open" to discussions that would start at the lowest levels and gradually build up to heads of state. The message was clear: we're having no luck diplomatically and the military option is extremely risky, so we're just going to wait for North Korea to fall apart. But it didn't.

Not only did the Kim regime prove remarkably resilient to all its problems over the years, but it also deftly handled the superpowers by making itself a thorn in the side of the global status quo. Nothing was off-limits, including funding its government operations through criminal rackets like counterfeiting $100 bills, hacking, and selling cigarettes on the black market around Europe and Asia. Whereas another small country might fear being pounded into the Stone Age by a rain of missiles for poking the American behemoth, North Korea recognized that American leaders had precious few options aside from a full-out war. And with such spotty understanding of what was happening in North Korea, outside powers like the United States couldn't guarantee that a nuclear missile wouldn't make it out of the North Korean hinterlands and hit Seoul, with its population of ten million.

South Korea didn't present a near and present danger to North Korea either. The security establishment spent twenty-four hours a day worrying about North Korea, but everyday citizens gave the subject little thought even if millions of dollars' worth of taxes they pay support defectors and escapees. The country's liberal politicians—the ones seemingly most inclined to push for human rights—were the least hawkish on North Korea.

North Korea's belligerent profile on the world stage was a reputation decades in the making. Over the years, North Korea had perpetrated such outrageous actions that it sometimes beggared belief that they had not erupted into a full-out conflagration. More hawkish North Korea watchers look back wistfully on those "opportunities," realizing that the cost of confronting the nation would have been much less in the years when North Korea's nuclear capabilities were at most elementary.

In January 1968, North Korea sent a contingent of special forces soldiers from its newly created Unit 124 to assassinate South Korea's strongman president, Park Chung-hee. The men penetrated the heavily fortified border, donned South Korean uniforms, and managed to talk their way to the Blue House, the official residence and office of the president. They were a hundred meters from the president's official residence when a South Korean officer became suspicious. Of the thirty-one invaders, twenty-nine were killed, one was captured, and another got back to North Korea. Twenty-six South Koreans were killed in fighting. Another four Americans were killed trying to stop North Koreans from escaping back over the border.

Just two days later, North Korea managed to seize the USS *Pueblo*, an intelligence-gathering vessel, as it passed alongside the eastern coast. One sailor was killed and the other eighty-two were held as prisoners of war, tortured, and beaten at times (especially when North Koreans realized the men were secretly signaling their resistance by giving the finger in propaganda photos). The *Pueblo*, permanently docked in the Taedong River in Pyongyang, has remained a major tourist attraction in North Korea.

In 1983, North Korea made another assassination attempt on a South Korean head of state. Learning of an impending visit by the

South Korean president, Chun Doo-hwan, a dictatorial leader, North Korean soldiers slipped into Rangoon and received explosives from the North Korean mission, which they hid in the roof of a mausoleum honoring the Burma independence fighter Aung San. On October 9, the South Korean state visit started with a wreath-laying at the mausoleum. As the group arrived, a huge blast cut through the crowd as one of the explosives triggered. In total, twenty-one people were killed, including four senior South Korean ministers and other advisers, journalists, and security officials. Chun survived only because he was late.

In each case, South Korea, the United States, and others decided not to escalate the matter into a full-blown conflict. They might have avoided greater bloodshed, but a whole generation of North Korean officials took away the lesson that they could carry out actions without fear of repercussion. In fact, the more dangerous the face they projected to the world, the less likely they would be invaded. It was a dangerous moral hazard that made North Korea stronger. "By not suffering the consequences, North Korea's calculus changed," said one longtime North Korea policy hand.

By November 2016, however, the Obama team, meeting with Trump's new advisers, had a message: The policy of strategic patience might no longer be viable.

FOR GENERATIONS, U.S. PRESIDENTS had avoided taking decisive action on North Korea, perhaps because they judged the North Korean nuclear program as a slow-motion threat. In 1994, during the Clinton administration, North Korea blocked international inspectors from verifying its adherence to the Nuclear Nonproliferation Treaty. U.S. intelligence concluded North Korea was processing plutonium to build two atomic bombs. Western intelligence agencies had underestimated North Korea's technical capabilities, only to find out its scientists had propelled their research program much more quickly than expected.

Bill Clinton later declared that he "was determined to prevent North Korea from developing a nuclear arsenal, even at the risk of war." But with each war-game scenario, the Pentagon planners reached the conclusion that the risks to South Korea and the U.S. troops deployed in the South were simply too high. Tensions mounted until Clinton reluctantly approved a public visit to Pyongyang by former president Jimmy Carter. Diplomacy, albeit unofficial, seemed to have saved the day. The United States and North Korea signed a deal known as the Agreed Framework in which Pyongyang would freeze operations and construction of nuclear reactors involved in its covert nuclear weapons program in exchange for two nuclear power reactors that couldn't be used for developing weapons. Under this deal, the United States, with help from allies, would supply the country with fuel oil until those reactors were built. Insiders privately thought it was a foolish, if not dangerous, deal. North Korea's real problem was transmission of power, not generation. Building the plants wouldn't actually light up the dark country.

When George W. Bush came into office in 2001, aided by hawkish advisers like John Bolton, the tone immediately shifted. Evidence that North Korea had never really abandoned its nuclear weapons program, even in the aftermath of the Agreed Framework, gave the new administration political cover to take steps toward tearing up the deal and halting construction. In his January 2002 State of the Union address, Bush infamously described North Korea as part of the "axis of evil," ramping up tensions even more.

In October 2002, Assistant Secretary of State for East Asian and Pacific Affairs James A. Kelly made the first visit to North Korea by a Bush official. During the trip, things really took a sharp downward turn. Instead of diplomatic niceties, Kelly immediately accused North Korea of continuing to secretly produce highly enriched uranium for nuclear weapons. At first, the North Koreans denied it. But the next day, North Korea's first deputy foreign minister told Kelly and his delegation that the country was "entitled to have nuclear weapons" to safeguard it from threats, the biggest being from the United States itself.

On and on the North Korea issue simmered in the background, flaring up from time to time but never really progressing. In 2003, North Korea formally withdrew from the Nuclear Nonproliferation Treaty. Despite prodding from some advisers to take more direct action with Pyongyang, Bush, too, opted for a diplomatic approach. That took the form of the six-party talks, a rolling series of meetings among North Korea, South Korea, the United States, China, Japan, and Russia. The talks went on for six rounds over six years, until just after the election of President Barack Obama in 2008.

In April of that year, North Korea pushed ahead with a satellite launch against the wishes of the superpowers who viewed it as a bullying display of its intercontinental ballistic missile program—something against the spirit of the talks and in open violation of the 2006 United Nations Security Council Resolution 1718, which prohibits ballistic-missile and nuclear tests.

The launch actually failed, but the United States led the UN Security Council to condemn North Korea's actions. North Korea responded the next day that it would "never again take part in such [six-party] talks and will not be bound by any agreement reached at the talks." International nuclear inspectors were expelled from the country. Just under two months later, on May 25, 2009, U.S. Memorial Day that year, North Korea detonated a nuclear device underground.

The following year, a South Korean patrol vessel called *Cheonan* mysteriously sank after an explosion near Baengnyeong Island near the Northern Limit Line—the disputed maritime border between North and South Korea. Of the more than one hundred sailors aboard, forty-six died. Western powers later concluded the ship was sunk by a torpedo from a North Korean miniature submarine. A South Korean admiral, Kim Sung-chan, vowed the country would not "sit back and watch whoever caused this pain for our people."

Yet South Korea and its allies did nothing other than express indignation and cut off aid.

Obama carried on with "strategic patience" but saw that the tired strategy yielded no results during his two terms. Upon Trump's election, the outgoing president warned his counterpart of the increasingly worrying nuclear capabilities of North Korea. He would likely need to confront North Korea very early in his tenure, Obama's top security officials told the incoming team.

"The North Koreans will up the ante," James Steinberg, who oversaw North Korea strategy during Obama's first term, told a *Wall Street Journal* writer. "The status quo, the steady as you go, is not sustainable."

ADRIAN HONG KNEW THE revolving door of North Korea policy makers well. He was a well-known person in the State Department's Bureau of Democracy, Human Rights, and Labor, having personally helped dozens of North Koreans connect with diplomats to seek asylum. LiNK, which Adrian often mentioned he founded, had saved more than a thousand people since he left the organization—a fact that gave him credibility even if he wasn't responsible for those rescues.

He still held some fragment of hope that the U.S. government might step up and confront the Kim regime before it was too late, and for years he pushed policy makers to take a harder line on North Korea, while also keeping guard about revealing too much about his own views on how to do it. By the mid-2010s, wearied from years of trudging around the Capitol and giving speeches at conferences and seminars, Adrian had dialed back the more public-facing side of his networking activities, but he carried on with his informal lobbying.

One thing that distinguished Adrian from some other activists is that he was as comfortable engaging with progressive, secular types as he was with conservative, even ultra-Christian human rights crusaders. He wasn't trying to win political points as much as attempting to put as many influential people as possible in play—in order to convince them that North Korea was playing the United States and its allies for fools—and succeeding.

One person who liked what he was hearing was John Bolton, the former assistant U.S. attorney general for Ronald Reagan who kept reappearing to hold positions around national security in each successive Republican administration, with his signature mustache and expansive views of how the United States should flex its geopolitical muscles. In the Bush administration, Bolton was among the most hawkish of the hawks, nakedly calling for regime change in all of George W. Bush's "axis of evil" countries, including North Korea.

In 2003, Bolton was removed from the team negotiating with North Korea because of belittling remarks he made about Kim Jong-il in a speech in Seoul. He called him a "tyrannical dictator," and went on to say, "While he lives like royalty in Pyongyang, he keeps hundreds of thousands of his people locked in prison camps with millions more mired in abject poverty, scrounging the ground for food.

"For many in North Korea, life is a hellish nightmare," he added.

North Korea retaliated, calling Bolton "human scum and a bloodsucker." (Bolton later said it was the highest accolade he received during his time in the White House.)

Adrian managed to snag a meeting with him in 2017, years after he left his position as U.S. ambassador to the United Nations. During the private meeting, Adrian opened up to Bolton about his grander visions for North Korea. He explained his view that there was no negotiating with North Korea, so the only option was helping foment an uprising. Bolton loved what he was hearing and heartily agreed with Adrian's vision.

Across Washington, D.C., there were others, like Bolton, who shared Adrian's views that North Korea was incapable of honest bargaining. They quietly prodded him on, promising help when the time came.

IN JUNE 2017, JUST a few months into Trump's term, Secretary of State Rex Tillerson had the grim task of overseeing the return of Otto Warmbier, an American college student imprisoned by the

North Korean security agents on January 2, 2016. Warmbier, a student at the University of Virginia, had entered the country, via China, as part of a guided tour. He decided to go on the tour just before starting a study-abroad semester in Hong Kong.

His group flew from Beijing into North Korea on December 29 for a five-day New Year's tour. After members of the group went drinking to celebrate the New Year, Warmbier allegedly tried to steal a propaganda poster from a staff-only area of the Yanggakdo International Hotel at around 2:00 A.M. on New Year's Day. A grainy video later presented by North Korea shows a male-looking figure take down a big framed picture from the wall of a hallway and gently place it on the floor against the wall.

At the airport the following day, as he was waiting to depart the country, two guards tapped him on the shoulder and took him away, according to a deeply reported article by *Rolling Stone* and others. The group boarded the plane, only for an official to come on to announce that Warmbier was sick and being taken to the hospital. He all but disappeared for several weeks until the Korean Central News Agency reported he'd been arrested for "a hostile act against the state."

Then, on February 29, Warmbier appeared on North Korean state TV reading a prepared statement at a press conference, confessing that he'd attempted to steal the poster. Bizarrely, his remarks said he had done so on behalf of a Methodist church in his hometown and the secret club called the Z Society at the University of Virginia, both of which, Warmbier said, were agents of the CIA.

Current and former U.S. officials lobbied North Korea for his release for most of 2016, while Warmbier went on trial in North Korea's Supreme Court. The North Korean "kangaroo court," as Human Rights Watch put it, ruled that Warmbier had committed the crime "pursuant to the U.S. government's hostile policy" toward North Korea and sentenced him to fifteen years of hard labor.

Then, suddenly, in June of the following year, North Korea announced it would release Warmbier from detention early. At first, it seemed like a gesture intended to butter up the new president, but it quickly became apparent that Warmbier wasn't well and North Korea wanted to get him off their hands before he died.

North Koreans quietly told U.S. officials that Warmbier had contracted botulism after his sentencing and had fallen into a coma after taking a sleeping pill.

A U.S. team, including medical personnel, flew to North Korea and found Warmbier in a "violent" vegetative state, with limbs contorted and in audible agony. They brought him back to the United States, where doctors at the University of Cincinnati determined that he had lost extensive brain tissue consistent with having an acute loss of oxygen to his brain. There was no sign of botulism.

Only days after his arrival, Warmbier's parents made the decision to remove his feeding tube, and he died in the hospital soon after at the age of twenty-two. That horrifying tragedy set the tone for the beginning of the Trump administration's interactions with North Korea.

With the enmity between the United States and North Korea growing in the wake of the Otto Warmbier tragedy, both sides began to escalate tensions.

In August, speaking to the press while seated in a meeting room at his Bedminster golf resort, Trump threatened "fire, fury, and frankly power, the likes of which the world has never seen," against North Korea if it continued its nuclear ambitions. A few days afterward, he claimed the United States was "locked and loaded" when it came to North Korea.

North Korea, claiming it was the victim of a smear campaign, ratcheted the tension up even more. In September 2017, it tested a hydrogen bomb in an underground facility. In a statement about the test, the government claimed it could load it onto an intercontinental ballistic missile. Following the usual playbook, the United States and its allies increased sanctions on North Korea in response.

Trump, speaking to the United Nations General Assembly not long after, told fellow world leaders that "no one has shown more

contempt for other nations and for the well-being of their own people than the depraved regime in North Korea." By coincidence, the
seating arrangement meant that the North Korean delegate was sitting in the front row, furiously scribbling notes as Trump talked about
Kim Jong-un as being surrounded by a "band of criminals."

At the UN, Trump invoked Otto Warmbier, and how he was returned to America, only to die a few days later, and the case of a
young girl abducted by North Korea from a beach in Japan as exam-
ples of the regime's brutality. "Rocket man is on a suicide mission for
himself and for his regime," he said, referring to Kim Jong-un. "The
United States is ready, willing, and able, but hopefully this will not be
necessary."

Threats bubbled for the rest of the year, and the North Korean
saga surfaced as big news again in January 2018, when South Korea
hosted the Winter Olympics in Pyeongchang. Vice President Mike
Pence famously stared down the North Korean delegation headed by
Kim Jong-un's sister Kim Yo-jong.

Pence's steely gaze notwithstanding, the North Korean visit during the Olympics thawed relations between the North and the South
governments and led to a meeting of their officials in Panmunjom on
April 27, 2018, where Kim Jong-un said he was open to more discussions with the United States.

On March 5, Kim Jong-un hosted a senior South Korean delegation for dinner. Kim reportedly said he was amenable to "denuclearization" and would like to meet President Trump. Three days later,
South Korea's national security adviser and spy chief, both of whom
had been in attendance at the dinner, brought the news to Trump
himself in the White House, with an "invitation from Kim Jong-un"
to hold a summit between the two leaders in May. Trump accepted
on the spot.

At one point in May, both Trump and Vice President Pence mentioned the downfall of Muammar Gaddafi in Libya as a warning for
what might happen to Kim Jong-un if he didn't relinquish his nuclear
weapons. They didn't seem to realize that Gaddafi fell *after* he volun-

tarily gave up his nuclear weapons during negotiations. The Libya model was precisely what North Korea thought was in store for it if it gave up its nukes.

Behind the scenes, Trump hoped his tough-guy showmanship could lead to a negotiation breakthrough. Throughout this period, he told advisers about how famous he might become if he could strike a better deal than his predecessors on North Korea. As he saw it, the best strategy was to threaten hell and damnation so that the other side would be persuaded to compromise rather than face a mortal threat.

Obama had "strategic patience" and Trump had "maximum pressure," though in reality they were two sides of the same coin. The key difference was that, thanks in great measure to Pyongyang's bluster barrage throughout 2016 and 2017 with dozens of missile tests, Trump had the incentive to enforce sanctions against the Kim regime and tried to get other nations to do their part. At the same time, Trump had no intention of launching an attack on North Korea either, as he would own up to after meeting Kim in Singapore in June 2018.

Adrian, living in Los Angeles by now, was watching this flurry of headlines involving North Korea with great interest. On the surface, the rhetoric seemed like more of the same wobbly diplomacy that has characterized North Korean relations for decades. But there was also something wild in the Trump administration's approach to things that could create openings for action. If the diplomatic gambit failed, as he knew it would, then hard-liners like Bolton might be given a bigger chance to set the agenda. Adrian knew he wanted to stay close to those developments, too.

AS TRUMP AND HIS team flew to the neutral meeting ground of Singapore in June 2018 for the scheduled summit with Kim Jong-un, the president was practically giddy at the possibility of striking a deal that no previous president could pull off. For the consummate dealmaker,

Adrian Hong's senior photograph at Bonita Vista High School near San Diego in 2001.

A page devoted to family photographs in Adrian's 2001 high school yearbook.

Kang Chol-hwan, author of *The Aquariums of Pyongyang,* about his experiences in the Yodok prison camp in North Korea. The book inspired Adrian and a generation of Korean Americans to devote themselves to helping North Koreans.

Kim Il-sung, the former guerrilla fighter who became North Korea's first leader, shaped the country's obsessive self-reliance and totalitarian government.

Kim Jong-un with his father, Kim Jong-il. North Korea is the only so-called communist country in the world that is ruled by a dynasty.

North Koreans are forced to worship members of the Kim dynasty as if they are deities.

Tickets for some of the earliest Liberty in North Korea events, in 2005. Adrian Hong was the founding leader of the group, which spread to campuses across the world.

Adrian had a knack for political networking and had connections on both sides of the aisle to people dealing with refugees and North Korea.

Escapees from North Korea often have to ford the Tumen River under the watchful eye of armed border guards. Even if they get to China, there is a strong chance they'll be discovered and sent back.

Joseph Kim was rescued by Adrian Hong in 2006. Kim later moved to America, where he learned English and spoke publicly about the horrors of the North Korean regime.

Adrian Hong became a TED Fellow who focused on how technology could help spread information in closed societies like North Korea.

The son of missionaries, Adrian frequently volunteered for humanitarian causes, including in Haiti in 2004.

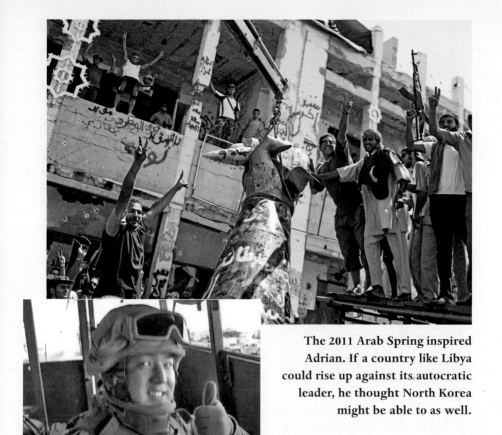

The 2011 Arab Spring inspired Adrian. If a country like Libya could rise up against its autocratic leader, he thought North Korea might be able to as well.

After graduating from high school, Christopher Ahn joined the U.S. Marine Corps Reserve and served in Iraq.

When Christopher was a teenager, his father died, leaving him and his brother to look after their mother and grandmother. Christopher married Grace, a teacher in Los Angeles, in 2018.

As his first big mission with Adrian's volunteer group to help North Korean escapees, Christopher met Kim Han-sol in Taipei soon after Han-sol's father was murdered in Malaysia.

Kim Jong-nam, eldest son of North Korea's second leader, Kim Jong-il, was unlikely to take his father's position, but he still represented a potential rival to Kim Jong-un. Kim Jong-nam was assassinated with VX nerve agent in Kuala Lumpur in 2017.

Adrian's group, Free Cheollima, later issued a video from Kim Han-sol that was viewed around the world. The CIA spirited Han-sol, his mother, and his sister to an unknown location soon after Adrian's team arrived to help them.

U.S. president Donald Trump attempted to strike a deal with Kim Jong-un to denuclearize in exchange for reduced sanctions, but the bid ultimately failed.

The North Korean embassy in Spain, where Adrian's group tried to rescue a top diplomat, sits in a leafy, wealthy neighborhood of Madrid.

Adrian arrived with gift bags, pretending to have a meeting with the official. The plan was to break into the embassy with his team to make the rescue look like a kidnapping.

After Adrian stepped into the embassy, Free Cheollima members waited outside until he opened the door to let them in.

Police arrived more than an hour later after a woman from the embassy ran into the streets screaming about an invasion. Adrian pretended to be a North Korean official and fobbed off the police.

Christopher Ahn was arrested in Los Angeles after Spanish authorities issued an extradition request, accusing him of attempted kidnapping and assault. As of April 2022, a judge has yet to rule on whether he will be sent to Spain.

it could be the deal of a lifetime. Inflating his ego even more was the South Korean president Moon Jae-in's public comment that he would nominate Trump for the Nobel Peace Prize.

One of the tricks up Trump's sleeve was a four-minute movie-trailer-style video created by the National Security Council that suggested Kim Jong-un could break the cycle of "history repeating itself" and achieve prosperity for his country. In the video, credited to Destiny Pictures, the narrator intones that "there comes a time when only a few are called upon to make a difference" and that "a new world can begin today."

"Out of the darkness can come the light," the narrator goes on to say. "And the light of hope can burn bright." At one point it shows North Korea lighting up at night—the inverse of the famous nighttime picture of North Korea from space.

Quoted in *The Guardian,* Ned Price, a former National Security Council spokesperson, said, "The whole enterprise reeks of amateurism and comes off as an attempt to check the box on a harebrained idea that presumably originated in the oval office."

The big summit took place at the Capella resort on Singapore's Sentosa Island, which has a colonial statehouse feel. After a grand photo op and ceremony, Trump and Kim Jong-un started bantering a bit about the press. Trump told Kim at one point that the press was "totally dishonest," which elicited laughter from the North Korean leader.

Kim Jong-un asked Trump how the American president assessed the younger North Korean, which Trump said was a great question. Trump saw Kim as really smart, quite secretive, a very good person, totally sincere, with a great personality, John Bolton later recalled. Though the two claimed to have much in common, including an interest in denuclearizing the Korea Peninsula, in reality there was no genuine overlap.

Feigning exhaustion, Kim told Trump how he was a mere politician and had to deal with the hard-liners in his country who were dead set against getting rid of the country's prized nuclear weapons.

What he needed, Kim preened, were concessions from the United States *first*. With those in hand, Kim could persuade his country's power brokers to make steps toward denuclearization. Impulsively, Trump agreed to hold off on joint military exercises with South Korea while he and Kim were negotiating in good faith.

As their talks wound down, Trump started joking with Kim about his insult "little rocket man" and asked if Kim had ever heard of Elton John. Trump was trying to convince Kim that "rocket man" could, in a new light, be seen as a compliment.

Speaking briefly to the press afterward, Kim told them the meeting was like a "day in fantasy land." Trump tweeted on arrival in Washington, D.C., that "everybody can now feel much safer than the day I took office. There is no longer a Nuclear Threat from North Korea. Meeting with Kim Jong Un was an interesting and very positive experience. North Korea has great potential for the future!"

But, of course, history repeated itself again. The empty statements led to no concrete actions on North Korea's part throughout the year. There wouldn't be much excitement again until the following year when Trump would make one last attempt at swinging the deal of a lifetime.

WHILE TRUMP'S EFFORTS SPUTTERED, Cheollima was ramping up. The group announced on its website in April 2017 that it had rescued two people. There were no details and no reports of North Korean officials defecting in any media, but for Korea watchers the posts were tantalizing. "Our gratitude to Mr. C, and to an unnamed government."

One North Korea nonprofit veteran told me that while publicly taking no stance, he was privately rooting for Cheollima to up the ante. The advocacy community could feel nearly moribund at times. There wasn't much fresh thinking, and there was a bias against action. Cheollima Civil Defense had made its name in helping out Kim Han-sol. "I was wondering what they'd pull off next," he told me.

To find truly exciting moments where the Kim regime faced a mortal threat, you have to dig deep into history. One such moment was the 1967 Kapsan Faction Incident. At this relatively early stage of North Korea's history as a nation-state, the dynastic aspect of the regime's power had yet to be established. Like Kim Il-sung, the members of the Kapsan Faction were veterans of Korea's conflict with Japan, but they had become disaffected with his encouragement of leader worshipping. The group sought to change the country's economic policies, undermine Kim Il-sung, and appoint a new man, Pak Kum-chol, as his successor.

The battle of ideas that played out in a series of grandiose speeches before Kim Il-sung and his twenty-six-year-old son, Kim Jong-il, launched a purge against the movement. Some were exiled to the countryside, and others were killed. But more important, it became the moment when Kim Il-sung's hold on power became unparalleled and the concept of dynastic succession took hold, according to the historical research of the South Korean academic Lim Jae-cheon. Without any concern, Kim Il-sung's allies called it the Monolithic Ideological System. Afterward, many of the features of modern North Korean autocracy crystallized: the ubiquitous Kim Il-sung pins on citizens' shirts, quoting of the Great Leader's shibboleths, and editing of all books for revolutionary "correctness."

Nearly half a century had passed with few overt challenges to Kim family rule. Within North Korea, the tattletale culture instilled in citizens virtually ensured that no serious attempt at challenging the regime from within could be established. But that didn't mean North Koreans—including government officials—were universally fond of the country's leaders and status quo. They just never expressed it outright, especially to outsiders.

Posting to its website in Korean in August, Cheollima made an overt offer to help more North Korean officials who wanted to escape. "If you contact us at the email address below, we will safely send you to the place you want to go, no matter what country you are in. We have already helped several North Korean officials and do not expect anything in return." Compared with their citizens back home, North Korean diplomats abroad were some of the few North Koreans who, plausibly, could log on to the internet.

Over the coming months, Cheollima continued to exude mystery with its murky online posts. The group thanked the U.K. government for "timely and critical assistance recently," without giving details, alongside cryptic posts such as "Black 70" and "3972745482." Were these coded messages, posted publicly, to the group's network abroad or to those it was trying to help escape?

Much later, I learned from a Cheollima official that the expression of gratitude to the U.K. related to the defection of a high-ranking North Korean man whom Cheollima rescued after assisting him in faking his accidental death in Europe. The man was spirited to the U.K. and then to South Korea.

Cheollima waded into politics, too. In November, it sent a screed out in Korean criticizing the Moon government for failing to help North Koreans in need. "Aren't you Korean?" the post asks. The group set up a special email address for volunteers, saying it was especially looking for people with experience in the military, first aid, policing, firefighting, nursing, medicine, and interpreting.

Then, on June 11, 2018, another intriguing post went up on the Cheollima site: "To comrades who want to escape from North Korea—I received your letter well. If you've already sent us an e-mail, don't send it anymore. We understand the difficult situation of our current comrades. Stay in shelter for the time being, be careful and be safe. We will see you soon."

12

THE ITALIAN JOB

Be mild with the mild, shrewd with the crafty, confiding to the honest, rough to the ruffian, and a thunderbolt to the liar. But in all this, never be unmindful of your own dignity.

—JOHN BROWN

ROME
NOVEMBER 2018

BY MOST MEASURES, JO SONG-GIL OCCUPIED A PLUM POSITION. Jo was among the most trusted and high-ranking diplomats abroad for North Korea. He was relatively wealthy, respected, and politically connected back home. He had arrived in Italy in 2015 as the number two official and rose to acting ambassador in 2017 when Italy ejected his boss in retaliation for a North Korea nuclear weapon test that year. Jo, a diplomat in his late thirties who spoke English, Italian, and French, had previously served in France and had a subtle whiff of the debonair about him. Among his interests was medieval art.

Not only did Jo hold the enviable position as acting ambassador to Italy based in Rome, but he was also charged with negotiating his country's food aid contracts with the UN's Food and Agriculture Organization. North Korea didn't like to admit it publicly, but such aid was critical for feeding the country and of huge importance to the government.

Yet Jo wanted out—at almost any cost.

Diplomats are almost exclusively chosen from the politically connected and intermarried top echelons of North Korea. They undergo extensive ideological training and learn to be extraordinarily fluent in all things North Korea. Even in a candid moment, in a meeting with a diplomat far from Pyongyang, it would be hard to detect even a trace of their personal view of things, according to Western and South Korean diplomats who have met them.

Defectors are among the most critical intelligence vulnerabilities for North Korea. Not only do they possess information about North Korea's cipher system used to send messages to its embassies around the world, but they have incalculable information about North Korea's criminal enterprises and its foreign policy establishment.

One sign of Jo's high status was the fact that he was able to live in Rome with both his wife and his daughter. Most diplomats, who hail from the highest "core" social echelon in the *songbun* system of political and economic classes, are required to leave one of their closest relatives behind as collateral. One reason Jo was permitted to have his teenage daughter with him was that she suffered from an unspecified mental illness that required constant attention.

The system isn't subtle: defect and doom your wife, child, or grandparent. Escapees or defectors, who commit a crime in the eyes of the Kim regime, suffer the infamous "three generations of punishment" instituted by the country's founder, Kim Il-sung. This would definitely mean imprisonment, but it could also mean death.

When Thae Yong-ho, a mild-looking, fifty-four-year-old, bespectacled deputy ambassador to the U.K. from North Korea, defected to South Korea in 2016, it was seen as a deep betrayal.

On the surface, during his years of service, Thae was a North Korean defender through and through, giving impassioned speeches before meetings of the British Communist Party and serving as the gatekeeper for British journalists visiting Pyongyang. But he also seemed to absorb the British way of life during his decade there, enjoying curry dinners and playing golf and tennis with acquaintances.

That a senior diplomat would defect to the South was a huge embarrassment. The actual defection wasn't something out of a spy novel. One day, as if nothing special were happening at all, he walked out of the embassy with his wife and son. They made their way to the South Korean embassy, where they were immediately supported and placed in a safe house with the assistance of U.K. authorities. The family were flown on a U.K. military plane to Germany and then on to South Korea.

The relative ease of Thae's escape was an example often given by Adrian to would-be defectors. The handcuffs you feel on your wrist are actually make-believe. The doors are wide open. All you have to do is step through them.

After the Thae affair, the Ministry of Foreign Affairs instituted a policy that at least one immediate family member—a child or spouse—would have to stay behind when a diplomat was posted abroad.

Even entertaining the desire to defect was exceedingly risky. But, one day, with Jo Song-gil's term in Rome expected to finish at the end of November 2018, he found a few precious seconds of time alone to dash off cryptic emails to the Italian and South Korean governments, as well as people close to Cheollima Civil Defense.

Diplomats were beginning to hear about Cheollima because of their role in the exfiltration of Kim Han-sol. Of course, for a diplomat to reach out to the group would mean committing a capital offense. Some North Koreans were even worried that the whole Cheollima group was a hoax created by North Korea itself to entrap would-be traitors. Such was the paranoia caused by the Kim regime.

The challenge with these diplomats is they need to at once completely embrace and believe the "truth" that North Korea disseminates to its people while also existing in the "real world," where none of these things are actually true. In a sense, one of the most important skills for a North Korean diplomat is to hold two contradictory views at the same time without it causing any cognitive dissonance. Orwell's "doublethink" was a fact of life, a survival mechanism, for North Koreans posted abroad.

Outgoing and talkative, Jo frequently surprised businessmen he met around Italy on trips to view factories and distribution centers. His formal manners were so precise, albeit mechanical, that many Italians he met believed he'd undergone extensive etiquette training.

The same couldn't be said about "Mr. Pak," a short and stocky companion for Jo everywhere he went. Pak spoke much less fluent Italian and had a crass demeanor. Italians meeting the two surmised Pak was there to keep an eye on the more senior Jo. For Jo to escape, he'd need to do so without raising the suspicions of his perpetual shadow.

At every junction, Jo appeared to follow all the rules to the maximum, even requiring documents of people with whom he was meeting to prove their bona fides. He and Pak would join lunches with Italian businessmen and politicians together, eating and drinking heartily but always conveniently looking away when the bill came, according to reporting from John Lyons in *The Wall Street Journal*.

Much later, Jo told interviewers in South Korea that he'd begun secretly studying the history of North Korea in non-Korean textbooks more than a decade before he opted to defect. Jo's position in Rome also gave him a rare window into North Korea's food situation. Despite the country's doctrine of self-subsistence, it actually depended heavily on handouts for its food security. Meanwhile, with illicit businesses around the world and factories full of employees working only for food, Kim Jong-un and his inner circle were able to live in luxury.

The revelations acted like a seed in Jo's mind, growing and tangling deeper with all his views of the world until he could see that everything he'd been taught was a lie.

FOR CHEOLLIMA CIVIL DEFENSE, rescuing diplomats wasn't only about helping individual families find a better life, though that was embedded in the unspoken contract between them. These officials had extraordinary amounts of information on the North Korean government and its secret operations abroad—information valuable for

Adrian and his team to have for themselves because of their more revolutionary plans for overturning the Kim regime, but also to bring to U.S. and other intelligence agencies. It gave Cheollima Civil Defense a reason to interact with spies.

Most of all, though, the propaganda value of senior officials defecting could be huge. The image of North Korea's senior diplomats betraying the regime sent the message that Kim Jong-un's hold on the elite was faltering.

When Thae defected, a South Korean government spokesman trumpeted that it was a "sign that some of the core elite in the North are losing hope in the Kim Jong-un regime" and that "the internal unity of the ruling class in the North is weakening." North Korea analysts were less sanguine about such defections, viewing them as more isolated incidents.

The risks with such defections are high, but not nearly as challenging as escorting North Korean escapees across China in the hopes that the U.S. embassy will help them leave the country and find safety in South Korea or elsewhere. One of the biggest risks for Cheollima Civil Defense was vetting the inbound emails. Since establishing their online inbox, they were aware that for every would-be defector there might be a dozen virus-laden emails from North Korean operatives trying to learn their identities. Even a seemingly real defector might be pretending in order to lure Cheollima volunteers into a trap.

Cheollima projected an aura of mystery, and speculation in blogs and among online commentators abounded that it was a CIA front organization. Even North Korea analysts at universities and think tanks struggled to conceive of the idea of a genuine underground organization dedicated to toppling Kim Jong-un.

In South Korea, there is a general skepticism toward activist groups focused on North Korea. The first question people ask is, who is funding them? For example, the activists floating anti-Kim propaganda and other information on balloons into North Korea receive funding from U.S. government sources, among others, which is often brought up to undermine their credibility.

The secret of Cheollima Civil Defense is it had almost no money at all. Nearly all of the donations were from members of the group—case in point, Christopher Ahn footing the airline bill for Kim Han-sol to escape Macau via Taiwan with his mother and sister. Adrian traveled the world working on North Korea, but mostly he was spending his own money and frequently he was spending more than he had. With a wife and plans to start a family, Adrian's lack of funds was a constant source of stress.

Cash was always a problem. Even donors sympathetic to Adrian's worldview didn't want to touch risky operations. They'd happily pay a monthly donation for supporting escapees once they arrived in America or to fund shelters on the border, but precious few wanted to risk being identified with an organization dedicated to toppling a nuclear state.

The more Adrian thought about it, the more he came to believe that he needed to appeal to the profit incentives of would-be funders of his revolutionary activity. In conversations with business executives he'd gotten to know well in Thailand, Japan, and elsewhere in Asia, he'd go so far as to ask for large donations that would be repaid once North Korea was liberated. The idea piqued interest, but there were no takers. Tempting, but still too risky. Adrian grew frustrated.

Once, in a moment of vulnerability, Adrian, looking deeply tired, confided to Christopher Ahn, "I don't want to do this."

Adrian intimated that he'd spent years looking for a leader but that he couldn't find someone else with the same level of commitment—someone who wanted to devote themselves almost entirely to the cause of destabilizing the Kim regime. He told Ahn that he felt constantly broke because of overspending and his tendency not to pursue commercial opportunities that came up.

Appreciating Adrian's moment of openness, Ahn said what a lot of well-intentioned ordinary people might say to a friend in need. "Hey, man, whatever you need," he'd tell him. "If you just want to hang out, blow off steam. We don't have to talk about North Korea."

But Adrian was not an ordinary person, and just as brief as his moment of intimacy, he'd close up again and flip open his phone to find dozens of messages on Signal from around the world.

With little funds, Cheollima Civil Defense needed to focus on operations that were relatively inexpensive, had an outsized potential to yield important intelligence, and could chip away at the myth of North Korea as an all-seeing, all-powerful regime. Of course, most people on earth didn't believe that, but North Koreans were inculcated from birth to see the Workers' Party and the Kim regime as deified and invincible.

The answer was high-profile defections. News of a defection from the senior ranks of North Korea's government went around the world. The footage could also easily be smuggled into North Korea on USB sticks carried by weather balloons.

Just as attractive were the troves of intelligence offered up by defectors. Not only were the diplomats trusted with many state secrets in their jobs, but they were tasked with making money for the regime. Most North Korean embassies also run side businesses to fund themselves, and some of these moneymaking schemes are illicit, according to UN reports and former intelligence officials. Diplomats moonlight as drug or arms dealers, or use their diplomatic immunity to import goods duty-free and resell at a profit. In 2015, a North Korean diplomat in South Africa was expelled for smuggling illegal rhinoceros horns into Mozambique. In 2016, another North Korean diplomat in Bangladesh was caught smuggling more than one million cigarettes.

A UN panel monitoring North Korean activity that tried to circumvent sanctions found extensive arms trading with Syria, gold and cash smuggling between Iran and Dubai, and other activity around Europe and Africa especially. But often the businesses run by embassy staff are not particularly lucrative or glamorous. The embassy in India used to sell beef on the down low, using its basement as an abattoir. Norwegian police found in a 1976 investigation that every

single member of the North Korean embassy in Oslo was heavily involved in the import and illegal sale of spirits and hundreds of thousands of cigarettes.

In Poland, there were forty businesses registered to the embassy,
including a yacht club, advertising agencies, and a pharmaceutical
company. A frequently rented event space for photo shoots and even
a reality television show in Sofia, Bulgaria, is actually owned by the
North Korean state.

One former North Korean diplomat told CNN in February 2021
that in addition to diplomats each embassy had "economic trading
workers" who were given a quota for how much money they needed
to make for the government back home. In some countries, such as
Kuwait, North Korea dispatched thousands of its low-class workers
who were rented out en masse to construction companies. All the
wages go to the North Korean government, of course. It's essentially
slave labor. The practice was largely stopped in 2017, except for in
China and Russia, after the UN published a resolution banning member states from employing North Korean workers in response to a
round of missile and nuclear tests.

The details of those side businesses are valuable intelligence because they could be used to shut down the flow of foreign currency
to Pyongyang, a chink in the Kim regime's armor that Adrian and
Cheollima Civil Defense wanted to exploit in their wider ambitions
to foment a revolution in North Korea.

WHEN ADRIAN AND HIS colleagues at Cheollima first learned about
Jo's efforts to defect, they began analyzing the North Korean embassy
in Rome, located on a quiet street dotted with larger homes and embassies in an area of the city called EUR, a neighborhood that had
once been earmarked by Benito Mussolini to host the 1942 World's
Fair. Just around the corner from the North Korean embassy is the
embassy of Bangladesh and a huge stadium called the PalaLottomat-
ica, home to the 1960 Olympic basketball tournaments.

If it wasn't for a small metal plaque that reads "Embassy of the Democratic People's Republic of Korea," the building, hidden behind a gate and leafy bushes, could easily pass as an older private residence.

A twenty-minute walk to the north is the Palazzo della Civiltà Italiana, also known colloquially as the Square Colosseum because it looks just like the famous Roman monument but in the shape of a sharp cube. The building was meant to celebrate Mussolini's Fascist regime.

Despite the global enmity between other Western countries and North Korea, Italy had markedly warmer relations with the North Koreans over the years. In 2000, it became the first of the G7 states to establish diplomatic relations with the country, and the two countries had numerous, though relatively low-profile, interactions over the years. North Korea was even permitted to exhibit ginseng-based beauty products at an expo in Milan in 2015. Italian researchers traveled to North Korea in 2010 to study volcanic properties of Mount Baekdu—the setting for many Korean legends and folktales.

Within the Italian political firmament, there are notable proponents of Italian–North Korean relations, including a former senator named Antonio Razzi and Osvaldo Napoli, an Italian member of Parliament, who even headed a commission trying to increase cooperation between Italy and North Korea. It was men like these whom Jo got to know best during his time in Rome.

In the eyes of the Italian businessmen and diplomats who met him, Jo Song-gil showed no signs of disloyalty to his government. Razzi sometimes tried to get a rise out of Jo by making extremely light criticisms of one of North Korea's founders—jokes such as Kim Il-sung smiled more than Kim Jong-il. Jo would immediately give a strident defense, almost as if by instinct.

On August 15, he invited two dozen Italian communists, lawmakers, and business contacts to the embassy on Viale dell'Esperanto for a reception in honor of North Korea's Independence Day. As the VIPs passed into the embassy, their eyes darted around, taking in this rarely seen space in their country. The overwhelming feeling was sadness:

the grand space was furnished with only the most basic and minimal furniture. The walls were nearly bare, except for a few pitiful North Korean landscape paintings and the usual hagiographic photos of Kim Jong-il and Kim Il-sung.

The North Korean embassy staff laid out a tiny sampling of Italian and Korean dishes on a table. Thimble-sized pours of wine in scratched, old glasses were handed to the visitors.

With an air of formality, Jo talked about his impending return to North Korea and said he was hoping to take one last trip to visit contacts around Italy before he left.

A MONTH LATER, ADRIAN, Christopher Ahn, and Sam Ryu—a younger friend of Adrian's who went to the same high school in San Diego—arrived in Italy for a reconnaissance mission, according to Spanish court documents later made public. They were scoping operations in Rome, but also in Prague and Kuala Lumpur, according to a Cheollima member.

They flew into Venice as a base of operations for the short trip, staying at the modestly accommodated Annia Park Hotel just a few minutes away from the airport. Many tourists from around the world go in and out of the Venice airport every day, so it's a cosmopolitan, diverse scene of people. With a camera around the neck and a fanny pack as your disguise, it's a perfect place to disappear.

Adrian had asked Ahn early on whether he wanted to be a leader in Cheollima, with his own responsibilities and missions. Ahn had given an emphatic "no."

"I've got to run a business, support my family," he told him.

Ahn was knee-deep in starting a company that would supply restaurants and cafés with special ingredients for premium drinks and other products. One of those was a cannabis oil supplement that could be used to make cannabis-oil-infused lattes and smoothies. With investors beginning to line up, he barely had time for Cheollima volunteer work at all.

But he found he couldn't quite close the door on Adrian. The one thing he was open to was situations where Adrian needed someone with empathy. No matter how busy he was, he still had a craving to be part of the "micro that led to the macro." He didn't want to do anything military related. "That doesn't define me," he said later.

Instead, Adrian brought him as a reassuring presence when they met with would-be defectors who risked their lives just to have a conversation with Cheollima members. Speaking Korean, Ahn would tell those men and women that he was "here to let you know that if there's ever a desire, we'll help you." In his own eyes, he was the "closer" in those scenarios—reassuring without coaxing, making people feel safe enough to take a step forward.

One quirk of the way Cheollima worked is that none of the members were fully briefed on an operation before arriving. They were there because they had placed 100 percent trust in Adrian. Arriving in Italy, Ahn found out the plans only a few hours later. This was to protect the security of an operation. All of the group's dynamics presupposed North Korean hackers would be after them, trying to get a hint of whom they were speaking to. Even the website of Cheollima, with its obscure codes and lists of numbers, was simply a system to distribute information to members without having to call or message each other directly.

To conduct intelligence gathering, Adrian acquired a fake Italian ID with the name Matthew Chao and created a fictional company in Dubai, Baron Stone Capital, for email exchanges with embassies and businessmen connected to North Korea. Over several years, Matthew Chao visited embassies across Europe and Asia under this guise. Sometimes the embassy workers didn't know who he was; other times, they—like Jo Song-gil—had reached out to Cheollima about escaping.

ON A COOL AND crisp November morning, it was go time for Jo and his family. The team that assembled for the operation included several people sympathetic to the Cheollima cause. They were among the scores of people around the world Adrian had recruited at different phases of his North Korea work. Some of them were themselves North Korean escapees who felt compelled to act. Others were from the sliver of activists in South Korea who were sick and tired of the status quo.

The rescuers arrived in two vehicles and parked about a hundred yards from the front gate. With engines running, they then waited, according to a Western intelligence official familiar with the escape.

Suddenly the gate opened and out came Jo and his wife, eyes darting around looking for the car—a moment of fear that no one would be waiting. Then they caught sight of the getaway car and rushed to get inside.

"Just go, please go," Jo told the drivers, according to the intelligence official. As they careened off, looking for the highway to get to Venice, he and his wife looked by turns frightened and upset.

Eventually, more composed, they were able to speak and explained that they couldn't get their seventeen-year-old daughter to come with them. She suffered from a disability (undiagnosed formally, but possibly a form of autism) and was often difficult to communicate with. But there had been no time to delay; a split-second decision had to be made, and the couple had left without her. Jo's wife was highly distraught.

Cheollima's role in the defection was reported by myself and colleagues at *The Wall Street Journal* in April 2020, citing people familiar with their movements. Jo eventually made his way to South Korea in 2021, where he denied any contact with Cheollima and maintained that he escaped on his own with his wife (they divorced after arriving in South Korea).

ANTONIO RAZZI, THE FORMER Italian senator, who had been among the guests invited to the North Korean Independence Day celebration in August, had made plans to see Jo one last time before his term as ambassador ended. They'd agreed right after the event to meet on November 20 at a trattoria called Lagana near Madama Palace, the fifteenth-century seat of the Italian senate, for a farewell lunch.

But instead only "Mr. Pak" arrived, accompanied by an unsmiling older man who spoke no Italian and was introduced as the new acting ambassador. The conversation was chilly.

A few days later, word began to spread among Italian officials about the diplomat's sudden escape.

13

I'LL BE GONE AWHILE

It is the unspoken ethic of all magicians to not reveal the secrets.

—*DAVID COPPERFIELD*

LOS ANGELES
JANUARY 2019

SAM RYU SHOWED UP FOR HIS FAREWELL DINNER IN DOWNTOWN Los Angeles buzzing with energy. His two friends had so many questions about this new venture: What *even* was it? Where? Whom would he work with?

But Ryu wouldn't spill any details. To his friends, the grinning twenty-nine-year-old was acting like some kind of spymaster, albeit one who wore his excitement for his new venture on his sleeve. It was all the more surreal for his friends because everything about Ryu's life until that point seemed rather tame.

After attending the University of Southern California, he jumped on the lowest rung of the Hollywood ladder. His first job was as an executive assistant—the underpaid grunt workers of the industry—at an outfit called the Traveling Picture Show Company in Los Angeles. The modern, loft-style offices were a few minutes around the corner from the Hollywood Walk of Fame.

Ryu rose a notch to become a film development and production manager for three years before becoming a producer at Portal A, a social media–focused production company. The work was often extremely shallow and related to the burgeoning field of online "influencers," a former employee recalled.

Ryu had picked up a lot of skills along the way. He knew how to oversee a film shoot and how to produce short documentaries. Yes, when he announced to friends that he was selling all his possessions, breaking his lease, and joining a mysterious, new project, he hadn't come close to breaking into the Hollywood big league. All he would divulge was that it was a documentary, one that was risky and globe-trotting—and one, he felt, that had the potential to change lives. Ryu told his friends he might be on the road for the better part of a year.

What he didn't tell those friends and co-workers was that his new boss and the chief funder on the project was Adrian Hong, crusading defender of North Korean human rights by day and operator of an underground rebel group dedicated to taking down the Kim regime by night. The documentary project they were planning would go inside North Korean embassies, including rare interviews with defectors, with the goal of serving as a galvanizing force for their plans to break the image within North Korea that the regime was all mighty and all seeing. By revealing the truth of the regime in a language and style understandable by North Koreans, they hoped to weaken Kim Jong-un's hold on power. It was a far cry from creating fodder for YouTube-bingeing teenagers.

Ryu was no stranger to Adrian. The pair knew each other from Chula Vista, where they attended the same high school about six years apart. Over time, Ryu, a boyish and polite young man, had become one of Adrian's ardent supporters. His skill set meant he could perform tasks such as editing video for the group, but, more important for Adrian, he was also a young, fearless lieutenant who was willing to jump on a plane to help on a project or mission at a moment's notice.

Twenty nineteen promised to be a big year for Cheollima. Just two weeks before Ryu's farewell dinner, the group wrote on its website, "This is the year everything changes." Inbound messages from

North Korean would-be defectors continued to arrive, and interest in the group and its work was increasing, too. The group had half a dozen rescues in different stages of development, all of them involving North Koreans abroad. Since the Kim Han-sol rescue, journalists had also been sending in a stream of interview requests.

Among the first journalists to approach the group was the *Wall Street Journal* reporter Alastair Gale. Adrian responded to his questions by email from the Cheollima email address, but Gale never knew the names of any members of the group, which he described as a "group of North Korean dissidents."

In his email to Gale, Adrian bemoaned that the group had met with refusals on the part of several countries earlier in the year to help with defections, including in connection with the Kim Han-sol escape, singling out Canada. Where others were refusing to act, Adrian wrote, "We came to meet an urgent need by North Koreans for protection of those in danger."

The article painted Cheollima in a good light, with interviews from anonymous defectors, human rights workers, and diplomats saying the group was well connected, moved quickly, and had participated in numerous successful rescues.

The same month as Ryu's farewell dinner, Adrian was traveling around the Middle East and Asia for another project. It was his best hope for making enough money to start properly financing Cheollima Civil Defense and paying his volunteers salaries. Adrian and Ousama Abushagur, his old friend from the Libyan civil war days, created in the summer of 2018 a company called Qwik.ly that had ambitions to become a global electric-scooter-sharing business. Their first market would be Dubai, a city open to trying out cutting-edge transportation ideas. Adrian was in Singapore in January, discussing Qwik.ly with potential partners there.

The company showed up on Twitter in July 2018 with the account @moveqwikly. Using Trikke electric bikes, Qwik.ly set up pilot locations around Dubai in that summer and autumn. Residents of the Jumeirah Beach Residence in the southern end of the city could use them to zoom across the full length of the promenade. Qwik.ly's website boasted that the company was "the first dockless micro mobility platform in cities and campuses around the Middle East, North Africa, Asia and Europe."

Sam Ryu and Christopher Ahn were going to be involved in the business, too. Adrian wanted to bring aboard trusted friends from his North Korea work, part of his ethos that business and nonprofit work could live side by side and even benefit each other. Qwik.ly had some seed funding to kick off operations, and there was the promise of more to come—money that they could use to expand across the Emirates to become the dominant electric scooter share brand.

Adrian was extremely bullish on the prospects for the company. As he saw it, the millions it could earn him would jump-start Cheollima in a way that nothing else had to date.

ARRIVING IN AN UBER on February 7, Adrian walked up to the red-walled compound of the North Korean embassy in Madrid in a suit and tie. His trusted deputy Sam Ryu was stationed at the Eurostars Zarzuela Park hotel just up the road.

After Adrian buzzed the door, a young man cautiously opened it and peered out at the man standing in the entryway. "Matthew Chao, Baron Stone Capital," Adrian said, stretching out his hand. He explained he was interested in meeting the ambassador about a business opportunity.

After a few minutes, the man returned to the door with So Yun-suk. Just inside the doorway, So and Adrian had a brief conversation. No details ever emerged about exactly what they said.

Before he left, "Chao" handed his business card to So, which included a Baron Stone business address and Adrian's actual mobile phone number.

This briefest of meetings was undoubtedly the beginning of a seminal event for So and Cheollima.

The process had kicked into motion several months earlier, in June 2018, when a message arrived at the group's email address

CCDprotection@protonmail.com from someone describing themselves as a North Korean diplomat in Europe. After some careful back-and-forth, the person agreed to reveal their name and location.

Cheollima had designed its website to be attractive to people like So. They stressed the promise of protection without expecting anything in return.

A testimonial had been posted from a "high-ranking North Korean official" written only in Korean. In it, the official describes first the terror diplomats can feel when they are positioned in embassies around the world. "When North Koreans go abroad, the first word that comes to mind is escape," he wrote, talking about the feelings of imprisonment and the fear of being summoned back to Pyongyang at any moment.

Then, calling Cheollima "a lighthouse by the turbulent open sea," the official goes on to say,

> When I was first contacted, I honestly had a lot of doubts. You were like a mysterious, amorphous shadow. From knowing my personal cell phone number to the luxury car and airplane used in the escape process, your passion and airtight preparation were astonishing. . . . It was by your miracle and grace that the far-off nightmare of escaping that I had foreseen until the end of my life came true in just a few hours.

In retrospect, it almost seems as if the official were addressing Adrian himself in his parting words: "Only you can approach them like a shadow and only you can make wishes come true."

Ryu and three other Cheollima operatives from South Korea flew to Madrid soon after So's first message to Cheollima. They stayed at the Eurostars Zarzuela Park hotel and used the trip to get a feel for the area and take clandestine reconnaissance photos of the embassy.

A big part of these trips was seeing what creative exfiltrations could be arranged considering the environment. What could they do so as not to arouse suspicion—what would look natural?

Their Koreanness was both a benefit in that some passersby innately seemed to think they were just tourists and a problem in that they could stick out especially if they behaved in odd ways. The embassy was located in Aravaca, a wealthy residential area in the northwest of Madrid, where several former presidents of Spain lived. There weren't many tourists passing through.

In February, Adrian arranged with So to stop by the embassy in person to prove his bona fides and confirm the operation was now live. When "Matthew Chao" would show up—that was the proof that Cheollima was genuine and ready to rescue him and his family.

There were multiple dimensions to the operation. Of utmost importance was rescuing So, and his wife and son, but there were other possibilities. So himself had even hinted at one outcome that caught Adrian's attention: it was possible that everyone in the embassy could join the defection together. The North Koreans inside included another married couple and two men on their own in addition to So, his wife, and his son. That was a total of seven.

Whether Adrian forgot or So never gave the exact number, Cheollima was under the impression in all its planning going forward that there were only six adults inside the embassy. Based on what he had learned from So, Adrian held out hope that perhaps these others could be persuaded to defect as well.

The chance of the whole embassy defecting at once, while not a guaranteed thing, would have made possible a longtime dream of Adrian's to create a de facto rebel embassy and headquarters for his opposition movement.

"We thought it was possible the whole thing would flip," he told a friend later. "We could declare it as the first embassy of the new republic, a launch point for resistance."

THE RECONNAISSANCE TRIP TO Spain also gave Adrian an opportunity to try to make headway with one of North Korea's strangest supporters in Europe, a Spanish man called Alejandro Cao de Benós.

Cao de Benós is the most high-profile of a very strange subset of people who can only be described as North Korean superfans, albeit with a more sinister edge. His interest in strongman dictatorships isn't completely random. He hails from a once grand family of pro-fascist aristocrats who lost their fortunes but retained their haughty mien.

A budding socialist and oddly affected by the myths of North Korea since his early teens, the young Alejandro Cao de Benós scrimped and saved enough money to fly to Pyongyang at the age of sixteen, where he found a "very clean society with very nice people," he later told a writer for *Bloomberg Businessweek*.

Inspired by his visit, Cao de Benós created the Korean Friendship Association on his return and presided over small meetings for much of the 1990s while working in IT. In 2000, he created North Korea's first official website, korea-dpr.com, which was the only such website for the entire North Korean government until it started maintaining its own websites in 2012.

When his employer confronted him about the website, Cao de Benós explained that it was a kind of hobby, according to *Businessweek*. "Whenever I go home, instead of playing football, or playing on the computer, I'm working for Korea from 7 or 8 P.M., until 2 or 3 A.M.," he said. "It's my passion."

Only three days before Adrian's visit to the embassy, Cao de Benós received an email from a woman called Elena Sanchez who identified herself as the associate director of a Dubai-based company called Baron Stone Capital. Sanchez explained that her employer, a certain Matthew Chao, had put aside up to $50 million to invest in "infrastructure, mining and energy," in North Korea, Mongolia, and Myanmar.

Chao was arriving in Madrid imminently, Sanchez explained, and wanted Cao de Benós's help in connecting with the ambassador. Distrustful of out-of-the-blue inquiries because they could be foreign intelligence operatives trying to use him to learn more about North Korea, Cao de Benós declined to make the introduction until he could get more information. Sanchez then got a bit pushy, offering to sweeten the deal for him: if he could help with introductions, Baron Stone would be happy to hire him as a consultant.

Cao de Benós told *Businessweek* that he notified the embassy of the request for a meeting, but didn't recommend they agree to it.

For Cheollima, Cao de Benós would have been helpful on multiple levels—creating a perfect pretext for Adrian to scope out the interior of the embassy without putting the blame on the ambassador for authorizing entry and learning more about whether Cao de Benós was just a harmless oddball or if he actually had access to senior officials and intelligence.

With growing attention and interest from businesspeople around the world, Cao de Benós had begun to take people into North Korea for meetings. His Korean Friendship Association set up in more than a hundred countries around the world, drawing in contrarian socialists, misfits, and other oddballs. A typical meeting involves pledges of support to North Korea, a discussion of North Korean ideology, and a very modest selection of cookies and coffee.

The North Korean government had recognized his fervor and even bestowed on him a Korean name, Cho Son-il, which means "Korea is one country."

In recent years, Cao de Benós counted among his achievements hosting North Korea's first cryptocurrency conference. North Korea's interest in alternative forms of money is not surprising. Severely sanctioned and barred from the global financial system, North Korea found the idea of using cryptocurrencies to trade with the world distinctly appealing. North Korean state hackers had for years been extorting people out of their cryptocurrency and stolen Bitcoin through computer intrusion techniques.

U.S. prosecutors later charged Virgil Griffith, a cryptocurrency designer and one of the attendees of the cryptocurrency conference, with violating U.S. sanctions. After initially trying to fight the charges, he agreed to plead guilty in September 2021 and was awaiting sentencing at the time of the writing of this book. In April 2021, U.S.

prosecutors charged Cao de Benós with conspiring with Griffith and another cryptocurrency expert to help North Korea evade sanctions.

Cao de Benós was also the proprietor of Pyongyang Cafe in his hometown of Tarragona, which sells Korean food, coffee, and beer but acts mostly as the headquarters for the original Korean Friendship Association. That's where he was spending most of his time, occasionally donning a uniform covered in medals with gold lapels and denying, to anyone who would listen, that North Korea conducts executions or violates anyone's human rights.

In 2018, Cao de Benós had given an interview in the demilitarized zone in which he expressed his disagreement with the U.S. presence in South Korea and vowed that he would take up arms to "push them out." Soon after, police raided his house and found two pistols. They fired only rubber bullets, but Cao de Benós still needed a permit for them. His passport was seized pending the outcome of the criminal case.

Such would be the summation of Cao de Benós—quirky, distasteful, but nothing more—if it wasn't for one incredible documentary film, *The Mole: Undercover in North Korea*. The documentary series, released in 2020 by the Danish filmmaker Mads Brügger, follows Ulrich Larsen, a former chef living on the edge of Copenhagen who infiltrates a branch of Cao de Benós's Korean Friendship Association in Copenhagen.

Over the course of ten years, as the film reveals, Larsen became fully immersed in the society and a close comrade of Cao de Benós's—secretly filming and recording all along. Over time, Brügger introduced another fictional character, a potential investor called Mr. James, to see how far they could push their way into North Korea. At one point, Larsen and Mr. James sign a deal with North Korean officials to produce drugs and weapons. At another point, they meet in Uganda to discuss buying an island to construct a luxury hotel that would be a front for a secret drugs and weapons factory.

Throughout, Cao de Benós is the key man in making the connections, boasting along the way about his power and influence in North

Korea. Later, after the series was released, he said he was "play act-ing" and that the entire film was "biased, staged and manipulate [*sic*]."

In one sequence, Larsen visits the North Korean embassy in Stock-holm, where he receives an envelope with plans for the Ugandan weapons factory from a diplomat described as Mr. Ri.

"If something happens, the embassy knows nothing about this, okay?" Mr. Ri is shown saying to Larsen.

Such dealings made Cao de Benós all the more attractive to Adrian. He could be a source of intelligence or unsuspecting bait for helping Cheollima Civil Defense gain access to a larger number of officials in Europe and beyond.

THE PREVIOUS AMBASSADOR AT the North Korean embassy in Spain was the type of person who might have easily been drawn into a sim-ilar scandal. He was highly trusted and held a key position in Europe. U.S. and European intelligence agencies long believed Madrid was an important component of North Korea's quasi-criminal diplomatic corps.

Kim Hyok-chol spent much of his diplomatic career in Ethiopia and South Sudan before arriving in Madrid to open the first-ever North Korean embassy in Spain in October 2013. He was a veteran of George Bush's six-party talks as well.

He stayed in that position until the Spanish government expelled him as persona non grata following a North Korean nuclear weapon test at its Punggye-ri site on September 3, 2017. It was the biggest test to date, with a quake magnitude of 6.3 on the Richter scale—at least six times more powerful than the bomb dropped on Hiroshima in 1945.

Kim Hyok-chol's expulsion only seemed to bolster his standing back home, and by the time of Adrian's reconnaissance visit to Spain in early February 2019, he was North Korea's highest-ranking official preparing for a second summit with Donald Trump's team scheduled for February 27 and 28 in Hanoi.

His counterpart on the U.S. side was Stephen Biegun, a career po-
litico and onetime businessman at Ford Motor Company who was
appointed by Donald Trump as U.S. special representative for North
Korea Policy in August 2018. A Russia expert, Biegun advised Sarah
Palin on foreign policy during the 2008 presidential elections.

Speaking at Stanford on January 31, 2019, Biegun vowed that the
Trump-Kim initiatives had a higher likelihood of success because
"neither leader is constrained by traditional expectations that might
doom their teams to try the exact same approach as in the past, with
no expectation of anything but the same failed outcome."

In the speech, he described how the United States was "prepared to
pursue—simultaneously and in parallel—all of our commitments our
two leaders made in their joint statement at Singapore last summer."

This was alarming to hawks like John Bolton, Trump's national
security adviser, who believed that the State Department was weakening the U.S. government's position because of their zealousness for
a deal. Bolton later wrote in his autobiography how he decided then
and there to try to persuade Trump with every argument he could
think of not to take a mirage of a deal with the North Koreans.

On February 12, in the White House Situation Room, the National
Security Council staff showed a film to the president showing four
previous presidents hailing great deals they got with North Korea. In
the next sequence, the film described North Korea's actual conduct
falling far short of its promises and included a clip of Ronald Reagan
stating that in deal making sometimes the best strategy is to hold firm.

The message from Bolton was clear: do not accept piecemeal denuclearization. In his eyes, North Korea would never denuclearize
unless it felt it was an existential matter. Any attempt to go about
things "action for action" was a recipe for North Korea to weaken
sanctions while retaining its nuclear arsenal.

IN THE FALL OF 2018, Adrian sent me a Signal message saying he was
passing through London. We agreed to get coffee. I'd now been com-

municating off and on with him for eight years, and right away something felt different about this interaction. He'd always been a user of
the best-in-practice encrypted apps and careful to make sure that
messages were automatically deleted after a short time—so short that
it was sometimes hard to keep track of a conversation because the
messages would delete after seconds. But this time, he seemed to be
operating an even more paranoid level of operational security.

We met inside Paddington Station and quickly found a back entrance to the Mercure Hotel, where we sat at a quiet table in the corner of the room. During previous meetings, Adrian had struck me as
businessman first and North Korea activist second. He'd show up
wearing a suit and tie and have his hair carefully slicked back. He
joked about how his own friends wondered if he was in the CIA.
(Anytime someone says something like that, it's a sure sign they have
no affiliation with the CIA at all.) I still couldn't quite decide whether
I thought he was doing interesting things or finding opportunities to
go along for an exciting ride. He seemed relatively wealthy, though in
retrospect that was based only on his attire and the frequency of his
globe-trotting travel.

On this visit, however, Adrian had an entirely different look. His
hair was long and tied up in a bun, and he had a scruffy beard. He was
dressed down and carried a bagful of phones, which he frequently
checked, shooting off brief messages during our coffee. There was a
trace of a new swagger in his demeanor—a mixture of confidence
and the air of someone with mysterious knowledge. At one point, he
showed me a folder with information about North Koreans using
companies in the United Arab Emirates to move money and other
material. But almost as soon as he pushed it across the table, he
quickly took it back. When I asked if the *Journal* could consider doing
a story on it, he replied, "Sometimes it's better to watch people than
expose them."

As a journalist, I found Adrian exceedingly frustrating. He was
always fascinating and charismatic, but never once in the time we'd
stayed in touch since Libya did he help me with an article. Most jour-

nalists would have long ago given up on a source like that. But I liked Adrian and enjoyed meeting him. He seemed to have bits of information all the time about things I was working on—a contact in Asia who knew about Jho Low from the 1MDB scandal, a friend in New York who might have an insight into another fraud.

It was always a tantalizing if irksome relationship. But the question on my mind remained: Was this guy actually doing things, perhaps even things of global importance, or was he just pretending?

I'd later learn I was glimpsing only the tiniest tip of the iceberg.

14

ANATOMY OF A FAKE KIDNAPPING

You can only become great at that thing you're willing to sacrifice for.

—*MAYA ANGELOU*

MADRID
FEBRUARY 2019

On THE LONG FLIGHT FROM LOS ANGELES TO MADRID, CHRISTO-pher Ahn's thoughts were consumed by his fledgling start-up business back in California.

He shouldn't have agreed to come. It was Friday and there were investor meetings on Monday. He needed to be well rested and prepared. After years of trying to find his way following his stint in active service in the U.S. Marines—business school, working low-paying marketing jobs to learn a new trade—he was finally on the cusp of a profitable venture. The company was in a sensitive but thrilling phase. With investor capital, Ahn was poised to start supplying cannabis-oil-infused mixes to cafés for use in their products. A café could charge $8 to $10 for a smoothie if it included one of his products.

A better income, Ahn believed, would help grow his family. He was hoping to start having children with his wife—a Korean American teacher in Los Angeles called Grace. For their honeymoon in July 2017, he persuaded her to fly back to the same hostel where he'd stayed when he jetted to Taiwan to help Kim Han-sol.

In addition to his all-consuming work with the start-up, Ahn was still recovering from a broken wrist. Even with a wrist guard holding it in place, the fracture point throbbed every time he lifted his suitcase. Considering Ahn's intimidating physique, friends assumed he had been working out or doing some heavy-duty house repairs. Actually, he slipped in the bathtub.

A month earlier when Adrian first asked if he'd join a mysterious mission in Madrid, Ahn had tried to marshal excuses for why he couldn't go. He told Adrian he didn't have time, but as the weeks ticked by, his curiosity grew and he finally agreed to join. He would be the last member of the group—the thirteenth man.

Ahn sensed that the operation was a bit bigger than the usual Cheollima adventure, given Adrian's persistent pitch for him to join in. But of course, according to the need-to-know secrecy Adrian had instilled in the group's operation, Ahn didn't know the venue, who was being rescued, how many of them there were, or how it would all go down. Ahn was still in the mindset of "if we can make a small, little positive nudge to help the momentum of change, that's a wonderful thing."

Just as Adrian Hong and Sam Ryu had been finalizing the plan for the exfiltration of North Korea's top diplomat in Madrid, So Yun-suk, and his family, on January 3, 2019, news of the country's ambassador to Italy Jo Song-gil's defection leaked in South Korea, thanks to loose-lipped intelligence sources speaking to local newspapers. The reports emphasized that the daughter they left behind in the embassy was quickly sent back to Pyongyang before Italian officials even realized Jo and his wife were out of the country.

Italian officials publicly raised concerns about the girl. Soon after, North Korea's embassy in Rome sent a letter to Osvaldo Napoli, the Italian lawmaker who knew Jo, saying the defections were the result of a "family quarrel" between Jo and his wife over how to care for their daughter's mental condition. Following an intense dispute, the pair walked out of the embassy, intentionally leaving the girl behind.

The daughter asked to return to Pyongyang to be with her grandparents, the letter said.

That experience emphasized the importance of creating an image that would reduce the chance of an escapee's family getting imprisoned or killed. The Cheollima team needed a way to confuse North Korea's security apparatus enough that it wouldn't know for certain or believe that the escapees had actually escaped.

The guilt of escapees who choose freedom despite potentially deadly consequences for their family can be debilitating. Substance abuse, marital breakdown, depression—these were common symptoms.

To rescue someone without those consequences would be a momentous achievement.

AS SOON AS AHN arrived in Madrid just after 8:00 A.M., it became clear that something different was brewing. Another group member picked him up from the airport and brought him to an Airbnb where the others were gathering. He had a quick shower while a fellow member cooked breakfast. Then Adrian strode in to explain the plans.

"This is our biggest operation yet," he began, going on to describe how by that evening they would be responsible for a North Korean family who had asked for their help. And the team had only a few hours before go time.

To Ahn, the moment felt similar to a pep talk on Thanksgiving morning at a soup kitchen: a mixture of idealistic, lofty talk ahead of what was going to be a physically challenging day of volunteering. Adrian emphasized that this was the kind of thing the group was evolving toward and that it was part of something bigger that could make a difference for North Koreans.

"Thank you for being a part of this," he told those assembled.

As Ahn spoke to the other team members, all of them men, he learned that many of them had already been in town for days. On

February 10, four South Korean members of Cheollima had flown in via Portugal and traveled the six-hour-long taxi journey over the border to Madrid. The maneuver ensured there would be no record of their arrival in Spain whatsoever because tourists with Schengen visas can travel freely around Europe without passing border controls.

On hand were Lee Woo-ran, twenty-six; Lim Chang-su, twenty-seven; Park Si-young, twenty-eight; and Kim Dong-hyun, twenty-eight; and four others. These were men who, like Ahn, played an on-and-off-again role in operations of Cheollima Civil Defense. They were all professionals in South Korea who'd met Adrian at one point and been taken in by his dream for something meaningful.

There was a single North Korean, Charles Ryu, twenty-seven, whose full name is Cheol-woo Ryu. Many of the men had similar hairstyles: long hair tied in a bun at the back as well as full beards. That served two purposes: making them harder to identify as individuals later and signaling they were a *different* kind of Korean. North Korean men invariably stick to short and tidy haircuts. Long hair and beards are forbidden.

Sam Ryu flew in on the thirteenth, booking three double rooms at the Eurostars Zarzuela Park, a quiet business hotel in a garden-like setting, until February 25. He also rented the nearby Airbnb where they were meeting. The hotel, located in Madrid's northwest outskirts, was the perfect base of operation for a small team who would be nearby with cars at the ready.

Adrian, being the most publicly recognizable person inside Cheollima, whose travel was far more likely to arouse the suspicions of intelligence services, was staying completely separate from the rest of the group at the Hotel Carlton to help protect the identities of the more anonymous members of the group. He later moved to another property in central Madrid, the Hotel Aitana.

Both hotels were operated by the Marriott chain. One of Adrian's quirks over the years was a nearly singular obsession with staying in Marriott hotels and affiliates during his travels—with so many nights, he became such a high-level member of its benefits program that he could check out late and as much as guarantee a room on short notice at any of the chain's hotels in the world.

The Airbnb, located just an eight-minute drive north, was the de facto safe house where So Yun-suk, his wife, and his child would be sequestered before being transported out of the country. Located in a purely residential area with a quiet alleyway behind, it was nondescript, private, and large. The house had three floors, a garage, and a garden.

Speaking to the assembled men in the Airbnb, Adrian explained a key component of the mission, one that Ahn had never heard before in the group's previous actions. Cheollima had staged accidents for North Korean defectors to protect their relatives from retribution, but this time they were going to be performing a much more elaborate play to confuse North Korean surveillance. They were going to pretend to be "kidnappers."

Adrian was raising the stakes. The sharper edge of the plan triggered a bolt of anxiety in Ahn, but his feelings were assuaged as Adrian filled the team in further. The operation, Adrian explained, had been months in planning, and members of the team had been going through the details for weeks before arriving. They'd even practiced how they'd move through the buildings, all the more important because few of them, outside Ahn, had anything close to formal military training.

If Adrian's confidence was reassuring for Ahn, seeing the assembled equipment wasn't.

A few days earlier, group members had gone to a hardware store called Ferretería Delicias to load up on gear: scissors, bolt cutters, thirty-three rolls of duct tape, pliers, ten metal crowbars, and a collapsible ladder. The ladder was lightweight and highly mobile—a backup plan in case they needed to scale the walls of the embassy.

"It was odd because they were buying the sort of things you need for breaking into somewhere, but they were smart-looking and didn't seem suspicious," the store's owner later told a reporter for *The Guardian*.

Adrian and Sam separately visited an army and police supply store called Tienda Shoke, where they bought balaclavas, five quick-draw pistol holders, four combat knives, six airsoft pistols that fired harmless pellets, four pairs of shooting glasses, five tactical flashlights, cans of Mace, and five sets of handcuffs. The imitation guns are so realistic they are most often used in Spanish films and TV shows. The bill was 833.15 euros.

They also bought candy and toys for So's son.

Playing the role of the technical wizard, Sam Ryu brought along GoPro cameras that could be mounted on Cheollima operatives to record proof that the operation was an elaborate ruse and not an actual kidnapping. The idea was similar to how Ahn had been tasked with recording footage of Kim Han-sol in the Taipei airport as proof that Cheollima helped him.

The weapons were purely for show, Adrian explained. They didn't even have to pull off a highly precise piece of theater. It needed to look good enough to get So into a room to make the final arrangements. Team members would then disconnect any security cameras and, if possible, take the hard copies of the recordings. Though they'd done some reconnaissance, they had no way of knowing how many cameras were inside and where they routed images to. The fear was North Korea's intelligence services had a system for observing the embassy from afar in real time.

Considering that possibility, whatever was captured on the embassy's security cameras needed to look as authentically like a kidnapping as possible, and any witnesses from the staff needed to feel as if their boss were kidnapped. If not, the extended families of So and his wife could end up in a gulag in days.

At one point in the midst of giving instructions, Adrian turned to Ahn and clarified his role: just as he had done in other operations, Ahn's job was to keep everyone focused and on task in what was sure to be an adrenaline-charged forty-five minutes. The idea was to get in and out quickly.

"You're the only one with experience of even doing things like this," Adrian told him, Ahn recalls. "You're there for oversight, to keep things calm."

They also planned for a possible contingency, the scenario suggested by So during his discussions with Adrian. If the whole embassy agreed to defect en masse, Cheollima, instead of fleeing, would opt to stay longer, increase security, and, eventually, announce that the embassy was the home of the opposition movement Adrian was creating—the so-called Provisional State of Free Joseon.

That plan for potentially taking over the embassy was truly startling in its ambitions. No one across their spectrum had veered even close to something like it in many decades of agitation and policy proposals about North Korea. It was too dangerous and the chance of success scarily slim compared with the range of things that could go terribly wrong. In Adrian's conversation with the team, however, he made it seem not just momentous but also possible.

It was a bold vision, powered by charisma and self-confidence, the kind of messianic "rule breaking" that had become commonplace and even celebrated in certain realms of modern society, like Silicon Valley, where half-witted business plans were routinely drawing in millions in venture capital funding. But here in Madrid, the stakes were much higher than a squandered capital investment. But no one seemed to realize it at that moment.

As they awaited go time, Ahn got to thinking about what other roles he could play on this trip. His thoughts drifted to what might be going on in the minds of the North Koreans they were about to rescue, and what he could do to welcome them, and celebrate their momentous decision to defect in the immediate aftermath.

His idea: a big barbecue. "I wanted to help celebrate that they made this brave decision," he said later. "For me that's a big deal. We needed to do something big and put effort into letting them know they are loved and cared for. The last thing we needed is for them to feel alone."

In the hours before the operation began, Ahn began writing down ideas for a fish barbecue at the Airbnb using the grill in the backyard.

While the team packed the scary-looking gear, he started writing a grocery list.

AT 4:38 P.M., ADRIAN, Ahn, Sam Ryu, and several other Cheollima members approached the door of the North Korean embassy. Others were waiting nearby in cars for the exfiltration.

The door to the embassy is near a bus stop on the street, where a handful of people eyed the assembled men with curiosity. Ahn, wearing all black and sunglasses, tried to look nonchalant, a pose that Spanish investigators would later deem to appear "defiant." The other Cheollima members were crouching next to the wall, which he thought was too conspicuous and could lead to a phone call to the police.

As the others waited, Adrian, wearing a black suit and a tie with white polka dots, pressed the buzzer, telling the groundskeeper he had an appointment with So, the commercial attaché. The grounds-keeper, Jin Choe, recognized him and let Adrian—who he believed was the returning Matthew Chao of Baron Stone Capital—inside to wait near the door.

Jin disappeared into the main building to find So, giving Adrian the opportunity to crack open the door for the rest of his crew to enter. If anyone had been watching the surveillance camera in real time, they'd have observed a group of men who appeared to be storming the embassy.

As the Cheollima members crossed inside, the balaclavas came out, and the men rapidly rounded up the embassy's personnel and placed them in an office with plastic restraints binding their wrists. Bags were placed over their heads.

"Get down!" Ahn blurted out in English, before switching back to Korean.

The North Korean embassy staff, who like the Cheollima opera-tors were also mostly in their twenties and thirties, folded instantly without resisting. The high speed and accompanying feeling of utter shock and surprise were highly effective. Just as Adrian had hoped, subduing the staff began and ended in a matter of minutes.

So was initially taken to a bathroom by Adrian and Sam Ryu, while several of the team members, including Ahn, went room by room to make sure they'd found everyone and restrained them. They found So's wife and son, who appeared petrified with fear at the arrival of the masked intruders. One of the Cheollima members stayed with her, saying calmly that no one was going to be hurt.

Word came back over a mobile-phone-based walkie-talkie system called Zello that the building was "clear and secure." Adrian turned to the men and, in English, said, "Transition, transition."

With all signs pointing to a smooth execution of the first phase of the plan—everything secure and no apparent video cameras inside the embassy itself—Adrian was using the prearranged phrase to signal they could relax their demeanor: they could go from posing as mysterious intruders to presenting as coolheaded rescuers. It was a moment to take a breath and focus on finishing up and leaving.

Speaking to the detained men in Korean, Ahn tried out a softer tone, telling them, "Please be patient" and "I'm sorry this is happening," while also explaining that no one would be hurt. They undid the zip ties and removed handcuffs after about half an hour. "This will all be over soon," he told them.

Adrian and Sam Ryu went with So into the basement to discuss the details of his defection and whether others from the embassy could be persuaded to join his family. (I later reviewed a partial video clip from the basement in which the would-be defector is laughing and appears to be relaxed.)

While the trio in the basement discussed their next moves, Ahn began to explore the building with other members of the team. It was surprisingly empty—like a beautiful mansion of a millionaire on the outside, but with almost no decorations and extremely modest furnishings inside. Even the refrigerator was mostly empty, a detail that

Ahn remembered struck him as particularly depressing. In a way, it wasn't all that different from the Potemkin villages on the North Korea side of the demilitarized zone.

The only room with a bit of character was the propaganda room, which was full of pictures of Kim Jong-un and mantras of the regime. Embassy workers would have been expected to study North Korean political literature daily in addition to attending frequent special discussions about the country's history led by So. A small group of North Korean students living in Madrid would also have attended some of these events in the embassy. This far from Pyongyang, it was all the more crucial to ensure unthinking obedience to the state and the "Great Successor," Kim Jong-un.

As they made their way through the building, two of the Cheollima operators found one of the secondary targets in the embassy, an intelligence center lined with foil to prevent eavesdropping and electronic surveillance. They swept up everything into backpacks and also removed a set of equipment they thought was connected to the surveillance cameras on the exterior of the embassy. It later turned out they missed another computer system with the recordings.

All these tasks were accomplished within the first hour of entering the building and the temperature and pace of the action slowed down quickly thereafter. The feeling at that moment was they were minutes away from walking out with So and his family, or having a bigger event with the rest of the staff.

Unaware of any issues, Adrian and other members believed the mission was nearly finished. It was poised to be a smashing success. Feeling relaxed, Sam Ryu took out his camera and started to record.

15

LONG LIVE THE GREAT SUCCESSOR

Leaving North Korea is not like leaving any other country. It is more like leaving another universe. I will never truly be free of its gravity, no matter how far I journey.

—HYEONSEO LEE,
NORTH KOREAN ESCAPEE

MADRID
FEBRUARY 2019

CHEOL-WOO RYU, KNOWN AS CHARLES, WAS THE ONLY NORTH Korean on the Cheollima team that had stormed the Madrid embassy. More precisely, he and two others were part of a subunit that had been tasked with waiting in a car up the street while the others secured the embassy. Mild mannered and kindhearted, Charles rarely gave new acquaintances an indication of the heartbreak he had experienced as a child in North Korea.

When he was a toddler, his father had abandoned him and his mother with huge debts. He had a Chinese passport, so was able to leave the country and live in a village not far from the border. Charles and his mother managed to eke by with some help from his grandmother. His mom traveled to other cities to try to earn money for two years. But one day, she turned back up in a terrible state—looking starved and barely able to communicate. Charles's grandmother used what little money she had to get her daughter into the hospital for a few months. For a while, things seemed to be getting better, but one day his mother collapsed on the floor. Charles dropped out of school and spent all of his time taking care of her, but her condition worsened until she died, another victim of North Korea's famine.

Too old and frail to take care of him, Charles's grandmother sent him to live with his aunt. He wrote fruitless letters to his father in China in the hopes of getting help. In another cruel twist, his aunt forged a letter from Charles's father, which purported to ask her to come to China. The fake letter helped Charles's aunt obtain a visa from the North Korean government. She then sent a letter to Charles's father, threatening to kill Charles or send him to an orphanage if he didn't send money for her to travel out of the country. The ploy didn't work.

After moving out of his aunt's home, Charles spent the better part of a year homeless on the streets, fighting with other homeless children for scraps of food and sleeping near a hot water boiler to survive the winter. Eventually, at age fourteen, he escaped the country with help from two stepbrothers. They gave him money to bribe some border patrol guards, and he made his way to the Yalu River on the border of North Korea and China under the pretext of washing up. After wading into the river, he swam across and on the other side found his father, who had been given advance warning of Charles's escape. His father, who took Charles on a twelve-hour trip into China to his home, had an emotional reunion with his son.

In a market, Charles saw his first banana and proceeded to take a bite without first removing the peel. Before then, he'd only seen bananas in cartoons. Life for Charles in China was good. He made up for lost time with his father—learning, in a sense, how to be a child again—and soaking in the experiences of good, plentiful food and playing games in local arcades. Then, one day, a Chinese neighbor reported him to the government.

The police came in January 2009 to his father's house and arrested Charles, refusing to accept he was his father's son because he had no records of it. Now, fifteen years old, Charles was hauled back to North Korea. One of the other people being deported, a woman, bit the vein in her hand to try to kill herself rather than face a North Korean prison camp.

In North Korea, Charles was interrogated for three weeks and thrown into a reeducation camp near Sinuiju. He worked sixteen-hour days, performing grueling construction and farming tasks, offered just 150 kernels of corn a day as sustenance. Desperate and hungry, Charles picked rice out of vomit on the ground one day to supplement his diet. At night, the guards drilled Charles and the other detainees with propaganda and endless repetition of the camp's myriad rules.

After nine months, Charles was wasting away. He could hardly lift his arms. In the eyes of the labor camp leadership, he was no longer useful. They released him.

He found a job working in a coal mine for a year. Most of the workers were fellow teenagers, tasked with hauling huge equipment and chipping away coal by hand. The workers were paid thirty kilograms of rice a month and given room and board. The work was highly dangerous: mine tunnels were known to collapse and coal carts could flip, maiming or even killing the workers.

To Charles, his situation in the mines was hardly better than the labor camp, and one day he decided to run away, caring little for the consequences. The guards didn't seem to care enough to chase him. Once again, Charles was homeless, wandering the countryside of the northern fringes of the country and its towns in search of bits of food.

As he rested atop a hill one day, Charles observed a train pulling into a nearby station. Thinking he might be able to steal a parcel of food, he moseyed down to the platform. The train, he learned, was heading for Hyesan, an industrial city and transportation hub, near the border with China. Charles slipped onto the train.

He managed to slip on but was discovered mid-journey and arrested. Locked in a room on the train, Charles managed to jump out of a window, hide, and then jump onto another train a few days later. He was on his way back to the Yalu River on the border.

One night, he snuck up to the river again and waded in icy-cold water. Slipping midway, he let out a gasp as a floodlight suddenly illuminated the water around him. North Korean border guards screamed for him to stop or they'd shoot. Swimming furiously, Charles made it to the Chinese side and managed to slink away, into the night, unscathed.

Still, a wandering North Korean in China is extremely vulnerable. With no money or food, Charles walked for three days without a clear direction, his feet bleeding. He had only his "dream of freedom," he later told an American podcast host named Jordan Harbinger.

Resting on the road, and near his breaking point, sixteen-year-old Charles prayed for help. Finally, a Chinese man on a motorcycle shuddered to a halt and asked if he was from North Korea. "Yes," Charles told him. The man told him to hop on and took him on a long journey, giving him food, clothes, and medicine. The following day, the Chinese man introduced him to a South Korean missionary who gave him money to travel to his father.

For months, at his father's house, Charles stayed indoors and didn't dare walk around the town to avoid getting rearrested. Finally, his father decided Charles had to leave China or risk being sent back to North Korea again. Charles found a broker to help him escape via Thailand on the other side of the country. After a tense series of bus rides, the broker helped a group of North Koreans get across the Mekong River by walking across on a wobbly log.

Thai police arrested Charles, but he had accomplished his goal, because he believed he would be free. Thailand recognizes North Korean refugees and allows them to travel on to South Korea even if they enter the country illegally. Even the food in a Thai prison was a massive step up from any experience he'd have in his life. Charles said he considered the day of his arrest in Thailand the best day of his life.

Thai authorities threatened to send him back to China because his father was Chinese. He felt suicidal with stress, refusing to eat for a week. Finally, a man he met helped him apply to the United Nations to obtain international refugee status, and Charles was immediately granted an interview. Days later, the United States agreed to accept him as a refugee in Los Angeles. His whole life was about to change.

In 2012, Charles finally arrived and settled in the United States, where he was able to finish high school and reunite with his friends from Thailand. At church, he received a second name—Charles—solely because it sounded similar to his Korean name, Cheol-woo. His new life in America was replete with hamburgers and Subway sandwiches, which he ordered with every ingredient he could. At his part-time job as a dishwasher, he was stunned at the amount of food thrown out. Later, while studying at a computer programming boot camp, he drove Uber and, in fluent English, would recount his escape story to passengers, who would often stick around after reaching their destination to listen to his story.

At one point, LiNK hired Charles as an IT intern in their Long Beach office, where he first exchanged emails with Adrian. Absorbing American culture like a sponge, Charles underwent a dramatic transformation. Watching television and spending time with Korean Americans, he soon transformed himself, adopting the chilled demeanor of a "SoCal bro," peppering his speech with "dude," and evincing a love for American pop culture and films while also spending time—and shocking audiences—telling his harrowing story of escape.

On his Instagram account, @freshprinceofpyongyang, Charles wrote up a cheeky bio: "In West North Korea born and raised, I'm just chillin in the State until I can go back the Hermit Kingdom to free my people."

Despite being miles away in a land of abundance, Charles never turned indifferent toward North Korea. And he was vocal about how the people, if united, could go against the government. This unfading idealism made him an easy recruit.

Charles later told the writer Suki Kim that he never actually met Adrian in person until he flew to Madrid for the Cheollima mission to strike a blow at the foundations of the Kim regime in North Korea. The details were worked out over Signal messenger; Charles didn't get a full picture of what was going on at all, other than it would involve a controlled visit to "North Korean soil" in Spain that would be used to crack the image of an infallible regime.

"It was an honor," Charles had explained. "For me, it was personal, this brotherhood I felt with Adrian."

AFTER ABOUT AN HOUR of waiting in the car up the road, Charles and the other Cheollima members outside the embassy received word from Adrian that it was time for Charles to come inside. He casually walked up to the embassy and knocked on the door.

Inside the gate, Sam Ryu was waiting with a camera, filming a shot of Charles entering the embassy—that is, entering "North Korea" for the first time since he escaped years earlier. It was just after 5:17 P.M., about forty minutes into the operation.

Sam Ryu asked Charles to walk through the door several times, filming multiple takes to make sure it was just right. In the unredacted version, Charles has tears in his eyes as he crosses the doorway, wearing a black zip-up jacket. (The group eventually released the footage in a video titled "Returning to My Homeland.")

In another clip released later, entitled "Recently in Our Homeland," another figure is shown smashing pictures of Kim Jong-il and Kim Il-sung. In Korean and English, the video finishes with two messages: "Down with Kim family rule!" and "For our people we rise up! Long live Free Joseon!"

North Koreans are inculcated with the belief that their leaders are godlike and undefeatable. The idea at the time was to release the footage later, as anti-regime propaganda, without mentioning where it was filmed to give the impression it was happening inside North Korea itself rather than "on North Korean soil" in another country.

BACK INSIDE THE EMBASSY, as Sam Ryu was filming his various staged scenes, Christopher Ahn was getting antsy. He felt alternately like they'd just arrived and also that they'd been there for hours—a bizarre feeling caused by the intensity and stress of the operation. By this point he was mostly just milling around the room where the North Korean embassy workers were tied up, occasionally loosening the bindings on their hands.

Adrian was still downstairs with So Yun-suk, emerging briefly to check on the situation. Every time he surfaced, Adrian seemed serious but confident and upbeat. "Everything's good," he said on one trip upstairs.

Before leaving the grounds, So wanted to understand the plan in more detail. Where would he be getting asylum? Would they be secure leaving the embassy? Where were they staying that night? What could the group offer the other diplomats? Was the operation safe?

Upstairs, So's wife, Jang Ok-gyong, appeared less calm. It wasn't clear he'd told her anything about the plans to defect. She later told police that she had been sitting in her room watching television with her young son when she heard a loud noise coming from the hallway as the Cheollima team stormed the building.

When she peered out, she told investigators, she observed embassy staff being "hit" as they were restrained. (All of the embassy staff later said they were beaten by the Cheollima team, but no footage I viewed depicted any violence. Cheollima members have denied hitting the hostages or using violence, and the group would later argue that the North Koreans had no choice but to report they were violently attacked to protect themselves from consequences in North Korea. One theory I heard from a Spanish journalist, who has followed the case closely, is that the North Korean male hostages hit each other in an effort, perhaps at the behest of superiors in Pyongyang, to manufacture false evidence they'd been attacked.)

Observing the frightening scene outside her bedroom, Jang Ok-gyong quickly closed the door and locked it. A few minutes later, there was a loud knock and a voice in Korean ordering her to open up and saying that nothing would happen to her. She looked out the window and tried to call her husband, but by then a Cheollima member had broken the lock on the door and opened it.

A tall man entered, with long hair in a bun and a suit. It was Adrian, who told her not to be afraid and that he had come to help her family. At one point, Adrian said to her he had previously been informed that her son was eleven or twelve but he seemed to be seven or eight instead. Another Cheollima member entered the room and Adrian left. This man told her that the action they were taking to help her was very dangerous for them and that they were taking a risk.

At one point, Jang Ok-gyong told police that she thought to kill herself and even tried to cut herself when she went into the bathroom, so worried was she that these men had terrible things in store for the captives in the embassy.

Eventually, a third man entered the room and relieved the second Cheollima member. Looking at the shape of his head and intonation of his voice, Jang thought he was likely born in North Korea before moving to South Korea. The Cheollima members brought her son a bag that included toys, crackers, and candy, but seeing his mother in such a state of distress, he stayed frozen.

BY NOW, IN AHN's mind, the "op" was right on the cusp of being finished. The team was amped up and ready to leave the embassy. The thought that it was time to get the barbecue going fluttered through Ahn's mind.

Then, at 5:50 P.M., the embassy front gate suddenly rang, sending a piercing chill through the Cheollima members.

A visitor?

One of the team members radioed Adrian through Zello, the communication app they were using that turns mobile phones into walkie-talkies over the internet. "Someone's at the door," he explained to their leader.

"The police are here," Ahn chimed in. Shocked, Adrian emerged from the basement and joined the others at a bank of television monitors where they could see the feed from the building's front-facing surveillance cameras. Clearly visible were three men, one with sunglasses. Their uniforms said "Policía."

Always quick to act, Adrian told the men he was going to answer the door: he would deal with it. Ahn dusted off Adrian's jacket and gave him a piece of gum. Then Adrian placed a "Dear Leader" pin that he had brought with him into the embassy. The pin clearly visible, he crossed the courtyard toward the front door.

AT THE OUTSET OF their operation to storm the embassy, the Cheollima members were relying on speed and the element of surprise to quickly detain everyone inside. Their goal had been to make it an "in-and-out operation." There was the more remote possibility of the whole embassy defecting en masse, which would have taken the whole project down a new pathway, but that was a distant Plan B.

Unbeknownst to the intruders, however, they had miscounted the total number of embassy staff inside. As they stormed the building, the wife of one of the deputies to So, a fifty-six-year-old woman called Cho Sun-hi, heard a ruckus she described later as "death fights between people," including blows and thuds on the floor.

She told Spanish police that hearing the voices, she could tell they were South Korean, even though she claimed she had never heard a South Korean accent before that moment. A bolt of sheer panic cut through her, and she decided she had to do anything to escape. Thinking quickly, she locked the door of the room she was in and grabbed her cell phone to try to call her husband or another one of the men working in the embassy. There was no reception.

Her mind reeling from what she thought were bitter fights to the death, she believed she was the only one still alive. It was up to her to escape, she believed. From a terrace outside her room, she decided it would be better to jump onto a patch of dirt rather than concrete. She clung to the wall with her hands and tried to use her leg to push herself away from the building, but she lost her balance and hit her head on the corner of a tile. Touching her head, she saw she was bleeding profusely. Her leg was also injured.

Instead of walking to the front door, she limped toward a less obvious side exit near a paddle tennis court on the northwestern edge of the property. In pain from her injuries and feeling panicked, she crawled on all fours into the road. A passing driver swerved to the side, seeing a woman covered in blood in the street. As soon as the car stopped, she climbed into the back seat.

The driver, who worked nearby, drove her to a health clinic just five hundred feet down the road. Two staff members came out and immediately began treating her injuries while simultaneously trying to calm her down. They kept asking her what happened and whether she was from China or the Philippines. Cho replied, "No problem," and said a few words in French.

Cho later told police she didn't want anyone to know she was from North Korea because she feared others were seeking her out to kill her, too, and that the people helping her might bring her back to the embassy. So when they asked if she was Chinese, she nodded her head.

Finally, uniformed Spanish police arrived, and she became more composed. Handed a phone, Cho dialed the Chinese embassy and said hello in Chinese, but the staff members realized she wasn't actually Chinese. "Are you from Korea?" they asked. She shouted "No!" when they tried to dial the South Korean embassy.

Eventually, she admitted she was from North Korea. One of the clinic staff members, a doctor, used an instant translation app on his mobile phone to decipher her words. It came through patchily, but the message was startling: South Korean attackers had assaulted the embassy and were killing people inside. They were "eating children," she warned, holding back sobs.

Police officers left Cho with the doctors, who patched up her head and secured her leg. They radioed what they heard to their commander; they weren't sure about diplomatic protocol with the embassy. He told them to approach the embassy and try to determine if there was a problem inside. Without verification of a criminal situation, they couldn't just barge in and arrest people.

APPROACHING THE FRONT DOOR of the embassy wearing his "Dear Leader" pin, Adrian sought to adopt the haughty demeanor of a North Korean apparatchik, as Ahn and the other team members watched nervously at the bank of TV screens. Ahn could feel his blood pulsing as he watched the surveillance feed. *This was definitely not part of the plan.*

As Adrian opened the door, the Spanish officers immediately introduced themselves, explaining that they had spoken to a woman who claimed she lived in the embassy and that it had been attacked. In an instant, Adrian responded to the men, in Spanish, that there were no issues and if they had any further communications they wished to share with the embassy they needed to go through appropriate diplomatic channels.

Ahn and the others couldn't hear him talking, but they thought his demeanor was perfect for a North Korean official. Arms crossed and thin-lipped, he looked annoyed to be disturbed.

Bemused by the whole affair, the officers thanked him and made their way back to their cars. Adrian headed inside, where the Cheollima members praised his performance. "You nailed it," Ahn told him. Sam Ryu, well acquainted with Hollywood performers, agreed. As far as they knew, the police had left the scene and were heading back to their vehicles.

But, his Spanish a little rusty, there was something Adrian didn't quite understand about what the officers were saying. They talked about a woman. Who could it be?

Possibilities racing through their minds, the team members thought out loud. Maybe it was someone with an appointment or a passerby who saw them bolt inside? Ahn had seen a woman eyeing them suspiciously from the bus stop, which had a clear view of the waiting group of Korean-looking men. Could it have been her?

Adrian went back downstairs to see So, where he asked him to clarify how many people lived in the embassy in total. "Seven," So told him. Adrian did the math. Cheollima had control of only *six* people. The missing woman was the seventh resident. When Adrian explained the discrepancy to So, the mood immediately changed. A bolt of fear shot through his face.

Could So call the woman and persuade her to come back? "No, no," So told Adrian, his face ashen. How could they have missed her? So was in despair. The North Korean government would know any minute now and was probably dispatching assassins, he told Adrian. There were more North Koreans in Spain than just the officials in the embassy, he explained, and threaded among them were dangerous men from the feared Reconnaissance General Bureau, the country's intelligence agency. Adrian tried to reassure him, explaining that the situation was under control; they just needed to leave as soon as possible.

Just as he appeared to be calming down, the phone line of the embassy started ringing. And ringing again, and again.

The cavernous rooms, with tiled floors and few furnishings, amplified the sound to the point where it was hard to think. It felt like the ringing went on for ten minutes at a time, pulsing every few seconds and reverberating in the whole building. Was it the Spanish police or Pyongyang?

With each ring, So seemed to become even more resolved not to escape.

Sounding more desperate now, Adrian once again rehashed the plan with So, telling him about other defections they'd handled. The hardest part was the beginning, when everything felt at stake, but things could quickly feel much safer. Every time So seemed to get closer to agreeing, his confidence collapsed and they had to try to rebuild. This went on for several hours.

One of the Cheollima members who was observing Adrian and So in the basement walked upstairs with a dejected look on his face. "He's totally turning," he reported to the others. So was also certain there were cameras inside the embassy, even though the men had determined there weren't. Thousands of miles from Pyongyang, So couldn't shake the paranoia that permeated every move within the North Korean system. That fear was instilled on purpose, and it was playing out better than any security alarm.

The Cheollima members let the phone ring and ring. But whoever it was would not let up. It was torture.

Finally, at about 8:15 P.M., Adrian came up from the basement with bad news. News of the escapee, as well as the hours of ringing phones, had deeply unnerved So, who believed North Korean authorities would soon be arriving.

"You can't keep me safe, Adrian," So had told him. "You have to leave. Now."

So told him to take the embassy cars, and he would take care of the rest. He'd convince the embassy staff that the attackers left after being spooked by the police, and everything would go back to normal. North Korea would know something happened but not suspect the staff of doing anything wrong.

It was dark out by now, and everyone knew they'd have a hell of a night ahead of them.

16

SOMEBODY PLEASE CALL THE FBI

History starts out as farce and ends up as tragedy.

—LESTER SIEGEL,
FICTIONALIZED CHARACTER
IN THE FILM ARGO

MADRID
FEBRUARY 22, 2019

PEEKING FROM THE WINDOW ON THE TOP FLOOR OF THE MADRID embassy compound, Adrian could see what looked like three police cars idling outside in the street. To test out reactions, he told several of the team members to summon Ubers at the same time and then cancel the ride requests shortly after they arrived. The resulting scene was confusing to the drivers, but truly perplexing to the Spanish officers sitting in their squad cars. They'd been ordered to watch out for any suspicious behavior until the story of Cho Sun-hi, who was still receiving medical treatment, could be properly investigated.

By now, the energy inside the embassy had plummeted. Police outside, phone still ringing nonstop, half a dozen North Korean officials still tied up: the team were starting to sweat. Plans A and B were off the table, so they were on Plan C: escape safely—with at least some intelligence gathering. With the risk of undercover North Korean officers in Spain, they knew they needed to move—and fast. No one on the embassy staff had picked up their cell phones or the embassy phone for hours. North Korea had to know something was badly amiss in its embassy.

With the hostages, save for So, still with bags over their heads in a room downstairs, Adrian summoned the Cheollima team to a room by themselves where they debated what to do. Resolved on Plan C, Cheollima members ransacked offices looking for useful paperwork and files. They grabbed two pen drives, two laptops, a cell phone, and two hard drives. One of them, they thought, was the only hard drive connected to the embassy's surveillance cameras.

Adrian called the team outside the embassy who had returned to the hotel and told them to start packing everything up for a rapid exfiltration. The mission was over and everyone needed to prepare for a lightning-fast journey across the border into Portugal within hours. They'd mostly arrived this way to avoid leaving a paper record of their entry into Spain, so they needed to leave the same way.

While Adrian was coordinating the logistics, Ahn's role as the keeper of calm became all the more critical. In his eyes, this was not a crime scene: it was the setting for a failed rescue, and he didn't want police or anyone else to later suspect otherwise. To him, cleaning up the scene was tantamount to admitting they shouldn't have been there. So instead of grabbing all the equipment they brought with them—handcuffs, pellet guns, scissors, cans of Mace—he told the team to leave everything exactly where it was. *We didn't do anything wrong,* he thought, *so let's not act guilty.* He also didn't want to get caught in a car with material used for kidnapping. Ironically, that decision would later make their situation even more challenging.

Once they'd decided to leave, the Cheollima members stopped talking to the North Koreans in the embassy altogether.

So Yun-suk told Adrian to take the embassy cars, directing him to a lockbox that had keys to an Audi A8, a Mercedes Viano, and a Toyota RAV4. Surveillance footage shows the group leaving in the cars by 9:40 P.M.

Ahn was tasked with escorting out the most vulnerable member of the team, Charles Ryu, the North Korean escapee. They rode in the Mercedes van with another Cheollima member driving. In the street, the Spanish officers watched as the gate opened and the cars sped out into the night. Calling their commander, they asked what they should do and were told to continue waiting outside.

Adrian and another team member chose to stay behind and take a riskier exit than the others. He ordered an Uber to a street called Valdemarín about 650 feet away behind the embassy using the name "Oswaldo Trump," a moniker he made up for one of his anonymous Uber accounts.

Minutes after the others zoomed off, Adrian and the other member scaled the embassy's back wall and traipsed through an overgrown and disused lot to get to the road. In a patch of trees and grass, he threw away his fake Matthew Chao ID card and some of the weapons they'd brought inside the embassy, including knives and one of the imitation guns. As the Uber arrived at approximately 9:46 P.M., Adrian picked bits of grass off his suit and climbed inside.

The Cheollima members had no idea just how close they'd come to a very dangerous situation. It turned out the people calling the embassy nonstop were a group of young North Korean men who identified themselves as students to the Spanish government. They'd immediately felt something was wrong when no one answered their calls. It's unclear what they were actually doing in Spain or if their education program was a cover for other activity. In testimony to police later, one of them, called Chol-hak Kim, said he was an architecture student at Nebrija University and that he and the other students were regular visitors at the embassy. (North Korea experts I consulted said they were likely required to attend regular sessions about North Korean ideology at the embassy to prevent them from becoming entranced by Western freedoms around them.)

Chol-hak, who was about forty years old at the time, told police later that they were ordered to the embassy after another North Korean official in Madrid called them to say they'd received a report about an injured embassy employee. Chol-hak would tell police that all of the embassy staff were injured with blood on their faces when he arrived—something Cheollima members completely deny.

Three of the "students," including Chol-hak, showed up at the embassy even before the Cheollima members had left. They witnessed them driving off in a hurry and immediately knocked on the door. When there was no answer, they jumped the fence and opened the doors to find several of the embassy workers still inside with handcuffs on. Everyone was freed immediately.

When police knocked again after seeing so much commotion, including the arrival of "students" hopping the fence, So came to the door after about half an hour, explaining little except that there'd been an invasion, and authorized police to come inside to search the premises for any members of the group. A crime scene photographer took pictures of all the material left behind by the Cheollima members as well as the broken frames on the embassy's doors.

IN THE STOLEN EMBASSY Mercedes van, Ahn told the driver to let him and Charles out along the way so they could start making their own plans for escape. The first thing the pair did was walk into a bar so Ahn could pee; he'd been so stressed he hadn't used the bathroom in hours and suddenly he couldn't wait any longer.

The driver left the van running on Galileo Street, about a twelve-minute drive from the embassy. The group in the Toyota dropped the car after about a ten-minute drive in a different direction, and the Audi was found by police days later about a fifteen-minute drive in yet another direction.

While still in the Uber, Adrian called the Hotel Aitana, where he was staying, and told the concierge he had a problem that meant he needed to leave the country urgently. He asked the staff to send his possessions to his home in Los Angeles. He radioed the Cheollima members to proceed to Portugal in small groups and fly to New York City immediately, where they'd reconvene to discuss next steps. The plan they'd agreed to while still inside the embassy was, after they arrived safely back in the United States, to inform the FBI what had happened and stave off any negative interpretation of the events. They still thought there was a chance that none of the day's events would ever become public.

One tricky issue was that the team members' passports were still with the Cheollima group who'd waited outside the embassy during the operation. One member of this subunit had sent a message to Ahn over Signal with an address where he and Charles Ryu could find their passports hidden in some bushes.

What proceeded was a series of comic events, even if the stakes were real. Ahn suddenly had the notion that he should shave his beard, so he went into a mini-mart to buy a razor. Using a bottle of water and a razor, he started shaving his beard roughly, leaving some cuts. All he had on his body was a wallet with 40 euros and credit cards and his cell phone. Charles had even less.

They hired a cab to go to the passport rendezvous location, but the taxi broke down. By now, Ahn looked at his phone and saw that it was down to 2 percent battery. One of the downsides of the Zello app they'd been using to turn their phones into walkie-talkies is it drains power fast. Rather than go straight to the passport location, they decided to buy an iPhone cable from another shop and then stop in Burger King to charge their phones.

Ahn still had the idea in his head that any action he took to conceal he'd been in Spain would be an indicator of possible guilt about a crime. So instead of using cash, he purposely paid for their burgers with his credit card to "leave a trail" for police to see later when they were piecing together what happened. Adrian had told all the members to do the exact opposite.

By the time they'd finished their meal, it was after midnight and Ahn's battery was still hovering close to 1 percent. He'd turned off all the apps, had darkened his screen, and was communicating with the team over texts. Ahn and Charles managed to find their passports in the bushes. But they were still faced with a challenge: How should they get to Portugal?

As two Asian men, one tall and husky and the other small and slim, standing around at 12:30 A.M. on the street in Madrid, they knew they looked suspicious. "We probably looked as out of place as a pair of unicorns," Ahn said later.

Across the street, they spied a cabdriver looking like he was counting up his wages for the day and about to head home. They ran over and started telling him in broken Spanish that they needed to get to Porto, Portugal—about six hours away. The driver stared at them with deep unease and suspicion.

Ahn, realizing that options were limited, invented a story of how they were late for his brother's wedding in Portugal and desperately needed to get there by the morning. "I lost my wallet, but my dad can pay you," Ahn told him. Pointing at Charles, he explained, "This is my little brother."

The driver relented.

At first, the driver refused to let Ahn plug his iPhone into the outlet in his car because he was using it for the GPS, but he eventually let him use it for ten minutes at a time. An hour and a half into the journey, they stopped for gas. Ahn overheard the driver explaining to the gas station attendant something along the lines of how he was driving these two suspicious Asian men to Portugal and how he "felt like these guys were international criminals."

With a tiny bit of juice left in his phone, Ahn managed to book airline tickets for Charles and him out of Porto. Their itinerary would then take them to Zurich and on to Istanbul, before a final flight to Los Angeles. Ahn refused to fly to New York because he had investor meetings to attend in Los Angeles on Monday. By about 7:00 A.M. they arrived at the Marriott in Porto. The driver, looking ill at ease, demanded that Ahn call his "dad" right away to get the money. Ahn got out of the car and went into the lobby, calling Adrian instead. Adrian, who by now was in Portugal as well, told him to find an ATM to pay him and get out of the country as soon as possible.

Back in the taxi, they drove to an ATM where Ahn withdrew the money from his own bank account. The bill amounted to more than

800 euros, with Ahn adding in a big tip on top. The driver let out a palpable sigh of relief when Ahn handed over the money, saying he was worried they would run away without paying. "I thought you guys were crazy," he told Ahn.

Word came through that the other teams had all safely exited Spain and were on their way to the United States, too.

By now, Ahn had been in Europe for just twenty-three hours. And he had to get back to Los Angeles for his Monday investor meetings for his start-up. So he flew all the way to L.A. on an exhausting three-leg, eighteen-hour journey.

When he finally got home, his wife took one look at him and said, "What the hell happened to your beard?"

IMMEDIATELY AFTER LANDING IN New York, Adrian booked rooms for the rest of the Cheollima members at a hotel in New York City.

Safely out of Spain, the team felt a giant sense of relief. But Adrian knew they could still be in hot water. In hopes of finessing the fallout to the failed extraction of So, Adrian drafted an unsigned, anonymous letter to the Spanish Ministry of Foreign Affairs explaining that the group had been invited into the embassy to facilitate an escape but that the person changed his mind.

Adrian also got in touch with his FBI contacts—agents from the same unit he first met when he was spending so much time in Libya. They agreed to meet right away. In the first of a series of meetings, Adrian explained to the agents in detail what had happened in Spain. The idea was that if the men were completely transparent with the FBI and they were identified somehow by the Spanish authorities, the FBI would protect them. Adrian still held out hope they wouldn't be identified at all.

The agents listened to the wild story, unable to conceal occasional wide-eyed surprise at just how audacious the Cheollima plan had been. When Adrian explained about the intelligence haul they'd obtained from the embassy, the agents immediately asked if they could have the files and drives. Adrian didn't actually know what was on them, because they were encrypted by a system his team couldn't surpass.

In a subsequent meeting, Adrian agreed to lend everything to the FBI agents for two weeks, and then they'd return the original files to him in New York. The agents agreed to strict confidentiality over the files and the meetings they were having. But they also pushed to know the names of everyone involved in the operation and to speak to others who were involved. Adrian refused to give up the names but agreed to try to persuade another team member to speak with them. Some of the Cheollima members involved in the Spain operation flew back to South Korea soon after arriving in New York. Somehow the group's actions had gone unreported.

Then, on Wednesday, February 27, Spain's *El Confidencial* newspaper broke the story of a mysterious group who took over the North Korean embassy a few days earlier. The bombshell report, based on interviews with unnamed sources in the Ministry of the Interior, revealed that an investigation had been opened into an alleged attack on the embassy. There were few details, but the ones included were eye-popping: a woman fleeing, bleeding and injured, and a well-dressed Korean man answering the embassy door to say nothing was the matter, only for police to learn hours later that the embassy had, in fact, been overtaken by a group of mysterious men who had allegedly beaten their hostages.

As for those alleged injuries, in fact, all of the embassy staff had been treated at the door of the embassy, and none were brought to a medical clinic or hospital. They were also not photographed, according to a Spanish journalist I spoke to. Cheollima members, including Ahn and Adrian, believe the men struck each other to create the illusion of violence not so much for the police as for their North Korean overseers to see that they at least put up resistance to the "invaders" and that there was no defection discussed whatsoever.

Back in California, Ahn tried to forget about Spain and focus on his start-up. But the botched operation would soon catch up with him.

About a week after the events in Spain, he got a call from Adrian, who said he was heading back to L.A., where they both lived, and wanted to meet up. Ahn picked him up from the airport, and they talked on the drive into town about the operation and how annoyed they were that they'd missed the seventh resident.

Adrian told Ahn that things with the authorities seemed to be stable. The agents were shocked by what Cheollima had done and wanted to know everyone's names, but Adrian had refused to give up his team members. But they were insistent that they wanted to talk to someone else, to corroborate Adrian's version of events. Ahn agreed to be that person.

A few days later, Adrian called with news that the FBI agents were ready to meet. With his wife at work, Ahn invited the same agents Adrian had been speaking to into his house and offered them tea and a plate of macadamia and white chocolate cookies he'd just baked— a new hobby. The agents asked to go through all the details of the day in Madrid and took extensive notes.

TWO WEEKS LATER, THE FBI called with a worrying message, explaining to Ahn that there were reliable threats against the lives of Adrian, himself, and others for their involvement in the operation.

"How the hell did that happen?" Ahn asked them, believing that their identities were still secret. They evaded the question, but the impression was that their names were already starting to circulate somewhere.

What Adrian and the rest of the Cheollima team didn't fully appreciate was just how bad the timing of their operation was. Donald Trump was preparing to fly to Hanoi for his second summit with Kim Jong-un, and the news was full of headlines about the possibility that the U.S.–North Korea relationship might be thawing, thanks to Trump's unconventional diplomatic overtures.

If there was one thing the Trump administration didn't want, it was any possibility of anyone thinking that the U.S. government supported—even tacitly—such a bold and infuriating move by a bunch of rogue operatives, led by an American green card holder. White House national security advisers believed any kind of North Korea deal was still a fairy tale, but Trump had high hopes that his unparalleled business negotiating experience would finally hit home with "rocket man."

The timing was remarkable. Most of the U.S. delegation were in the air on their way to Hanoi as the Cheollima Civil Defense team were on their way back to New York. The timing made it look like the Spain embassy mission had been precisely coordinated to put pressure on the Kim regime or, worse, had been set in motion by forces within the U.S. government security apparatus opposed to Trump's reconciliation efforts.

The coincidence would have been even more explosive if people had known that Adrian had met John Bolton, Trump's top security adviser, years earlier and received a welcoming reception for his aggressive ideas for toppling the Kim regime.

But strangely, the events in Madrid didn't come up at all. No one from the North Korean government contingent mentioned Madrid to their counterparts. "We were worried it would throw a spanner in the works," one member of the U.S. team said. "It was a wild card."

Unbeknownst to Adrian, behind the scenes in U.S. law enforcement, a curious directive had come down regarding Cheollima. As the FBI agents handling Adrian explained to their superiors about the unbelievable things Adrian was telling them, they received an abrupt message: these guys are on their own, and we can't have anything to do with protecting them. By this point, the bureau already had the purloined intelligence materials in their possession and were potentially copying them for dissemination within the U.S. intelligence establishment. They were turning their backs on Adrian and Cheollima, but they couldn't tell them either.

At the Hotel Metropole in Hanoi, Trump and Kim Jong-un met again to see if they could make progress on a deal for denuclearization in exchange for sanctions relief. But this time, the reality of the impasse between the two sides became clear right away. Sitting in a kind of air-conditioned greenhouse at the center of the hotel courtyard, the leaders were growing frustrated with each other. Kim's sister Kim Yo-jong stood stoically outside in the hot humid morning.

The next morning, during a wider meeting at 11:00, they tried to recapture the historic nature of the moment. Trump even offered to fly Kim back to North Korea on Air Force One, which made Kim chuckle and decline what was a hugely symbolic gesture. Kim continued to press how much they'd already given up by agreeing to close the Yongbyon nuclear facilities. But the United States was unwilling to relieve sanctions for that single move. Goaded by John Bolton and others, Trump pushed for a full declaration that North Korea would dismantle its nuclear weapons altogether.

When it was clear no acceptable deal was possible on this trip, they tried to find a way to make it seem as if progress had been made. In reality, however, Trump's North Korea gambit had wilted away. There had been some hair-raising moments when Kim could have agreed to one of Trump's fleeting—and, in the eyes of security officials, reckless—offers, but constrained by his own advisers and hawks, he'd held out for a better deal, believing Trump needed this deal for his legacy and would agree to something even more advantageous.

A little more than a month later, North Korea started testing missiles again. The standoff returned to just about exactly where it had started, with no progress whatsoever. It was only the latest failure of a U.S. administration to deal with the threat of North Korea; ten previous U.S. presidents had also failed to stop the rise of an unexpectedly powerful hermit kingdom that threatened superpowers without retaliation.

AFTER NEWS OF THE Madrid operation started coming out in Spanish newspapers, bigger outlets from around the world began to pick up the story as well. There was something so outlandish about it. On one level, it looked as if a crack team of intelligence operatives had broken into a foreign embassy and stolen material. But there were fissures in that image, too. Were they inept? Were they amateurs?

To try to shape the narrative, Adrian decided to use the Cheollima Civil Defense website to make a statement taking credit for the operation without giving much detail.

On February 25, the group wrote on its website, "Our organization received a request for help from comrades in a certain Western country. It was a high-risk situation, but we responded."

A few days later, they added a message implicitly for the North Korean ambassador: "Don't worry if you keep your promises to us." In other words, they were forgiving him for pulling out of the escape mission he'd initiated in the first place and implicitly saying they would try to protect the truth of his outreach.

Finally, Adrian's secret organization decided to take an aggressive step into the light. On March 1, the anniversary of a protest movement by Korean people and students calling for independence from Japan in 1919, Cheollima Civil Defense made its declaration for a "Free Joseon," named after the Joseon dynasty, a Korean kingdom that stretched over five centuries. The announcement involved a grandiose mission statement and a video of a woman reading out the text from Tapgol Park in Seoul, where the movement was launched a hundred years earlier. Cheollima Civil Defense, the secret underground network of risk-taking activists, had become Free Joseon, the self-appointed stewards of a revolution against the Kim regime.

Cheollima Civil Defense, like the Joseon Institute, was meant to be almost apolitical—a group of volunteers helping people in need. But Free Joseon was the final step in Adrian's radical transformation: this was a group not only agitating for change but asserting itself as the legitimate government of North Korea.

The launch had been planned for before the Madrid mission went pear-shaped, but it took on new meaning amid international media interest in the group. Interview requests had been flooding into the ProtonMail email addresses the group had mostly used for dealing with would-be defectors and volunteers.

Adrian and his teammates had worked on it for months, drawing inspiration from other declarations of independence and call-to-arms writing around the world, even a quotation from the Chinese national anthem. The document included highfalutin passages:

> Today, we hear the twin calls of both our ancestors and our descendants. Our spirits demand that we wait no longer. Do we not also deserve joy, dignity, education, health, and safety? We, too, claim liberty as our bounty. We hereby take into our own hands our destiny and duty.

The goal had been to create something inspiring, but also palatable to a wide range of constituents—North Korean citizens, European sympathizers, people on the left and the right of the issue. The statement addressed different constituencies with separate messages.

To North Koreans within the system, it called on them to "defy your oppressors." To the Korean diaspora, "join our revolution." For "those who would continue to legitimize and empower the regime: History remembers where you stood when you were offered this choice."

In more practical terms, the declaration included the creation of a "provisional government in exile," a concept borrowed from Adrian's friend Ousama Abushagur's father and his fellow anti-Gaddafi revolutionaries. "We declare this entity the sole legitimate representative of the Korean people of the north," it said. In the history of North Korea, there has never been such an approach taken by a group seeking the liberation of the country. The idea of a provisional state was also provocative to South Korean officials, who believed South and North Korea should be reunified as a single state.

On March 11, someone spray-painted "Free North Korea . . . we are rising!" and the Free Joseon logo on the wall of the North Korean embassy in Kuala Lumpur. On its website, Free Joseon wrote, "Courage in Kuala Lumpur," adding, "We're lonely now when we're longing for freedom quietly. But we'll meet one by one through courage."

What wasn't publicly disclosed in news articles at the time was that the flag within the embassy itself was changed to a Free Joseon flag, proof of the group's reach even within the diplomatic corps itself.

Adrian also kicked off a new fundraising strategy inspired by the global fascination with cryptocurrencies that the group had been working on for months. Their perceived anonymity could be a benefit to groups such as Free Joseon, he believed. In March, they debuted a "Post-Liberation Blockchain G-VISA" that would allow any holder to visit the country of "Free Joseon" established after the fall of North Korea.

The announcement even included an authentic-looking visa from the Provisional Government of Free Joseon. The stunt wasn't a wild success. Blockchain records show it earned only about $30,000 worth of cryptocurrency.

In an echo of Adrian's discussions with businesses about buying permits to work in "Free Joseon," the rules for the visa asked for anyone seeking "to establish commercial activities" to contact the group via its encrypted email address. "Ownership of one or more G-Visas should be considered a contribution to the movement and should not be used for speculative or fiduciary purposes," the group wrote.

Ironically, during this time I was texting with Adrian about the mission in Spain, wondering if he had any idea who was behind it. I thought it would be an interesting case to explore in *The Wall Street Journal*. He responded to me in short bursts, acknowledging nothing of the operation. By that point, he was still hoping to stay anonymous with the help of the U.S. government. They hadn't given him any explicit promises, but he had faith that they knew Free Joseon was trying to do a good thing.

UNBEKNOWNST TO ADRIAN AND the members of what was now known as Free Joseon, the Spanish authorities had succeeded where the international press had so far failed: they had identified most of the men involved in the Madrid mission and gathered testimony from the North Korean diplomats, who told prosecutors that the Cheol-lima volunteers had beaten and terrorized them. So, the top diplo-mat, told prosecutors several days later that the men had raided the embassy and tried to force him to defect, in part by telling So that the North Korean government was about to collapse.

When So came in for the interview, he had a large fresh bruise on his face. So told the police that one of the invaders had hammered him in the face with the butt of his fake handgun. (Ahn and others I spoke to categorically denied any acts of violence had occurred in the embassy.) Interestingly, Spanish authorities included no information about the destruction of the portraits of North Korean leaders in their investigative reports. So and others in the embassy denied any-thing had ever happened to the portraits.

Spanish National Police called their investigation Operation Nol-lam, using the Korean word for surprise. Two things helped Spanish police almost instantly come up with a list of the men: they used their real names, and they used American Express cards for all their trans-actions. American Express is rarely used in Spain, so the transactions stood out like a sore thumb.

By the end of March, the Spanish court had removed a secrecy order on the case revealing their names and a startling detail: the FBI had been cooperating with the Spanish investigation *from the outset* and had informed them that Adrian had handed them embassy mate-rials.

The revelation of Adrian's name caused a flood of messages onto his phone. People from across his whole past—university days, LiNK, nonprofits, church communities, political advisers—wanted to know if it was true he infiltrated the North Korean embassy in Spain. It was almost too crazy to believe for many of these contacts. He didn't re-spond to most of them, but he did speak to a former U.S. government official who recommended he get a lawyer as soon as possible.

Not long after, Adrian was introduced to Lee Wolosky, a former government lawyer who had gone into private practice during the Donald Trump presidency, by Sue Mi Terry, a former CIA officer and senior fellow at the Center for Strategic and International Studies. Terry had taken a shine to Adrian even if she also found his spy-movie behavior to be a bit over the top. She was an *actual* former intelligence officer focused on North Korea, so it was all the more silly. In several years of knowing him, she frequently wondered if he was making things up or at least exaggerating—so extraordinary were the stories.

"He used to annoy me a little bit with the whole super-secretive act," she said. "Phones have to be put in a special bag to block signals. Like *Bourne Ultimatum*. Come on. I'm former CIA."

At the same time, she found him fascinating. He was putting every penny he made from his consulting company into this work. "He's not a normal person who's just happy with something simple," she said.

When he came to her after the failed Spanish mission in February 2019, she could immediately sense he was telling her a true story. When she heard the details, she knew he needed a lawyer to help him tell his story to the authorities. She'd known Wolosky from her time in government and reached out to him to set up an introduction.

Wolosky had a history dealing in edgy public interest cases connected to national security, such as serving as the U.S. special envoy for Guantánamo closure in the Barack Obama administration. Seeing the incredible tension of Adrian's position, an idealist trying to oppose a tyrannical regime systematically torturing citizens who ran afoul of Spanish law, Wolosky agreed to take on the case pro bono.

TO ADRIAN HONG AND Christopher Ahn, back in Los Angeles, it was clear Free Joseon was in hot water. News reports were focused on the allegations of violence. The idea that So requested the group's help to escape was not accepted by the Spanish government, at least publicly, and Free Joseon itself couldn't outright say that without putting him, his wife and son, and their extended families in immediate danger. Depressingly, they were having to pull back on their Dubai electric scooter company; investors would never pour more money into the project if their names were associated with an international incident.

Spanish authorities didn't appear to find any meaning in the fact that North Korea recalled all of the staff from the embassy except So soon after they gave testimony. (It's unknown whether his wife and son were allowed to stay with him there.)

Meanwhile, photographers and journalists were knocking on the door of Adrian's apartment in Los Angeles. Adrian feared his wife and their young toddler would be publicly identified and targeted by North Korean assassins. After the FBI told him he was a target, Ahn started carrying a concealed pistol, for which he had obtained a permit.

One day, Adrian called Ahn with an update. Adrian told him he was breaking his lease on his apartment and moving out to avoid the press and anyone else seeking him out. Ahn offered to help him pack his house. Adrian had always kept Ahn at arm's length over the years, even as he had relied on him to perform increasingly risky tasks on behalf of Cheollima. But now there was a sense of new comradeship as they packed toddler toys and books at Adrian's apartment.

Adrian also mentioned he had bought a load of surveillance cameras for protection. "Want one?" he asked Ahn. Thinking he was referring to a Ring front-doorbell camera, Ahn agreed.

A day later, Ahn picked up the box of cameras from a store, realizing they were more expensive outdoor security cameras, not the kind he thought they'd be. He told Adrian he'd drop them off at Adrian's apartment in Koreatown after he went to the barber.

But when Ahn opened the door to Adrian's apartment with a key Adrian had left him, he saw a group of burly men. "Who the fuck are you?" he shouted. They jumped up and pulled their guns out, shouting back, "Who the fuck are *you*?" They identified themselves as officers with the U.S. Marshals Service and demanded his name.

When he said Christopher Ahn, they looked at each other with the realization that one of the men they were seeking had walked right into their laps. On the spot, Ahn was arrested on an extradition warrant from Spain.

All the way to the police station and hours into processing, Ahn remained calm. It was a Friday afternoon, but he thought he'd be released immediately after the mix-up was cleared up. Never in any of their discussions did Adrian and Ahn think about the real possibility of getting arrested while in the United States.

"I kept saying, 'Can somebody please call the FBI or State Department to clear this up? There's obviously been a mistake,'" Ahn remembered. "I thought I'd be home for dinner."

Hours into the process, he was booked and detained at the Metropolitan Detention Center in Los Angeles. That evening he finally spoke to a public defender, who gave him the bad news that he'd definitely be held for the whole weekend. "I was shocked," he recalled. "It dawned on me that it isn't just a small thing."

He wasn't able to call Grace, his wife, until the next morning. A public school teacher in a low-income area of Los Angeles, she was accustomed to keeping her cool and holding her emotions in. The whole previous day she'd kept her calm, talking to the U.S. marshals and the public defender. When Ahn finally called, she completely broke down. All the stress and fear came pouring out.

"I need you to come home," she told him.

17

JAILHOUSE KIMCHI

*It is said that no one truly knows a nation until one has been
inside its jails. A nation should not be judged by how it treats
its highest citizens, but its lowest ones.*

—NELSON MANDELA

LOS ANGELES
APRIL 2019

As THE INMATES SHUFFLED TO THEIR TABLES FOR ANOTHER GRIM
dinner, Christopher Ahn spotted his quarry: coleslaw.

In jail, Ahn realized that there were two culinary worlds. There
were the universally despised meals served in the mess hall, where
rotten ingredients are not uncommon. Then there were the inge-
nious concoctions inmates created using a mixture of real ingredients
stolen from mealtimes and various fast foods or processed foods pro-
cured from the outside. The Mexicans could make a mean posole—
a traditional stew that calls for hominy and pork—from such components as corn nuts soaked for days, meat purloined from dinner,
and a variety of spices and hot sauces harvested from other pre-
packaged products. Everything from cooking tools to work-around
techniques—including a sous vide system that involved hot water in
a trash can—required imagination and clever use of whatever could
be found in the very small world of Pod 6 West at the Metropolitan
Detention Center in Los Angeles.

Most of the jailhouse recipes were handed down from one generation of prisoners to the next, a kind of oral tradition. Biding his time in the bleak 1980s tower in the center of the city, Ahn was craving the familiar punch of kimchi, the traditional pickled cabbage dish available in every Korean kitchen. As of yet, the small group of Asian prisoners had not been able to invent a hack for that. Ahn wasn't deterred, however. He'd made it at home many times. All he needed was clean, simple vegetables, vinegar, sugar, time.

Time was a given. After the U.S. marshals arrested him weeks earlier, Ahn initially thought he'd be out of custody in hours or days at most. When he was finally interviewed by a court clerk the day after his arrest, Ahn demanded to know what exactly he was being charged with. Confused by the documents, the clerk mistakenly told him he was accused of aiding a fugitive.

An immense feeling of relief washed over him. This, he thought, could easily be cleared up with an explanation. But a few hours later he met his public defender, only to find out he was accused of a whole raft of crimes in Spain and was facing an extradition request. His heart sank as he realized the documents revealed that the FBI themselves had helped the Spanish confirm Ahn's involvement in the operation. He felt foolish for having naïvely invited those agents into his house for cookies and tea with no lawyer present. It was meant to be a chance to help them understand the truth, but instead he'd utterly incriminated himself.

In a conversation one day not long before the Madrid operation, Ahn had discussed with Adrian how they should always make sure they didn't do anything that jeopardized the possibility of them coming home and having a simple life.

Just a few days before his arrest, however, Ahn told Adrian and other Free Joseon members that he felt bad that Adrian was taking all the heat for what happened in Madrid. One of the members replied to not worry about it. "You weren't even really part of the op," the member told Ahn. "You showed up at the last minute."

Now, however, it seemed that Ahn was the one taking all the heat. The thought was dizzying, absurd even. "I briefly questioned whether or not this was a reality," he recalled. "Then I realized my worst night-mare was coming true."

As the weeks passed, the very concept of time was warping in his mind; minutes felt like hours, and there was no clear end in sight. He'd deployed to Iraq and seen some scary things in his life, but he lacked the ruthless cunning and strategizing that surviving jail or prison in America seemed to require. "The machine inside the prison system is designed to constantly remind you that you're worthless," he said later. "You have no one to rely on for your safety other than yourself or alliances you make in the general population."

Until now, Ahn had never had any kind of run-in with the criminal justice system whatsoever, barring a visit to traffic court in college where he contested a ticket for not wearing a seat belt. He ended up paying a small fine.

In that way, Ahn wasn't so different from the other members of the Cheollima, and now Free Joseon, team. The men involved in the Madrid operation were putting on a brave front, but they'd spent their whole lives eager to be upstanding citizens with good careers. These were not mercenaries or rogues, by any means. They were good at playing by the rules. The truth was they were also naïve, be-lieving the U.S. government would sanction their work after the fact because it was the right thing to do. What happened next would shat-ter that idealism.

Pod 6 West at the Metropolitan Detention Center was purport-edly the nicest of the jail facilities in Los Angeles. Even still, Ahn found the experience so "appalling and dehumanizing" that he vowed he'd eventually spend part of his career working on criminal justice reform once he got his life untangled from the fallout from Spain. "The inmates I met were by and large decent people who made mis-takes, yet they were all being treated inhumanely," he recalled. "I would rather be in Fallujah on the worst days than be in jail."

One of the first shocks Ahn had in jail was wrapping his head around the severity of the racial pecking order in prison, where Asians were often considered the bottom rung. While the guards were nominally in charge, they left inter-prisoner relations to the gangs. Whenever Ahn stepped out of the cell, he put on a game face. The pod was riven with gangland and racial tension. Violence could erupt at any point over something as small as a disrespectful look.

By sheer luck, the pod where Ahn ended up had recently had an influential Asian "shot caller," who was respected as a mediator of problems and viewed as particularly tough after beating up a Black prisoner who was trying to extract "taxes" from the Asian cohort. As a result, Asians in this particular part of the jail had a relatively stronger position.

Arriving in the general population of the jail, Ahn ping-ponged between cells where there was a spare bed. But soon he was assigned to share a cell with an older Korean man called PK accused of fraud. The man wasn't violent or well versed in jail politics—a relief to Ahn. They became friends, turning their cell into a Korean refuge at night, listening to Korean radio, which featured talk shows, traditional music, and commentary about Dodgers baseball. These pleasant diversions helped the men forget where they were. "Inside we had a totally different vibe," Ahn recalled later. "Outside it was gangs and crazy stuff."

Ahn's wife, Grace, who visited each week, sometimes bringing along Ahn's mother, started sending a stream of books to him. Years earlier, Grace had read the bestselling novel *Life of Pi* and filled the margins with notes about her feelings as she read the book. Now in prison, as Ahn read her copy, he was filled with emotion. He and Grace also read *The 5 Love Languages* at the same time and traded emails with their thoughts to each other.

Ahn also read books from the jail library, including one novel that he found unexpectedly poignant. The novel revolves around an old English grandmother searching for meaning in her life now that her children were off having their own lives.

"It was a chick-flick-type book and so dramatically different than where I was," he said. "It made me feel like I was on the couch watching some terrible Hallmark movie with my wife 'cause that's the movie she chose."

One day, when Ahn was feeling particularly forlorn, he said out loud, "How did I get here? I shouldn't be here." He wasn't blaming anyone else for his predicament, but he was still in disbelief that the situation in Spain could be so badly misunderstood. His cellmate told him then that he couldn't let that kind of thinking take hold. "If you keep asking, you're going to go insane," the cellmate said. It was communicated with a matter-of-fact tone, but helped him snap out of it.

As the days went by, Ahn began absorbing jailhouse knowledge and cultural norms. For instance, spitting in your sink is considered uncivilized. For mysterious reasons, when you brush your teeth, the only acceptable place to spit the toothpaste is the toilet. Another skill: turning a blanket into a rope to hold up a makeshift bookshelf. Grace and Ahn's brother, Daniel, started sending a steady flow of books and comics, which were particularly popular, especially Ahn's collection of works from the Game of Thrones franchise. The Game of Thrones books helped Ahn forge surprising bonds with fellow inmates, including members of the Bloods and the Crips. A shot caller for the Bloods, universally feared among the prisoners, would "nerd out" over the book with Ahn, asking for help with some of the vocabulary.

On the Fourth of July 2019, Ahn was drawn into a cell block dispute. Guards rewarded the organizers of basketball tournaments with a "goody bag" that included highly desirable items like Snickers bars and hot sauce. "In the real world these are mundane things available at any gas station, but in jail they are prized possessions," Ahn said.

Joining with a Mexican mafia leader and the Bloods shot caller—the Game of Thrones aficionado—Ahn helped broker a peace that involved splitting up components of the goody bag carefully among two men who believed it should rightfully be theirs.

Just as he had for Cheollima during tense operations with defectors, Ahn found himself looked to in jail to help keep peace and calm. Thanks to his skillful negotiation that day, Ahn, near the end of his time in jail, began to be considered the new Asian shot caller of Pod 6 West.

———

AHN AND HIS WIFE, Grace, were deeply loyal to his first lawyer, a thirty-year veteran of the Office of the Federal Public Defender called Callie Steele. Despite having no real familiarity with the North Korea or extradition cases, she told Ahn she believed his story and would fight hard to get bail for him.

Not long after Ahn's arrest, Adrian Hong's lawyer, Lee Wolosky, contacted another attorney in Los Angeles, asking for volunteers to serve as Ahn's pro bono lawyer. A name was soon recommended: Naeun Rim, a Harvard-educated, high-powered lawyer at the white-collar firm Bird Marella who previously served in the same Office of the Federal Public Defender as Steele, Ahn's public defender. Rim was overloaded with casework but instantly drawn to the case along with another Korean American lawyer at her firm, Ekwan Rhow.

Like other Korean Americans, Rim felt compelled to play a role in addressing the situation in North Korea. The conflict struck a "deep chord of grief" in her gut, Rim said, explaining, "There is a sharp political divide amongst South Koreans on how to deal with North Korea, of course, but the root of it is the same—there is this grief that the country was torn apart less than a century ago, that the North Korean people, many of whom share bloodlines with us, are suffering and inaccessible to us, and there is no easy or neat solution to mend that rift."

Rim felt that Ahn had been trying something brave to address the "tortured history" of the Korean peninsula and was a good person. "I felt a personal responsibility to help Chris," she recalled.

With Steele's blessing, Rim and Rhow came on board the legal team. She and Rhow immediately started poring through the details of his case and extradition law. Their conclusion wasn't good. Extradition between allies largely boiled down to a simple test: Does the United States have an extradition treaty with the country, and would the crimes allegedly committed there be crimes in the United States, too? In Ahn's case, the answers were yes and yes.

Still, the trio of attorneys put together an ambitious and aggressive legal strategy that involved arguing strongly that he was a humanitarian caught up in a misunderstanding that could see him executed by North Korean assassins. They weren't going to lose the case against Ahn, "A Fugitive from the Government of the Kingdom of Spain," as his extradition request put it, for lack of hard work.

THE MAKESHIFT COOKING PROVED to be among the most exciting parts of jail life. Getting the hang of it, Ahn invented a jailhouse pad thai involving ramen, peanut butter, and vegetables. Kimchi required more creativity. The fellow inmates called the concoctions they made "spreads."

One of the worst dishes in the mess hall was the coleslaw—at least the way it was served. Ahn thought he could do better. Asking for fellow inmates to "donate" their coleslaw to him, Ahn stored it in a plastic bag, which he brought back to his cell. There, he washed the mashed mess thoroughly using a hairnet as a sieve and squeezed as much water out as possible.

Then he took peanut butter jars, completely cleaned out with soap, and put the remaining coleslaw vegetables inside, adding garlic powder and a squeeze of sweet-and-sour sauce. Sugar, or even ingredients that contained sugar, was hard to come by inside because it could be used to brew alcohol. But the sweet-and-sour sauce had just enough to kick-start the fermentation process. Ahn stored the jars filled with his concoction in bread bags under his bed. After a week, he revealed his creation of jailhouse kimchi to the other prisoners. It was a hit.

FINALLY, THE WORK OF Christopher Ahn's legal team seemed to be paying off.

On July 16, 2019, Judge Jean Rosenbluth, of the U.S. District Court in Los Angeles, granted him bail despite the opposition of the U.S.

Department of Justice, pointing out that much of the evidence against Ahn was provided by officials of a country, North Korea, that doesn't have diplomatic relations with the United States. Some of Ahn's family members put up their homes as collateral on a nearly $1.3 million bond. The judge issued a stern condition for Ahn's bail: absolutely no contact with Free Joseon.

Still, Ahn was overjoyed. As soon as he stepped outside on a warm Los Angeles day, Grace handed him a goody bag including yogurt, candy, and soda. "I was overwhelmed with relief and thankfulness," he said.

For the next year and nine months, Ahn lived under full house arrest. He couldn't even help his wife bring groceries from the car. The situation was hard on his family. Finally, in 2021, Judge Rosenbluth modified his bail so that he could travel in a restricted zone from 8:00 A.M. to 8:00 P.M., which allowed Ahn to care for his mother—who has a disease called trigeminal neuralgia that causes extreme pain in the face—and his ninety-nine-year-old grandmother, who lived together in their home nearby.

However, as of May 2022, more than three years after the operation in Madrid, Ahn's life was still being upended without any end in sight. Judge Rosenbluth still hadn't ruled on his extradition. Ahn's career was on hold; even some friends had turned their backs on him. He and Grace had decided to put off having children until his situation was resolved.

"I try not to feel bitter," Ahn said. "What it comes down to is if someone asks for help and I have the capability of helping, then I don't want to be the type of guy who says no."

18

ON THE RUN

The voice of passion is better than the voice of reason. The passionless cannot change history.

—CZESŁAW MIŁOSZ

LONDON
APRIL 2019

JUST BEFORE A MEETING WITH A JOURNALIST FRIEND IN LONDON'S Borough Market, I started scrolling through Twitter, when an image stopped me in my tracks. Someone had retweeted a wanted poster with Adrian's face.

Distributed by the U.S. Marshals Service, the notice was for "Adrian Hong Chang, a.k.a. Matthew Chao, a.k.a. Oswaldo Trump." The six-foot one-inch, 220-pound man was "wanted for his involvement in the February 22, 2019, raid of the embassy of the Democratic People's Republic of Korea in Madrid, Spain. Adrian was last seen driving a white 2017 KIA Soul 4D, license plate number 'ARDENT.' Adrian is considered to be armed and dangerous."

My jaw dropped. Months earlier, I had read news items about the Madrid embassy break-in, but I had been completely unaware of Adrian's involvement. I had even contacted Adrian over Signal to see if he could shed light on who might have been behind the storming of the building.

Not only had I just seen Adrian in London before the Spain

mission, but weeks *after* the mission—with no knowledge of his involvement—I'd introduced him to a like-minded contact who was investing his wealth in things like combating misinformation in politics and building refugee camps around the world. In my greeting to them, I said they were both members of what seemed like the international "justice league," spending their time and money to fight against the darker forces at work in the world.

Now, seeing the image of Adrian in the wanted poster, I began wondering if I truly knew anything about him and how on earth he could be described as armed and dangerous when the person I'd come to know never gave even an inkling of having a violent side. Within seconds of seeing the tweet, I sent a message to Adrian over Signal—the encrypted messenger of choice for journalists, officials, and activists looking to avoid prying eyes. But my messages went unread. Adrian had already disappeared.

I'd known Adrian for eight years by this point. Now it was dawning on me: I didn't know much at all.

I went into overdrive to try to find a way to do a story about Adrian. Working to fill in the picture of the Yale graduate turned wanted man alongside two of the most intrepid reporters at *The Wall Street Journal,* I quickly realized how narrow the access was that Adrian had granted me into his life. He was so cloistered and compartmentalized. I discovered he was married only because he let it slip to me during a conversation in December 2011 that his wife was asleep in the next room.

The close friends of his that our reporting team at *The Wall Street Journal* managed to track down knew next to nothing about his work for North Korea. Those who knew about his North Korea advocacy knew next to nothing about his personal life. Later, I would discover that even members of Free Joseon who were considered at the top of the organization had no real visibility into what their own group was doing. It was Adrian who was running the show.

In a way, I realized it was all purposeful: this structure that had allowed Free Joseon to get itself into so much trouble. As an institution, it was able to take on an unbelievable amount of risk because the "chief risk officer" and "chief executive" was Adrian himself. Fellow members were in it for the idealism, but they didn't have an equal vote in how much danger they'd get into.

Sometimes, as with Christopher Ahn or Charles Ryu, they wouldn't know the plan until they had flown halfway around the world at Adrian's behest.

WHEN CHRISTOPHER AHN LANDED in jail, Adrian Hong and Sam Ryu set in motion a long-brewing plan to disappear. Adrian had no idea that U.S. marshals were getting ready to arrest him, but he happened to be on a separate errand in town when it happened.

One of the last things Ahn heard while he was with the U.S. marshals was an officer getting a report from a colleague at a house where Adrian's wife was staying with their child. She was refusing to help them find Adrian.

But the original plan wasn't to evade the U.S. marshals; it was to hide from possible North Korean assassins, the possible threat having been formally disclosed to lawyers for Adrian and Ahn by the FBI.

The problems facing the Free Joseon members involved in the Madrid operation were compounding. At first, their problem was only the Spanish authorities, who didn't understand what had happened. It was also the North Koreans, who sought vengeance against them for the symbolic invasion of their territory and the embarrassment of the resulting global headlines. There were also photographers and journalists showing up at Adrian's apartment for several weeks. If they had once believed they could leave Spain and return to more or less a normal existence, now they were having to hide from a much more adept authority monitoring borders, credit card spending, and phone calls. The stakes were already high, but they went up another ten notches.

The FBI was still talking to them until near the arrest. Adrian, in particular, was blindsided by the arrests. Only later did he and the others find out that after he handed them the USB drives and other material, the FBI had held on to it for an unknown period of time before transferring it back to Spain in a sealed box, which was returned to the North Korean embassy soon after. It's unknown whether any U.S. intelligence agency copied the materials before returning them, or whether anyone from the White House, who had been involved in diplomatic overtures to the Kim regime, had played any role in the return of the materials.

It seemed that So managed to convince his superiors in North Korea that the embassy was invaded and they'd valiantly fought off the attackers, sustaining injuries in the process—a complete fiction. He remained as the commercial attaché in the embassy, according to Alejandro Cao de Benós, but all the rest of the staff were returned to Pyongyang.

The same day as Ahn's arrest, the Department of Justice unsealed an arrest warrant for Ahn and Adrian based on an extradition request from Spain. The attached investigative material from the Spanish authorities detailed everything they had discovered about the case and a surprising addition: footage.

It turned out that in the Madrid embassy the Cheollima members had missed a key piece of the North Koreans' surveillance system. They hadn't found the separate computer that stored video from the cameras at the front door and in the embassy courtyard. It caught many of the crucial moments of the operation in detail, including the dramatic entrance, the capture of several of the North Korean officials and staff, the arrival of the police, their escape, and the arrival of the North Korean students.

What both the Department of Justice arrest warrant and the Spanish extradition request failed to include anywhere was any mention of the letter Cheollima sent to the Ministry of Foreign Affairs immediately after their return to New York, seeking to clarify the group's intentions and any discussion of the claim that So had asked to escape. The documents were framed entirely around the allegations that the men broke into the embassy, beat the staff, and tried to force the commercial attaché So Yun-suk to defect. When he refused, the document claims, they beat him, too, and stole intelligence and the embassy cars to escape the country. That document then set the tone for all the coverage in the mainstream media.

In their investigative summary, Spanish authorities pointed to the kidnapping paraphernalia that Cheollima left behind, including balaclavas and fake guns, as proof of their violent activity. These were the same materials Christopher Ahn had insisted they leave behind to prove the opposite, by showing that they weren't trying to cover anything up.

The Spanish authorities had also obtained sworn testimony from North Korean diplomats inside the embassy, including the would-be defector, who said the Cheollima men attacked the diplomats and that he had not given consent for the mission and had never harbored any desire to escape his country.

A picture of Christopher Ahn wearing sunglasses and black clothes outside the embassy was used to reinforce the idea that this was a paramilitary operation. Headlines referred to him as a "former marine" involved in the operation, lending further credence to the idea of a violent assault.

A hidden dimension of the case, according to a person familiar with the Spanish prosecution, was that Spanish authorities genuinely believed Cheollima was acting on behalf of or in concert with U.S. intelligence, even while their American counterparts denied any connection. Those denials helped precipitate a decision to bring charges, with some on the Spanish side believing the United States wouldn't allow any Cheollima members to be extradited, which would prove that they were intelligence agents.

That created a convoluted situation where the U.S. government, despite their knowledge of Adrian's history of rescuing North Korean escapees and having some element of contact with him over the years for intelligence sharing, couldn't intervene in the case without making it seem as if they supported the Free Joseon cause, which the U.S.

government didn't support. And the Spanish couldn't drop charges without looking as though they acquiesced to American pressure to protect intelligence assets, which wasn't actually happening.

In Europe, the events were also tainted by the bitter memory of CIA extraordinary renditions in the post-9/11 era, which were considered deeply outrageous incursions on state sovereignty. France, Germany, Italy, and other countries had all opened investigations into activity on their soil.

In conjunction with "War on Terror" CIA activities in Europe, Italian prosecutors had gone so far as to try twenty-six people, mostly CIA officers, in absentia and convicted them in the only trial involving the U.S. government's extraordinary renditions program. The Italian case, in particular, involved the kidnapping in broad daylight of the Muslim cleric Osama Moustafa Hassan Nasr from the streets of Milan.

The lingering effect of those cases was antipathy to anything even faintly suggestive of U.S. intelligence officers conducting operations on the ground in Europe without going through the proper channels. Invading an embassy is a particularly bad red line because it suggests a country like Spain can't protect diplomats from attacks.

The consequence: each member of Cheollima faced up to twenty-four years in prison in Spain on charges of illegal entry, assault, illegal confinement, and being part of a criminal organization.

THE RELEASE OF THE U.S. Marshals Service's wanted poster was an extraordinary turning point. The same man invited into the White House for photos with the president, feted as a leading North Korean human rights campaigner, and praised as the creator of what had become an international organization to help North Koreans was now "armed and dangerous" and wanted on felony crimes.

In the weeks prior to the arrest, Adrian sent out a last round of messages to close friends. The messages were mostly brief: he was facing serious issues because of the Spanish case, and the situation might require him to go off the grid. After Ahn was arrested, his communications went silent. He and Sam Ryu severed ties to everyone.

Within Free Joseon, members had been working to establish a protocol for exactly this situation. The plan had been fine-tuned in the weeks since the Spain operation as the relationship with the FBI had gone south and details about the storming of the embassy had begun to trickle out in the international press. Rule number one was that no one in the group would have direct access to Adrian so long as he remained belowground. If they needed to reach him, they could use only a prior arrangement known as Silver Bullet to get in touch— a system that involved no direct messages sent between the parties.

This protocol was effective at blocking efforts of authorities, or anyone else, to identify Adrian's whereabouts, but it also meant the group was as good as headless. Free Joseon had been painstakingly built up over years, piece by piece, by Adrian's relentless networking. Many of the members operated as cells without knowledge of the others. If Adrian was removed from the structure, the group itself shuddered to a halt. Adrian later told a friend that several other rescue operations that had been in the works were summarily halted.

The silence of the group harmed them in the crucial early days of the crisis. It meant that they had no way of communicating with the world what they were really about. In the absence of comment from them, except the high-minded rhetoric on the Free Joseon website, the narrative of violent assaulters cemented in the media narrative. The fact that they were anonymous people with lofty-sounding goals involved in something out of a spy movie actually hurt more than it helped. In the information vacuum, the idea that they were puppets of a foreign government began to seem not just possible but likely, in the eyes of commentators and observers.

In time, I made headway in establishing sources within the group. In my discussions with Free Joseon members, they almost invariably referred to Ahn's arrest and Adrian's disappearance as a tragic fate they needed to shoulder. They were deeply bitter about what they saw as the U.S. government's betrayal, but were reluctant to speak out, knowing it could jeopardize members and the people they'd rescued.

In those early days of my exchanges with them, the members of Free Joseon I spoke with all predicted Adrian would have to go underground for only a matter of weeks or months at the extreme end of possibilities. Just as Ahn thought that surely someone would realize this was a terrible mistake, the Free Joseon members believed reason would prevail and someone in power would realize the colossal mistake that led these self-sacrificing do-gooders to face decades in prison. It was a bias toward optimism.

Surely, someone would realize So had asked to be rescued even if it wasn't obvious from the Spanish evidence, they thought. Why on earth would a group of Korean Americans and South Koreans choose the North Korean embassy in Spain and risk everything to literally kidnap the commercial attaché? Would there be anything more dangerous and completely ridiculous?

But they were wrong. Nobody stepped up because nobody wanted to put their neck on the line. Just like in China in 2006, Adrian hadn't asked permission for what he was doing, so he had no umbrage—no protector. Members like Ahn had gone along with the plan, thinking it must be airtight, when in fact it was full of holes and there was no protection if things went badly. If the North Korean students had encountered the men in the embassy that night—they missed each other by mere minutes—there could have been a serious fight. A Cheollima member could have been killed. They could have been arrested on the streets of Spain and been sentenced to prison.

Even influential people who knew instantly that the image of Adrian as "armed and dangerous" was completely false felt they couldn't put their heads above the parapet. The mission was just too far over the line—invading an embassy, fake guns, allegations of violence. Lee Wolosky, Adrian's lawyer, appearing on Fox News, did his best to try to explain the group in short sound bites, but nothing took hold.

Sung-Yoon Lee, a professor at the Fletcher School at Tufts University, who'd stayed in touch with Adrian and invited him to speak to his class years earlier, became one of the only public defenders of the group. He explained Free Joseon's actions as intrepid and brave, but most of all actually impactful. They shattered the image of the all-powerful Kim regime with their daylight embassy mission and involvement in rescuing Kim Han-sol, he told interviewers.

He also wrote an op-ed in the *Los Angeles Times* arguing the United States shouldn't extradite Free Joseon members to Spain. "For the U.S. to accept what is essentially a North Korean version of the events is to effectively defend the Kim regime," he wrote. "It sends the message to Pyongyang that its egregious crimes lie beyond the concern of the world's presumptive champion of freedom and democracy."

On June 25, 2019, the group tried one of their last efforts to change the narrative. Charles Ryu, the North Korean who was filmed entering the embassy in Madrid, wrote a pseudonymous testimonial on the website of Fox News about his life and the episode. Free Joseon members believed throughout 2019 and 2020 that appealing to Fox News viewers was the best way to influence the Trump administration to intervene politically in the case.

"When I learned of the existence of the North Korean dissident group Provisional Government of Free Joseon, I was overwhelmed with joy and relief," he wrote. "Finally, I had discovered a group of people who felt a personal responsibility to stop the crimes against humanity in my homeland."

He described entering the embassy for the first time as a North Korean escapee and how he'd smashed the portraits of Kim Il-sung and Kim Jong-il. Most important, he described how they were there to help a diplomat defect.

"We took huge risks to help others reach freedom. Why is the U.S., Spain punishing us?" he asked.

IN DECEMBER 2020, WITH the world still in the throes of COVID-19, I finally had the chance to meet Christopher Ahn over Zoom. It would be the first of countless hours of mostly late-night discussions.

At first, I couldn't believe how different his personality was from the impression I'd had looking at the pictures and reading the court case against him. Almost all of his stories had a sensitive, emotional dimension to them. It was an instantly revelatory experience and emphasized just how dramatically wrong Free Joseon's public image was in all of the reporting so far.

One of the things Ahn explained to me was that everything about Free Joseon felt more like a start-up than some Weather Underground or Baader-Meinhof cell of armed agitators. There weren't really any rogues or mavericks or extremists in the group, he explained; these "kids" were *chakhae*—a Korean term used to describe good, undefiant children who stay out of trouble. In fact, they had actually been incubating the scooter start-up together in Dubai at the same time as they were arranging rescues of North Koreans.

I was also moved by Ahn's personal story and his strong connection to his family. Everything about his involvement in this affair seemed to be a tragic mistake, but with the threat of extradition and a criminal trial in Spain still looming, there didn't seem to be any off-ramp for him. In the meantime, his life had been ravaged by the case. The food start-up he had been working on at the time of the Madrid incident had been ruined by his stint in jail, and his entire life had been completely upended.

Over the course of 2021, I followed Ahn's court case closely and wrote an article about him in *BuzzFeed*. It felt as if there were almost no chance that Judge Jean Rosenbluth could find a way to not extradite him considering the seemingly bulletproof treaty with Spain. But in court, her pointed questions and detailed comments showed how hard she was trying to find a way not to do it.

Before a bail hearing in 2019, after a flood of letters had been submitted to the court from people vouching for his character, including the co-founder of Vets for Freedom David Bellavia, the judge remarked that Ahn appeared to be a "good and honorable man."

His wife, Grace, too, had written a moving letter to the judge talking about their dedication to their parents and how Ahn would never run away from a lifelong commitment to take care of his mother and grandmother. She also recounted a story in hopes of better conveying his loving nature:

> I remember last winter was particularly cold. . . . He had become friendly with a homeless man always outside of our local Ralphs. One very cold night, we saw that man passed out and shivering violently. We tried to wake him up, but he was incoherent. So Christopher rushed home and brought several of our blankets to wrap him up in. Christopher asked the store for cardboard boxes and built a sort of wind blocker and left some money in his pocket. This is the real Christopher Ahn. He is a big ball of love, generosity, honor and service. He is a gentle soul.

In 2021, Judge Rosenbluth showed remarkable signs of believing Ahn's story and the altruistic nature of the group. At a hearing on May 25, the parents of Otto Warmbier even flew in to show support and, if given the opportunity, speak on his behalf. Lee, the Tufts University professor, spoke as an expert witness.

During back-and-forth with the federal prosecutors arguing to extradite Ahn immediately to Spain, the judge expressed her views more expansively and captured the apparent contradiction of the decision she was required to make:

> You know, back in the day we prosecuted people for being members of underground railroads and then, you know, a hundred years later we were giving them medals. I just— I don't know. I'm going to follow the law because I have to. I'm going to look at the cases that— I took an oath to do it and I will, and I will come out with whatever result I think is warranted by the law. But I have to say that I don't understand what's going on here, and it does not seem that justice is being done.

As of May 2022, the judge had yet to rule on the case—an almost unprecedented delay in making a decision in an extradition case like this. If she eventually does rule for extradition, Ahn can appeal. And even if he loses that, he can lobby the executive branch to not fulfill the extradition—a process that could take years. Spanish authorities have maintained in public statements that they intend to try the men before a Spanish court.

AS FOR ADRIAN HONG and Sam Ryu, the story of their lives after they went into hiding in 2019 will have to be told one day in the future. Like the government authorities from whom they are running, and even some of their closest friends, I couldn't find out the details of where they were or how they were managing to survive nearly three years on the run.

I did manage to make contact with one person with some knowledge of what had happened to them after they disappeared from their homes in California. This person, who spoke to me on the condition of anonymity, told me that the pair had suffered a lot from the lack of connection to their loved ones, whom they couldn't contact for fear of giving away their location and potentially putting a target on their backs.

Adrian's child, now a walking, talking toddler, hadn't seen their father for most of their life.

THE PRICE

NEW MALDEN, U.K.
FEBRUARY 2022

ONE DAY AS I WAS WRAPPING UP MY REPORTING FOR THIS BOOK, I decided to take a drive to New Malden in South London. This neighborhood's high street is lined with Korean restaurants and shops. It is the home of London's Little Korea as well as a nonprofit group called Connect: North Korea that helps escapees build new lives far from the all-seeing eye of the Kim regime. At one point, New Malden had more North Korean escapees than anywhere on earth other than South Korea and Japan. The area had a peak of more than seven hundred escapees in the mid 2000s, but with many dispersing around the country and the world over the years, it has only about three hundred left now.

Michael Glendinning, the organization's Scottish founder, started the group after working with North Koreans in Seoul. After graduating with a degree in English, he'd traveled to Seoul looking for opportunities to see that part of the world. Eventually, he started working with North Koreans and felt staggered by their stories of hardship in their home country. The systematic way the regime kept people underfed and exhausted for their whole lives felt like a dystopian novel. He was also struck by how, for South Koreans, it wasn't a topic people liked to discuss.

Returning to London, he set up the first version of what would become Connect: North Korea, which helps North Koreans in the U.K., and its more muscular sister organization, Korea Future, which investigates crimes against North Koreans and advocates for staunch penalties to be levied against the Kim regime.

I wanted to know if people like Glendinning felt as Adrian did. After years of advocating, did it feel like any progress was being made? Did he, too, feel like taking direct action so that North Koreans could experience something better within their lifetimes?

I'd spoken weeks earlier to Nicolai Sprekels, chairman of a German nonprofit, Saram, who'd told me a startling number he used to motivate himself all the time. At any moment, there were approximately 100,000 to 120,000 inmates in political prison camps in North Korea with a life expectancy of between six and seven years. That number really puts the regime's brutality into perspective.

Sprekels had been advocating for North Korean human rights for about nine years, meaning that at least 100,000 people had died during that time. "You can't really feel that, what that means," he told me. "We are too far away, especially the young generation, from these crimes against humanity."

For Glendinning, the deaths were only one part of the full picture. The North Koreans in New Malden were carrying immense survivor's guilt and trauma from their experiences there. They frequently expressed depression about the fate of their parents, siblings, extended relatives, and friends who weren't lucky enough to escape.

He admitted that many involved in his line of work experienced burnout from the lack of progress on the wider objective to make life better for North Koreans while the world fixated on Kim Jong-un and his nuclear weapons.

Glendinning had met Adrian at a conference in London in the 2000s, remembering him as an impassioned speaker during closed-door discussions. He understood Adrian's desire to do more, even if he didn't agree with the path he'd taken.

"What I keep coming back to is it's important to take a stand defending human rights, even if it doesn't bring quick results," he said. "You have to focus on the worst situations in the world. If you can't defend human rights in that context, then all is lost."

AT THE OUTSET OF this project, my goal had been to answer a simple question: Who is Adrian Hong? And for as much as I learned about him, and about Free Joseon, the edges of his character still do not feel fully defined.

One persuasive perspective on Adrian's motivations came from Soobin Kim, a reporter who helped conduct research for this book. She herself had briefly worked as an intern at LiNK, the organization Adrian founded, long after he'd left the group.

Just as I was finishing work on this book, she sent me a message with her views after reading the near-complete draft. She perceived something from the story that hadn't occurred to me in my own experience, but seemed spot on when I reflected on it. Adrian, she wrote, had

> a shaky sense of citizenship—Mexican in passport but culturally American, Korean in appearance (but most Koreans will not think of him as Korean either)—and working on this cause gave him the power to effect change in not just one but three countries. He's going to the White House and meeting with politicians in a country he can't even vote in. And, of course, it's kind of hard to just accept US history as his own because it's almost entirely black-and-white, so I think he turned to Korean history. While I believe that this did give his life meaning and purpose . . . I think it also became a substitute for his fragmented identity.

Whether Adrian's extraordinary commitment to the North Korean cause was catalyzed by a fragmented identity, or something else, there is an aspect of his journey that I can relate to. What attracted me to tell Adrian's story, in part, is the compulsion I also feel within myself to do something bigger than my day job—a sense of longing that I think many people share. That Adrian and the others in Free Joseon actually did something about that, at great personal risk, is to me admirable even if their strategy itself is ripe for criticism. That they are on the run and facing prison time is, to me, a stark injustice.

ONE OTHER MESSAGE ARRIVED in March 2022, in my final days of writing. As I was trying to finish the book, the world had become consumed once again by a war, begun by another of the world's modern-day autocrats—Russia's invasion of Ukraine, at the behest of Vladimir Putin.

Living in limbo, out on bail in California, and still waiting for a ruling on his extradition case, Christopher Ahn reached out to me about the conflict with a poignant message, one that also struck a chord with me. I thought it would probably resonate with many people who felt compelled to *do something* about such an egregious assault on civilians:

> Hey Bradley, I wanted to tell you something. One of the main questions and critiques I have had has always been, "why did you get involved?" For the overwhelming majority of people, they just don't get it. Why get involved with people you don't know thousands of miles away, just cause they're Korean.
>
> I try to explain, but most simply just don't get it.
>
> But now . . . with all this Ukraine stuff happening . . . I think people will start to get it.
>
> I just read a *New York Times* article about American Vets volunteering to go fight in Ukraine, and the things they are saying to explain their reasonings why, are virtually the same as mine of why I got involved.
>
> Also, I think white people who see people who look like them going through such a terrible and violent situation, and

having a deep feeling of wanting to do something, creates a moment of empathy for people to understand why someone like me would volunteer to help people who look like me going through something tragic and terrible.

That's all.

Two months after sending me that message, Ahn received some bad news. Judge Jean Rosenbluth, the federal magistrate judge who had been reviewing his bid to stop his extradition to Spain, ruled against him.

The ruling didn't mean Ahn would instantly be transferred into Spanish custody. He still had the ability to file a claim that would force a higher court to review the case again. But the claws of the Spanish criminal justice system were getting closer.

Even though she did not rule in favor of Ahn, there was something noteworthy about Judge Rosenbluth's decision. In remarkably personal and even pained language, she expressed a sense of heartache over Ahn's fate. Lamenting her own lack of power in the case, she called on a higher court to set a new precedent with regard to the extradition of U.S. citizens facing criminal prosecution abroad, and to issue a ruling overturning her own. She alluded to the possibility that, once outside the United States, Ahn would face an unknown fate, including the possibility that North Korea could find a way to assassinate him on Spanish soil.

"Although I conclude that the law requires me to certify, I do not think it's the right result, and I hope that a higher court will either tell me I'm wrong or itself block the extradition," Judge Rosenbluth wrote. "Yes, Ahn should have to face a court reckoning of some kind for possibly violating at least the letter of the law. But he should not be cast off to face an uncertain fate at the hands of a despot, perhaps sacrificed to advance a foreign-policy agenda. If I thought I could, I would require any trial of Ahn to be here in the United States, and I hope that a judge or judges tasked with fixing law instead of simply following it will do just that."

In the ruling's concluding remarks, the judge cites Cindy Warmbier, the mother of Otto Warmbier, who had spoken in support of Ahn at a previous hearing.

"Cindy Warmbier said that Ahn needed a 'strong woman' to 'stand up to North Korea.' I regret that I am too weak, in power if not in will, to save him from the threat of torture and assassination by that outcast nation."

MY LASTING FEELING IS that there's something about the entire story of Adrian, Ahn, and Free Joseon that feels like a fairy tale; there's something elemental about human society and personalities embedded in the entire journey. Putting all the details aside, the experience raises a deep question about whether people can change the world. What does it really take?

So much of what Adrian said to me and others over the years goes to the heart of this. He told me once that the American dream itself is fictional, but he still believes in its power to transform lives. He frequently talked about how everything—start-ups that become behemoth companies or activism that leads to an uprising—started with a single act of faith that nothing is too big to achieve. Whether you admire him or find him pretentious or even dangerous, there's something powerful in that belief. As to whether he made a difference with his underground organization, it will take a long time yet to fully know the answer.

ACKNOWLEDGMENTS

THERE IS ONLY ONE BYLINE ON THE FRONT OF THIS BOOK, BUT IT was very much a team effort with contributions from people around the globe.

I always like to start by thanking the people, many of them unnamed, who gave their time and trust to speak about Adrian Hong, Christopher Ahn, and Free Joseon. Sources are the unsung heroes of journalism, and some of mine took big risks to help me understand their world better.

In 2021, my longtime friend and collaborator Tom Wright and I left our jobs at *The Wall Street Journal* to found a journalism start-up company called Project Brazen. This book was one of the first two projects we launched at the company, with all of the proceeds used to kick-start the business, hire staff, and invest in storytelling. My thanks to Tom for reviewing parts of the manuscript and offering his friendship and support always. Many thanks also to Project Brazen's advisers, Stefano Quadrio Curzio and David Giampaolo.

Paul Whitlatch, the talented editor who commissioned Tom's and my first book, *Billion Dollar Whale*, in 2018, as well as a second book, which I co-authored with Justin Scheck, *Blood and Oil*, convinced me that I had it in me for a third book project in only six years. His guidance and editing, first at Hachette and now at the Crown imprint of

Random House, have propelled Tom and me on our new path in ways we never could have expected, so we offer him our deep gratitude and hope for future collaboration.

At Crown, I would also like to thank Katie Berry, David Drake, Gillian Blake, Annsley Rosner, Stacey Stein, Dyana Messina, Sierra Moon, Melissa Esner, Julie Cepler, Mark Birkey, and Amelia Zalcman.

Jake Levy, of Levy Law, has been an extraordinary guide to Project Brazen and me, as well as a champion of this book. Taking on this project during the COVID-19 pandemic was a unique challenge, but I benefited from the assistance of an amazing group of reporters and researchers in different geographic locations whose contributions allowed me to push forward despite the inability to travel as extensively as I might have during normal times. This book would not have been possible without the extraordinary research and reporting help from Soobin Kim, a reporter in London; Mackenzie Hawkins, a student and journalist at Yale University; Lucy Woods, the head of research at Project Brazen; and Grace Moon, who conducted research before joining *The Washington Post*. All of them helped deepen the journalism and find details to bring alive the story.

Sung-Yoon Lee, a professor at Tufts University who knew Adrian, and Chad O'Carroll, the founder of NK News in Seoul, served as sounding boards for much of my reporting and soul-searching about Free Joseon.

Most of all, I thank my wife, Farah, who always has confidence in me and who helps me see the world in all its complicated glory. She is like the keystone of an arch.

PHOTOGRAPH INSERT CREDITS

Page 1, top	Courtesy of Bonita Vista High School
Page 1, middle	Courtesy of Bonita Vista High School
Page 1, bottom	Andrew Caballero-Reynolds/Getty Images
Page 2, top	Bettmann/Getty Images
Page 2, middle	Kyodo News/Getty Images
Page 2, bottom	Kim Won Jin/Getty Images
Page 3, top	Courtesy of Cole Carnesecca
Page 3, middle	Courtesy of Hong family
Page 3, bottom	Lucas Schifres/Getty Images
Page 4, top	*The Washington Post*/Getty Images
Page 4, middle	Courtesy of Hong family
Page 4, bottom	Courtesy of Hong family
Page 5, top	Benjamin Lowy/Getty Images
Page 5, middle	Courtesy of Ahn family
Page 5, bottom	Courtesy of Ahn family
Page 6, top	Courtesy of Christopher Ahn
Page 6, middle	*The Asahi Shimbun*/Getty Images
Page 6, bottom	Jung Yeon-Je/Getty Images
Page 7, top	Handout/Getty Images
Page 7, middle	Javier Soriano/Getty Images
Page 7, bottom	From court documents
Page 8, top	From court documents
Page 8, middle	From court documents
Page 8, bottom	Courtesy of Phil Cheung

BRADLEY HOPE is the *New York Times* bestselling co-author of *Billion Dollar Whale* and *Blood and Oil*. He is a Pulitzer Prize finalist and Gerald Loeb Award winner. Formerly a reporter for *The Wall Street Journal* and a correspondent in the Middle East, Hope is co-founder of Project Brazen, a journalism studio and production company. He lives in London.

ABOUT THE TYPE

This book was set in Dante, a typeface designed by Giovanni Mardersteig (1892–1977). Conceived as a private type for the Officina Bodoni in Verona, Italy, Dante was originally cut only for hand composition by Charles Malin, the famous Parisian punch cutter, between 1946 and 1952. Its first use was in an edition of Boccaccio's *Trattatello in laude di Dante* that appeared in 1954. The Monotype Corporation's version of Dante followed in 1957. Though modeled on the Aldine type used for Pietro Cardinal Bembo's treatise *De Aetna* in 1495, Dante is a thoroughly modern interpretation of that venerable face.